SHOWING THE FLAG

A Report from
Inside a U.S. Embassy

Marguerite Michaels

SIMON AND SCHUSTER
NEW YORK

Very special thanks to Walter Anderson, editor of Parade *magazine, without whose support this book would have been impossible.*

Copyright © 1982 by Marguerite Michaels
All rights reserved
including the right of reproduction
in whole or in part in any form
Published by Simon and Schuster
A Division of Gulf & Western Corporation
Simon & Schuster Building
Rockefeller Center
1230 Avenue of the Americas
New York, New York 10020

SIMON AND SCHUSTER *and colophon*
are trademarks of Simon & Schuster
Manufactured in the United States of America

10 9 8 7 6 5 4 3 2 1

Library of Congress Cataloging in Publication Data

Michaels, Marguerite.
Showing the flag.

I. Title.
PS3563.I2735S5   813'.54   81-23336
ISBN 0-671-25616-5   AACR2

For my mother and father
my sister, Lauren
my brother, John

Author's Note

I spent six months in early 1980 in Bogota, Colombia, observing the daily operations of the embassy and conducting repeated interviews with personnel concerning their duties, private lives and personal perceptions. Events where I knew my presence had the effect of shaping reality have been reconstructed with the help of those involved. There are some telescoping of time and a few shifts in chronology. The recording of people's thoughts is a product of extensive interviews with those people. One composite character was created and a few names and identities were changed when I thought it possible to protect people who requested protection without damaging the integrity of the material.

Cast of Characters

CLAY ALLISON, *customs agent*

DIEGO ASENCIO, *ambassador*

NANCY ASENCIO, *his wife*

RICHARD BACA, *country director, Peace Corps*

CHUCK BOLES, *security officer*

DAVE BURNETT, *country director, Drug Enforcement Agency (DEA)*

JUNE BURNETT, *his wife*

FRANK CRIGLER, *deputy chief of mission (DCM)*

BETTIE CRIGLER, *his wife*

PHIL FERRIS, *junior officer, political section*

ELLIS GLYNN, *general services officer*

JERRY HARRISON, *junior officer, consulate*

MICHELE HARRISON, *his wife*

EILEEN HEAPHY, *desk officer*

MRS. CHARLOTTE JENSEN, *mother of Richard Starr*

KEN KELLER, *consul general*

MIKE KRISTULA, *country director, United States International Communications Agency (USICA)*

MIKE KUHLMAN, *DEA agent*

JEANNIE KUHLMAN, *his wife*

PATT LINDSEY, *secretary, political section*

JOHN McINTYRE, *narcotics coordinator*

MIGUEL, *Colombian staffer, General Services Office*

BOB PASTORINO, *commercial officer*

FRANK RAVNDAL, *administration officer*

MARILYN RAVNDAL, *his wife*

DON ROBERTS, *political officer*

HADIA ROBERTS, *his wife*

EMILY ROTH, *secretary, economics/commercial section*

JOHN SIMMS, *political counselor*
RICHARD STARR, *Peace Corps volunteer*
GEORGE THIGPEN, *economics/commercial counselor*
DICK WEEKS, *budget and fiscal officer*
JIM WELCH, *junior officer, USICA*
FRANK WHERLY (TOP), *Master Gunnery Sergeant, U.S. Marines*
COLONEL CARL WITTENBERG, *Military Group (Milgroup)*
BRUCE WITTER, *assistant security officer*

SHOWING THE FLAG

1

EMILY ROTH felt great. Outside the plane there were mountains as far as the eye could see.

"Romantic, sunlit, velvet green hills wrapped in ribbony dirt roads that wind with purpose and then disappear . . . mysterious dark—no—dark, mysterious, snow-topped ranges in the distance sliced by flat purple clouds . . ."

Emily read what she had just written in the diary on her lap. Ugh, too many adjectives. But Emily loved adjectives. That was why she had joined the foreign service. Not just to travel, but to travel to "exotic," "exciting," or even just "beautiful" and most certainly always "interesting" places.

It wasn't that her own adjectives were bad. They were just boring. She was a pretty, skinny thirty-four-year-old-divorcee-with-no-children. She had been living with her married sister and working in the front office of a Chicago high school, when her brother-in-law challenged her to answer a foreign service ad in the newspaper: "Looking for secretaries to go overseas. Positions not available right away."

Emily glanced out the window again. Still mountains. Soft and green close up. Craggy and gray far off. It was as if the plane were floating. She let her mind do the same.

She had stood in line six hours—that's how many people had shown up—just to apply. Emily took the foreign service test a week later, January 14, 1975, and thought frankly that she had done very poorly.

Two pages had stuck together and she was sure her right answers were in the wrong place. At the end of the steno she was the only one still sitting there. What she had after five hours was a headache.

It was weeks before she picked up the phone at work and heard her sister stuttering: "Em-Em Emily! Wash . . . Washington just called. MY HOUSE! They called HERE! They said they wanted to talk to you about a job. They left you a number to call back—COLLECT! Emily!"

"Quiere una cobija y un cojín?"

"No, *gracias*," Emily answered. The stewardess wanted to know whether she wanted a blanket and pillow. She must have looked as if she were sleeping.

"Oh God!" Emily blurted. "She spoke to me in Spanish—and I understood!" Six weeks of language training at the Foreign Service Institute in Washington wasn't really much. But then three weeks was all the training she'd gotten altogether for her first post.

It had taken two years to get an assignment from Washington—a person could die waiting to get into the foreign service. There was security clearance, and forms and more forms. She was asked for twelve recommendations. Her divorce was not final; they said she couldn't go overseas with legal matters pending in the States. There was a series of physicals. Then the call came. They said, Okay, now you have to either accept or not accept without knowing where you're going. She remembered how excited she'd been. That was the beginning of 1977, January. Two weeks later Washington called and said, You got your first choice—Europe. You're going to Greece. Emily could see that she had a lot to learn about the government if they considered Greece part of Europe.

Those were wonderful days. There were lots of

farewell parties. The government came and packed her up. They even put your stuff in storage if that's what you wanted. They sent her a "post report."

The post report was a maze of information about the history of Greece, the history of the U.S. Government in Greece, the weather and taxi situation in Athens, the number of employees in the American embassy and how they were housed. It was about fifty pages long and Fodor couldn't have done it better.

Emily smiled when she remembered the three-week "orientation" course in Washington. There were herself and about ten other girls living in the Ramada Inn on a government per diem. Everybody was going to a different part of the world. It was so exciting. You felt so special. You're going to be a diplomat! It wasn't going to be just another job. There was some typing and shorthand—and abbreviations, a three-day course on abbreviations. There was records management—"tags." If a cable has "EFIN" on it, that means it has something to do with economy and finance. There's an "official formal letter," there's an "unofficial informal letter". . .

The two years in Greece had been wonderful. She'd felt part of the embassy and found the city of Athens fascinating. She'd fallen in love with a Greek. Emily's eyes filled with tears. The Greek, as it had turned out, had not fallen in love with her. It had not been a pleasant parting.

But that was past. Emily prided herself on her lively personality and natural optimism. Bogotá was going to be wonderful. Colombia, the land of the legend of El Dorado. Naked Indians covered in gold dust. Beplumed Spanish conquistadors.

Bogotá had not been her first choice, but then, as her personnel officer in Washington had explained often, assignments were really just a matter of the embassy that had the right kind of job opening at the right time. She had worked in the economics section in Athens and when it was time to move to another post Bogotá had a secretarial slot open in its economics section. She had always wanted to learn Spanish, and Colombia was so much closer to the States. She'd only been able to get home once in two years from Greece.

Bogotá's post report was depressing. The altitude, 8,700 feet, causes health problems; the city is rainy and dreary, and there is a lot of theft. But that was all right. Greece's post report hadn't been altogether upbeat and Emily had loved it anyway.

In an hour the plane would land at El Dorado airport in Bogotá. The mountains outside were crowned with rainbows now. Emily counted three. A good omen.

The Colombians in the plane looked attractive. The women were well dressed, the men too—especially the attractive one sitting to her left.

She must have been staring.

"Señorita?" he asked, as if she'd said something. There was just a slight pause. And then he spoke in excellent English. "Please allow me to introduce myself. I am José Palacios Bonillo. My friends call me 'Pepe.' Have you been to Colombia before? Are you here for work or for pleasure?"

"My first trip," said Emily. "For work and for pleasure." He really was good-looking. Shiny black hair that curled up at the collar. Silk collar. European-cut gray suit. Silk maroon tie. A slightly decadent-looking forty.

"If I may ask," Pepe asked, "where will you work in Bogotá?"

"At the American embassy," Emily answered, quite proudly.

"Ah," Pepe murmured, almost to himself. "Please, you must allow me to show you a little of my city and perhaps you will have dinner with me tomorrow."

Emily smiled and accepted, "although tomorrow may not be possible. You could call me at the embassy. My name is Emily Roth."

"Delighted," said Pepe promptly.

Emily had such a feeling of well-being and good fortune. This was going to be a great tour.

The ambassador slammed the phone down with no feeling of well-being or good fortune.

Goddamn Washington.

When the State Department wanted to hang someone's ass in the wind they sent cables. When the State Department wanted to cover its own ass they picked up the phone. Old cables never die. It's the phone calls that fade away.

Ambassador Diego Asencio sat at his desk and stared straight ahead at nothing, waiting for the fury to pass. Eighteen years in the foreign service and here he was, still having trouble with the incessant contradictions between "foreign policy" and getting the job done.

This Richard Starr thing was a perfect example. He was a Peace Corps volunteer who had been taken hostage by the FARC almost three years before. Colombia had five guerrilla groups of uncertain following and questionable impact. Every once in a while one of them made itself a nuisance. The FARC—the Revolutionary Armed Forces of Colombia—was a rural, Moscow-oriented group.

The FARC raided villages regularly for provisions and it was in one of these raids that Starr had been caught. They figured they had an American spy. The poor bastard was a botanist who spoke almost no Spanish.

When Asencio had been appointed ambassador to Colombia two years earlier, he had looked at the

Starr file and talked to the anti-terrorism task force in Washington. There had been reports in the Colombian press that Starr had been tried by a kangaroo court and executed. There had been no ransom request from the FARC.

The U.S. Government, he had been reminded, does not pay ransom.

Nothing happened until Starr's mother, Charlotte Jensen, made her first trip to Bogotá. She had been stonewalled at the State Department and the Peace Corps, but she turned out to be a tough little old lady who would tell the task force boys the ambassador was a schmuck and then tell him they were schmucks.

After Mrs. Jensen had pleaded for her son's life over radio and TV, the first note from Starr was delivered to the embassy.

"Dear Mother"—Asencio remembered the poor Spanish—"I am alive and in good health and in the hands of FARC. Contact the embassy or the Peace Corps to negotiate my liberation. I want to return home. Dick."

The ambassador had been amused at the State Department's first reaction—a handwriting analysis that showed "no indications of mental or emotional disturbance or weakness . . ."

It was not until Starr's mother had made her second trip to Bogotá that terms were finally offered for her son's release. The FARC would swap Starr for an imprisoned revolutionary leader named Jaime Gauracas.

The Colombian Government refused any prisoner exchange with the FARC.

"So what?" Mrs. Jensen had said.

This is not the United States, the ambassador had explained.

"What about sending in the Colombian military then and getting him out?"

He had explained to her that the jungle area where her son was held was so wild, so immense and so unpopulated that an army raid would just be a sure way of getting him killed.

There had been only one intermediary who seemed truly connected to FARC and Starr. Jorge Villamil was a *bogotano* composer who owned a ranch near the jungle area where Starr was supposedly being held. Asencio had talked to him three or four times already in the embassy and many more times on the phone. The guy said he was not a FARC sympathizer. He was simply cooperating to help save a life. Villamil was the one who had delivered the letter from Starr. And although Asencio and his deputy chief of mission at the time, Ted Briggs, had looked for other routes to Richard, all feelers had led back to the composer. It was spooky.

Then came a demand for ransom. Two hundred fifty thousand dollars. Asencio couldn't believe it. He had 160 other Peace Corps kids roaming around the countryside. Everyone had been pulled out of the known guerrilla territories long ago, but he still woke up in the middle of the night multiplying 160 times $250,000.

Once again Washington reminded him that the U.S. Government does not pay ransom. Don't touch any money or deliver any money. Don't negotiate any money terms. When the FARC refused Mrs. Jensen's offer of $11,750—all the money she had been able to scrape together—he felt sorry.

And then Villamil brought another note from Richard. "I ask you again to do everything possible with the governments to obtain my early departure from here. My release will not be worth anything if I have gone crazy."

Lots of bureaucratic back and forth followed about how to placate Mrs. Jensen. What about getting the kid out of hock? Asencio had answered. Washington was not amused.

Two years after Starr's 1977 capture, if he remembered it correctly—the Starr file was immense—he and Briggs got a group of Americans to put up $50,000. The FARC turned it down.

Then a Bogotá newspaper printed a story about a couple of peasants who had seen Starr hanging from a tree with a "CIA Spy" sign tacked to his chest. After a few phone calls Asencio's embassy boys determined that the story was a fabrication, but Mrs. Jensen was furious, and frightened.

Her congressman, Washington Democrat Lloyd Meeds, who had been trying to get some help from the State Department, sent Mrs. Jensen to the columnist Jack Anderson. Anderson had already intervened in a hostage case involving an American businessman, William Niehous, who had been held captive for three years by Venezuelan terrorists.

Anderson's boys had gone to the State Department and had gotten all the way up to the deputy secretary, Warren Christopher, who had offered the department line, "There's nothing we can do." And then Anderson's first column appeared. Richard Starr had now been two and one half years in the jungle. *Having failed to make any progress through official U.S. and Colombian channels, Mrs. Jensen has appealed to us for help. . . .* Something like that.

This morning the cable had come. "Give Anderson your sources." And then the phone call had followed. One of the boys in the anti-terrorist office had wanted to warn him about all the publicity Anderson would bring—as if Asencio wasn't already unhappy about that aspect—and of course "the ambassador would be careful" to make sure that everything went "right" because if it blew up it would be "hang Asencio" time in Washington.

That had been the phone call he had just unceremoniously cut off. Time to quit fuming and call the Peace Corps director with the news.

The ambassador's call awakened the Peace Corps director. His glasses were still on his chest. His book had fallen face up on the floor.

Such is life in the tropics, thought Richard Baca, as he grabbed his glasses, swung his feet over and down, and grunted his way off the couch. "Yes, sir?" he said, surprised at how alert his voice sounded.

"Can you get over here?" the ambassador said.

"Yes sir," was clearly the correct answer.

It had to be Richard Starr. He hoped to God it was Richard Starr. He needed some excitement.

Baca had been in Bogotá for about six months. It seemed like years. By the age of forty-two he had taken himself from token Mexican lawyer, to head of California's legal aid program, to executive director of the Civil Rights Commission in Washington. But he had gotten tired of lawyers and tired of the hours and tired of the contentiousness. Mainly tired of the hours. He didn't know his wife and kids.

Well, he sure knew his wife and kids now. He lived five or six blocks from the office. He got home for lunch. Every weekend there was some kind of family outing.

The Peace Corps job had turned out to be a sort of placement service and he agreed with Asencio that fewer volunteers should be placed in Colombia. The job just didn't absorb him. Neither did the idea of the Peace Corps itself. He didn't believe in it anymore. It was mired in the sixties, when a B.A. in English Literature and being American was supposed to be enough qualification to raise cattle in the Sudan. You had to wonder about an agency that was still trying to cling to its glory days.

If he were in Washington he would tell the volunteers, Look, you can go down there and you can work real hard and what you get out of it is you get to come back to the United States bilingual, which makes you infinitely more employable. Plus you have two years of experience working in some very trying circumstances. It was time to quit talking about peace and harmony and making friends for America. Why do we Americans feel we have to save everybody else's souls along with our own—via democracy?

"Christ," Baca said, "I'm beginning to talk to myself." He walked over to pick up his book, Tom Wolfe's *The Right Stuff*.

Ironic. That was another thing about the Peace Corps, at least here. Most of his people in Colombia were overaged adolescents. Generous of spirit maybe, but superfluous. And because of security problems they were for the most part in cities of over 50,000, where they were just competing with the Colombia work force. Colombians were not exactly pro-American people. They'd get a better impression if they'd see us doing something useful. This was not an underdeveloped country. It was a country with a high unemployment rate.

Baca wondered what Richard Starr thought of the Peace Corps now.

"Who in your family lives here?" Phil Ferris asked.

"Just my mother," the girl answered.

"How much do you earn?"

"It's there in the papers."

Phil was reading her papers. She had an employment verification letter from Avianca Airlines but he knew the name of the employer was out of date. He looked up through the plate of bullet-proof glass. There were two plates, overlapping midway to provide an opening to drop papers and passports into the visa officer's bank teller-like trough. She was very pretty. And a liar.

"If you've worked for over eight years," asked Ferris, "why don't you have a bank account or an income tax form?"

"I give all my money to my mother," she answered.

"I'm sorry," Ferris said, "I can't give you a visa until you can show that you have some money here." His Spanish still needed some work. What he wanted to say was if you don't have proof of economic ties to Colombia then there's no reason to believe that you're going to the States on a tourist visa to do anything but take a U.S. citizen's job away from him.

"Oh, but señor, I have my airline ticket already," the girl cried.

"Señorita," Ferris answered, "just because you have an airline ticket doesn't mean you get a visa."

He cut her off with a loud "Next!"

Phil watched a confident-looking middle-aged gentleman get up from the rows of chairs and approach the window. Five hours of this a day, five days a week. Faces and names melted interchangeably into one another. The visa section was nobody's favorite job, but every junior officer had to start there. It was unfondly called the "conveyor belt" of the embassy. While visas meant power—*palanca*, Colombians called it—for the U.S. Embassy, because almost every Colombian wanted one sooner or later, the people in the visa section had no power at all.

As soon as the gentleman dropped his papers and passport through, Phil could see why he looked confident. His passport carried visa stamps from three other countries. When another country accepts a

Colombian, he's gotta be good. No problem with this guy.

The fluorescent ceiling lights flickered and died. Nobody even noticed. In a few minutes either half of them or all of them would drone back to life. If they all did, a "miracle" would once again have saved Bogotá's ill-run electrical works. If half, then the embassy's emergency generator had kicked on. The visa section was only half lighted during emergencies. Full power went to the embassy's fifth floor communications area, and, of course, to the ambassador's office on the fourth. The embassy also had its own water supply. An underground tank held enough water for two or three weeks, Ferris had been told. Easy on the toilets.

All the lights went back on.

The next man's papers showed that a visa had been denied just a few months before. Incomplete information.

"Has anything changed since last time?" asked Phil.

The man nodded.

"Okay. I'm going to keep your papers. Come back in two weeks."

Phil didn't like the look of the old or new stuff. Better get them checked. Counterfeiting was big business in Bogotá. Colombians were such good forgers that the embassy had two part-time Secret Service men and two full-time Colombian F2 policemen, the equivalent of the American detective.

He'd been at the window for just two hours and he had a stack of eight rejections. Not bad. Although the idea was to issue visas if at all possible—let 'em spend their money in the States—every person interviewed was presumed to be a potentially illegal alien until proven otherwise. In a country like Colombia, where life is difficult and people are desperately trying to change their status, Phil had been cautioned to watch for the person who is going to the States to stay and work and send his wages back to his family.

Still and all, the consulate in Bogotá had issued 54,000 non-immigrant visas last year. Welcome to the U.S. Travel Service, Department of Commerce. There were diplomatic visas and correspondent visas and intra-company transfers and temporary employment visas and student visas.

Phil Ferris was just filling in in the visa section for the morning. Lyn Curtain, the consul in non-immigrant visas, was short a man. Curtain was always short. There weren't enough junior officers to go around, and even when there were, visa was the last section to get them. Curtain was a mild-mannered man who'd been a consular officer for seventeen years. But Phil had watched him work into a rage a half-dozen times when an economic or political officer grabbed one of his junior officers for "something more important." Each time, Phil would watch him go back to his office, find the inevitable request for a diplomatic visa that an economic or political officer had submitted—there was always a pile of them: "important" Colombians whom embassy officers didn't want to have to wait in the visa line—stick it at the bottom of the stack, sit back, and smile.

Phil Ferris slid off his waist-high stool and took a break. He filled a cup at the water cooler and walked down the consular stairs out into the back parking lot of the embassy. It was a formidable-looking building. Five floors of concrete in an L-shape. Only the first four floors had windows, and most of the curtains were drawn. La Embajada de los Estados Unidos occupied a city block in downtown Bogotá, and was surrounded by a fourteen-foot steel bar fence. A small lawn and a few trees softened the effect, but Phil remembered someone telling him that the Colombians had been insulted when the building was finished in 1972, it looked so like a fortress. Even with the sun shining directly on it, Phil had to admit it looked unfriendly. But that is what Phil thought the Colombians were, with or without the sun shining on them.

He took a sip of water. He knew that it wasn't good business to think bad thoughts about the locals when you were working the visa line. He'd been in Bogotá about a year and he really didn't know what he thought of the embassy, or the foreign service for that matter.

Ferris had been in his last year of college in New York when he decided to take the foreign service test. That was in February, 1977. In June he went to Washington for his oral interview. It had turned out to be a day of role-playing: he was given an in-box of consular work to deal with, and then tested on his negotiating tactics. During the last days of July the department started the security check. There were questions about his sex life and about drugs. He was asked for six references. The next February, the State Department called and said, Report to Washington in one month. There was a six-week orientation course—everything from Name the capital of Ecuador to reading Gabriel García Márquez's short stories; there were thirteen weeks of language training, and a six-week course in consular work. He had been very impressed.

One morning he was assigned to Lima, Peru. That afternoon he was reassigned to Bogotá, Colombia. It seems that a consular officer's wife had gone after her husband with a knife. They were both removed from the scene immediately.

Phil Ferris found the embassy a toss-up between a bureaucratic behemoth and a middle-aged high school. Most of the people behind those formidable walls he had found unformidable, plugging away unimaginatively, unnoticed—they hoped—eight to five with two fifteen-minute coffee breaks, until pension time. It was a strict class system. The lower classes were the FSRs, foreign service reserves, who worked in embassy administration—lights, phone bills, cars, security and like that—and the FSSs. The secretaries were FSSs. The real thing, FSOs, foreign service officers like himself, were divided all the way from FS8s at the bottom to FS1s at the very top. The ambassador was an FS1. Everybody made it his business to know exactly what FS everybody else had, and what number went behind it. The embassy in Bogotá had a weekly newspaper that looked like a high school's: meeting and picnic announcements, greetings for new arrivals, lost-and-found columns, and items for sale. Phil's favorite feature was the medical officer's monthly piece: "Ask Dr. Miller." It didn't matter what the question was—from nerves to hemorrhoids—Dr. Miller always said, "Don't worry. It's the altitude. You'll get used to it."

The worst job in the embassy was the "blue furniture"—the Colombian "escorts" dressed in dark blue suits who loitered around the front door, moving only if they were in somebody's way. He'd never seen them escort anybody anywhere. The second worst job in the embassy was the marines.

And, Christ, there went one now running toward the consular section with his .38 in his hand. Phil dropped the cup of water and ran after him.

The marine, it looked like Sergeant Blake—hard to tell, they all looked alike—was already walking out when Phil arrived at the door.

"False alarm," the sergeant said and looked at Phil accusingly.

"Hey look," Phil said, "I've been out here the last five minutes. Besides, you know there must be a short in the consular section alarm system somewhere. That's the fourth time one of you guys has run over this week and nobody's ever pressed the button."

"Right," Sergeant Blake answered and kept

walking. He doubted the goddamn highfalutin State Department types even knew where the alarm buttons were.

Ferris went back and perched himself on the stool, but he waited a full minute before he yelled, "Next."

He had spent the last couple months in the American Services area of the consular section. He'd liked the work well enough—everything from tourists in trouble to notarizing. Next week he would start his second-year specialty. He would be the junior officer in the political section.

John Simms, the political counselor, had told him he could begin by writing the first draft of the annual human rights report. Phil had been around long enough to know that that was not exactly considered an honor.

Two men sat across the table from Mike Kuhlman and Bob Howard. It was the second meet for Kuhlman and this time a café wouldn't do. He'd brought along Howard, his pilot, and Howard had brought along some maps. They needed the privacy of a hotel room. Mike hated even to think the word, it was so trite, but this place was seedy. The walls were either green or gray; the bedspread matched. Cigarette burns decorated every flat surface. The bathroom was easy to find. You could smell it from anywhere in the room. No tourist had ever seen the inside of the Bogotá Plaza.

"Are you sure you're not DEA?" one of the men, a chemist, asked. He had described himself as a Colombian with U.S. citizenship and a wife and four kids in New York. He knew his cocaine chemistry.

"I already told you I'm not DEA," Drug Enforcement Agent Kuhlman answered. "If you're so fuckin' nervous about it, find yourself a Colombian buyer."

"No," the chemist answered. "I prefer dollars to pesos. And Colombians fuck things up."

Only he spoke. The second guy just sat. He was five foot eight, a hundred fifty pounds. His black hair was greased and long. No facial hair. Forties. Mike had checked him out with the Colombian police after the first meet. They'd never heard of him, or the chemist.

The first meet had been set up by a fairly reliable informant. "CIs" they were called now, "cooperative individuals." There was no mystery about any CI's motives. They were in it for the money. If this deal went down, the cooperative individual could get five thousand dollars easy.

"All right then," said Mike. "I've got my pilot here. Let's run through what he missed last meet. You've got a thousand kilos of cocaine base in Bolivia. You're selling at seven thousand dollars a kilo."

"Eight thousand dollars and we'll deliver the stuff to a strip in Colombia," the chemist said.

"We don't have a clandestine strip in Colombia," Howard answered. "We'll pick it up in Bolivia. We've got three aircraft. One in Mexico. Two in Texas. We have access to Colombian air semi-legitimately. . . ."

"Why?" interrupted the chemist.

"That," said Mike, "you don't need to know. What you need to know is that we only want to do a hundred, a hundred fifty kilos for the first buy and we are not paying any seven thousand for it, that's too damn high."

Thirty minutes later, the chemist and his silent partner left. The price hadn't been settled but the chemist had agreed to let Mike inspect the stuff next week at a *finca* near Santa Cruz.

What he'd do is get the CI to go. Then he'd call the DEA office in La Paz and let them know the time and place. If the CI could get them to bring all one hundred fifty kilos instead of just a sample, it'd be a pretty good bust.

"What do you think?" Mike asked.

"Highly unlikely," Howard answered. "That's a lot of stuff. We've never heard of them. There's no sign they're even trying to check us out. And worst of all, the CI doesn't know them that well either. It's too big a deal to just stumble into. Too easy. It's not gonna go down."

Mike had to agree. Not many deals went down in Colombia. That the DEA got their hands on, that is. Plenty went down.

There was no point in paying attention to the numbers. Everybody had his own set. It didn't matter if it was one billion or eight billion dollars a year. Colombia exported a lot of cocaine and marijuana. All of it went to the States and that's what mattered. Mike worked with eleven other agents. They covered the country, but were all based in Bogotá.

Mike Kuhlman had arrived from Seattle with his wife and two kids more than a year ago. At five foot eleven with bright blue eyes and a big blond beard, he was every Colombian's idea of what an American drugger looked like. But he rarely went undercover—none of them did. One bust, and they were burned.

And, of course, there was the Mansfield Amendment. The Mansfield Amendment says U.S. law-enforcement officials working overseas can collect information but they cannot make arrests or fire their weapons, except in self-defense. In other words, as it had been explained to him, you can hold the Colombian policeman's hand until you get to the door. He has to kick it in. Now that was nice, Mike had discovered, if the Colombian didn't duck right after he kicked the door in.

For the record, Kuhlman had not violated the amendment. "The law is gray," he had become fond

of saying; and there was always the eleventh com-
mandment: Don't get caught. There was a way to
write up the reports so that when the amendment
was violated, and it was, nobody had to know.

As Mike understood it, U.S. Embassy people had
talked the Colombians into letting the Drug Enforcement Agency come in sometime in the mid-sev-
enties when the country was beginning to get a lot
of critical publicity about its drug traffic. But they
hadn't gotten much support until Ambassador
Asencio had arrived. He was a real police buff. He'd
gotten the President of Colombia to involve the
country's army, for chrissake, in a "war on
drugs."

Mike thought he was some piece of work.

2

AMBASSADOR DIEGO ASENCIO'S car was stuck in traffic in the narrow streets somewhere near the Plaza Bolívar.

An old dark-green Chrysler LeBaron, with no front fender flags flying, the ambassador's car was quite unremarkable. "The better to be unremarked," as Asencio would say. There was always one bodyguard in the front seat with the driver. Both were armed. And there was a follow car, same make and color, with another two or three armed bodyguards. They were all Colombians.

It was no secret that the American ambassador was at the top of the M-19's kidnap list. The M-19 was Colombia's urban guerrilla group. They had been almost fondly described as "bourgeois revolutionaries" until they successfully tunneled five thousand weapons out from under the army arsenal in the northern part of the city. The army, much embarrassed, was in the process of rounding up suspects.

Asencio winced, thinking about the human rights flack that was on its way from the Colombian desk officer in Washington. At the moment, however, he was on his way to make a courtesy call on the newly elected president of the senate, Hector Echeverri Correa. He was taking along T. Frank Crigler, his new deputy chief of mission, to "get his feet wet" with the Colombian boys.

There are only two things an ambassador gets to pick, Asencio thought, staring absentmindedly out the back window at the mass of people squeezing down the sidewalk; his nose and his DCM. The guys he had wanted were not available, so he'd gotten Frank Crigler. Frank looked all right. Looked all right—Christ, he was beautiful. They couldn't have been more different. Diego would have to describe himself as round. Round of face, rounder of body. A respectable forty-eight-year spread. Horn-rimmed glasses. No hair on the top of his head and a gray goatee at the center of his chin which was cover for an irritating, unattractive skin infection. Crigler did a three-piece suit justice, the ambassador had to admit, even if it was some sort of green. He was tall, slim and square-faced with lots of blown-dry hair and tinted aviator glasses. He could have been cast as the Lone Ranger; instead, he had just been a U.S. ambassador in Rwanda, a little African country. One of the fast-track State Department boys they'd run out of track for. Asencio wondered if he'd have trouble being Number Two.

"Hey Frank," the ambassador said, pointing, "see that building? That's the Palace of San Carlos, where Simón Bolívar lived. A bunch of guys came to get him one night and his mistress, Manuela, shoved him bare-assed out of that first-floor window there. Interesting lady, Manuela. All kinds of books have been written about her, even a soap opera. There's a fascination for her that goes with the mores of Colombian society. Public mistresses are a given here.

"You'll like Echeverri," Asencio went on. "He's a little prickly, but he's a sharp guy who's been around awhile—every politician in Colombia has been around awhile. In ten years the faces and names haven't changed. Just the titles. Echeverri is a liberal, just like the president. Not that it makes any difference. Have you heard the description of the difference between a liberal and a conservative in Colombia? A liberal goes to mass at six A.M. A conservative goes at eight."

Crigler laughed, although he'd heard the joke already.

"There's not much difference," Asencio said. "And a liberal here would be considered a conservative in the States. Congress doesn't matter as an institution. The president runs the country. But there are a handful of guys who are influential. Echeverri is one of them."

The car started to inch forward. It really should have been a lovely neighborhood, Asencio thought. It was the only part of the city where you could still find the carved doors and graceful grillwork left from the Spanish colonial architecture of the eighteenth century. But only recently had there been some effort to save the quarter from rampant decay. Mixed in with the elegance and the history—he pointed out the house where Antonio Nariño had printed his translation of *The Rights of Man*, which triggered the movement for independence in 1794— was real squalor. Dark, dirty, rundown buildings housed five families in four rooms with bad water and no sanitation. Garbage littered the streets. There were as many dogs around as people. Everything looked mangy.

They were getting close to the Capitol. Small groups of olive-garbed, machine-gun-toting soldiers lounged on the corners.

"Diego," Crigler asked, "how would you describe the feelings here toward the United States?"

"I think it varies," and Asencio settled back into the rear seat. The car had stopped again. "There's obviously a segment of Colombian society, the bourgeois set, who are very identified with the United States and very pro-U.S."

"Bourgeois?"

"The upper-middle class. The butterflies at cocktail parties. The wealthy. Those who have condominiums in Key Biscayne. For the politicians, we are the only game in town. The technocrats dealing with trade and economic issues object to things like textile quotas, but they negotiate them because the U.S. is forty percent of Colombia's export market. There's a set of intellectuals who use the United States as a sort of abstract ideological target, as a didactic tool to show what is wrong with Colombia, in terms of economic theory. Capitalism is bad, that sort of thing. Colombia is an elitist, hierarchical society. That's true. My argument is that it isn't our fault. It's theirs. Then you have the radicals—the FARC, the M-19—who obviously are ideologically predisposed to use us as the enemy. Below that, you have the guys who want to come to the United States," Asencio started to laugh, "and that's eighty percent of the population.

"There are also those Colombians," he was serious again, "who were affected by the Alliance for Progress and the Economic Development Programs, who still have a sense of dependency, and who sort of yearn for the good old days and the Kennedy crowd. Our sharpest critics and our weakest effort is among the students and university crowd."

Asencio made a mental note to bring that up at the next staff meeting with Mike Kristula, head of the embassy's PR contingent. Was it USIA or USICA now? "Communications" was the new neutral word.

Traffic was moving again.

"Echeverri is going to talk about drugs," Asencio said. "You'll get a chance to hear the Colombian line. Have I ever told you the story about how I got this drug thing going?"

"Uh—" was all Crigler got out.

"The drug mandate had been Pete Veckey's too, before me, but no one expected anything to work."

Asencio packed and lit his pipe. "About the policy I have no feelings. If the government wants to protect the young, infirm and stupid then that's that. Personally I think people ought to have the right to go to hell in a handbasket of their own choosing. But if the government says marijuana and cocaine are dangerous, then it's my job to try and stop the traffic. Besides, druggers are very worthy adversaries.

"I had a speech I ran around giving to any Colombian who would listen about the drug traffickers forming a separate class with great liquidity and no scruples, which would eventually threaten the stability of the boys in power. I pulled numbers out of a hat. Said that eight points of their thirty percent inflation rate was due to drug money. That drugs were bigger than coffee. I pointed out that if they let things go, pretty soon their guerrilla groups would start dealing drugs for guns. That's a lot of guns. I wanted to shake them up. Who knew if any of it was true?" Diego laughed.

"Well, the turning point was the presidential election in '78. I had my eye on Julio César Turbay. I figured from everything I heard that he was going to win. And when I met him I told him that. I said I've come to the conclusion that you are going to win and I want to be your friend and he said Very wise, very wise." More laughter.

"So we had a little confidence in each other. I met with him several times before he was president. The first time he came to see me he was worried. There had been rumors raised during the campaign that he was involved in the cocaine trade. Turbay asked for a letter from me that he could publish—a sort of certificate of dignity. I asked the opposition candidate if he minded. He said no, it was for the honor of the country. So my bases were covered."

Asencio was grinning. "I said, Okay, I'll write a letter that says you hate drugs and drug trafficking, and that if you are elected president we will do great things together to fight narcotics. I looked at him and said, We will, won't we? He said yes. The letter was written, printed and made fun of by the left. But he won and was as good as his word. One month after his inauguration he sent me over to the minister of defense to put together a narcotics program. Best deal I ever did."

Asencio switched his attention to the best sight in Bogotá, the Plaza Bolívar. It was entirely stone, not a tree anywhere, and he found its massiveness an impressive sight. To the north there was the brand-new Ministry of Justice. It had been dubbed "the comb" because of its vertical stripes of light stone and dark glass. To the east there was the imposing cathedral, a flat-faced mix of Ionic, Doric and Tuscan architecture built on the site of the first simple church of the sixteenth-century colonists. The municipal building faced the square on the west side with two stories of graceful columns and arches— the first floor open, the second floor enclosed by windows. The Latin American omni-present equestrian statue of the Great Liberator, Simon Bolívar, was in the center of the square. Asencio had never seen a South American city without a Bolívar square. The Capitol building took up the south side. A product of the nineteenth-century Romanticism that had followed independence, there was no sign of any Spanish influence. It was a huge square-shaped building wrapped around a courtyard with a rather fine neo-Greek facade.

Asencio's door was opened by one of his guards almost before the car had come to a stop. He headed for the Capitol, trailing two unobtrusive Colombians and Frank Crigler.

This was the part of the job that the ambassador relished. He would say, with due immodesty, that probably he was one of the best outside men in the foreign service. Born in Spain, Asencio was bilingual and bicultural. Brought up in Newark, New Jersey, in the days when you could have a real spaghetti dinner and then go to a German beer hall and drink with the Irish, he considered himself naturally trained as a cultural relativist. His high-school yearbook read like the League of Nations roster. He didn't consider foreigners strange, just different and interesting. Even in the foreign service, he had found that that was not the ordinary attitude.

His reverie had taken him right up to Echeverri's handshake. Slight bows were exchanged, Frank was introduced, and the three men sat down at a long glass-topped wood table. Coffee was served, photographers recorded the event, Crigler got out his notebook to do the same, and Echeverri scored first:

"So I read in *El Tiempo* this morning that the sixteen million you promised to get us from your Congress for the War on Drugs is being held up while they look at our human rights violations."

"Yes, I saw Daniel Samper's column," Asencio answered. This was not going to be a meeting filled with the usual flowery Spanish rhetoric. "Such a good writer. Too bad about the quality of his reporting." Asencio thought he'd better leave it at that. There hadn't been time to check it out with Washington. And anyway he knew that most Colombian politicians thought Samper something of a gadfly communist.

"You know his brother, Ernesto Samper, just spent some time in New York," Echeverri continued, and his face, more American-looking than Asencio's, lit up with the fun he was having. "Ernesto says that everyone in the United States is smoking marijuana. Why must we have a 'war' on it here?"

"Ernesto only went to Central Park," laughed Asencio.

"Defense Minister Leyva thinks you should shoot down the narcotics planes in Florida if our army must capture marijuana truck caravans on our coast." Echeverri was grinning now.

"Thank God he is not the president," Asencio replied. Echeverri and Crigler laughed. Asencio added: "Of either country."

"And why can't you stop the contraband Marlboros coming into Colombia?" asked Echeverri. "Our cigarette market is ninety percent contraband now."

"Well," Asencio conceded, "I haven't been able to get the tobacco boys down here to discuss it with you. I'm trying. It's not my fault we make better cigarettes. What brand are you smoking these days?" More laughter.

"Seriously," Asencio continued, "I think we are doing well with narcotics. The price for marijuana has tripled since your boys started the interdiction program. You know all we need to win the 'war' is to make life unpleasant enough so they'll move to another country. Maybe Venezuela." Echeverri laughed with Asencio. Frank's smile, Asencio noticed, looked more like a grimace. Washington hated it when the ambassador said he just wanted to move the traffic out of Colombia and he didn't care where. Diego had promised not to say it anymore, but he meant it.

If Echeverri had scored first, Asencio was going to score last. The courtesy call was coming to a close:

"Not to worry. The traffic will shift—maybe back to the States where you all would love to see it go anyway. The stuff Hawaii is putting on the market is much higher quality than yours."

Echeverri acknowledged the barb with a nod and announced a little surprise of his own. "The Foreign Relations Committee is meeting. I told them you would be by to say a few words."

Asencio knew it was a set-up. The press would be there, and it would be grill-the-American-ambassador time. That was fine. He enjoyed the Colombian pols and he knew the feeling was mutual.

The Senate Foreign Relations Committee was sitting, waiting, right next door. It was a small room, packed with a jumble of office furniture in no particular order. File cabinets with stacks of yellowed dusty papers were jammed into what had once been graceful window bays. Metal desks lined the walls. A beautiful old crystal chandelier hung in the center of the room. But since it was capable of lighting no more than a black-tie ball, fluorescent light bulbs had been stuck midway on the walls between each window. Oil portraits of knobby-kneed Spanish "ancestors" looked as forlorn as the floor-length red draperies that hadn't been cleaned since Independence.

Eight committee members were seated around two tables that had been shoved together to form a T. Each senator had a cup of coffee, an ashtray, a nameplate and a microphone in front of him. Asencio fondly hoped the mikes weren't on. They would all be blasted to hell. Their nameplates faced in, rather than out. Odd.

Asencio sat down next to the committee chairman at the head of the T. Echeverri followed Asencio in, and sat down to his right.

This was going to be a pipe session. Asencio packed his and lit up, and by the time the chairman had finished asking the first question, the ambassador had surrounded himself in smoke.

"So I read in *El Tiempo* this morning that the sixteen million dollars you promised to get us from your Congress for our War on Drugs is being held up while they look at our human rights 'violations.' "

To keep from laughing, Echeverri lit a cigarette.

Asencio gazed at him good-naturedly through all the smoke, shifted his pipe to the left side of his mouth, and whispered, "How's your Marlboro?"

Nancy Asencio did not feel great.

It was pitch black outside the plane. Thank God she couldn't see the mountains. Colombia's mountains . . . Colombia . . .

She wanted another glass of wine. She never drank, ordinarily, but the thought of coming back to Bogotá . . . Mrs. Asencio had spent a month in Florida with the kids, cooking her own meals, driving her own car, not having to be guarded, or on guard twenty-four hours a day. She and Diego had a little house in Port St. Lucie. Her own home . . .

Colombia had been such a disappointment. Oh, she liked the country and the people well enough, but she had thought Diego was going to be sent back to Washington. She had been finally going to get a degree in psychology at the University of Maryland. With the kids all grown, she could have done all sorts of things.

Diego had asked her if she wanted him to take the post. If she had hesitated, she wouldn't have understood at all what Diego had stood for all these years. Ever since they had become engaged she had known what he wanted. He'd been a protection welfare officer in Mexico, a political officer in Panama, special assistant to the assistant secretary of state for Inter-American Affairs in Washington, political officer in Lisbon, political counselor in Brasilia, deputy chief of mission in Caracas, and then they had asked him whether he would like to be ambassador in Colombia. It didn't matter where. He was going to be an ambassador.

Nancy wondered if there had ever been a successful man who had considered his family as much as himself. She was of the "Father Knows Best" vintage. Maybe she was wrong, but she thought Diego was the sort, if his wife had not gone along, whose marriage would have ended in divorce, and who would simply have continued his career. His career was the thing. In his kind of job the man is sent and the woman goes along. There's a new trend now, where wives want to stay in Washington. Women are more sophisticated now. In a few years they'll probably find out that they had other problems. You can't be without problems.

Here was the stewardess with the glass of wine to help her with today's problems. Looking out the window at the inky blackness she had the feeling she was in a time machine.

She'd been nineteen when she married Diego. That was in 1953. He had already taken the foreign service exam. When he'd gone for his orals, after their wedding, they had told him that since he was eligible for the draft, they wouldn't take him in. He'd had no job when they got married. No—he had gotten a job with Prudential as an underwriter two weeks before the wedding.

Two years later he went to Texas with the army. It had been like the beginning of foreign service. All the Easterners would gather together. After the army he contacted the State Department as he'd been told to do. Diego had asked the FBI please not to let Prudential know that he was going into the foreign service because they'd been so nice and given him a subsidy those army years. So right away the FBI figured there was something wrong and they went right to it. Prudential offered him another job with more money. She was expecting her third child. They were living with her in-laws in New Jersey.

Diego asked her, What do you think of the State Department? What do you think of Prudential? Her response was always, I can make a home in Timbuktu, but it's your career. What you want to do is most important. Don't worry if the kids' shoes aren't tied right. They don't know any better. The main thing is for you to be happy in your work. She'd never to her knowledge influenced him in a post. Anybody crazy enough to have five kids in five years . . .

The wine was making her melancholy.

Finally they called him and said, Okay, name three places you want to go and, of course, he said Madrid, Argentina and Paris. They assigned him to Washington because she was pregnant. Diego was so disappointed. After number four was born, they went to Mexico and produced number five. Diego was making $5,700 a year. Actually the foreign service made bringing up the kids easier. She'd had maids everywhere, and she could say that her children had opportunities for wider horizons. Different countries. Different values. She hoped they'd benefited by it.

Nancy thought they had a strong family unit compared to her sister, who was married to an executive who traveled for months at a time, leaving her all alone in Ohio. At least overseas her husband had been with her.

Things had changed in the foreign service. Nancy remembered the first post in Mexico. It was like arriving at a new school. You were given the rules and told what to do. You take out your little white gloves . . . She had four babies when she arrived in Mexico. One of the embassy wives would come over to babysit while she made her calls. First, you called on the ambassador's wife. She'd received Nancy and it was lovely. Then you went to see the DCM's wife. A long list followed. Mexico was a huge post. She'd put on her gloves and hired a cab.

The list included all the wives of section heads, which days they received, at what time. Since she was Cuban-born, Nancy was Spanish-speaking. She would ring the doorbell, the maid would come to the door and say, I'm sorry, the lady says she is not in—*La señora dice que no está*. You wrote on the proper side of your calling card, in pencil, your address and phone number and turned in the right-hand corner. She remembered a friend who said she used to turn both corners and punch it full of holes. By the end of day, no one had received her. Then she'd come to the consul general's house. His wife was wearing slacks, the maid was off, she was making cookies or something. She opened the door herself, took her into the kitchen, sat her down, and Nancy had almost wept.

She'd never seen Diego in Mexico. He'd get home at 9:30 at night, want just a sandwich, read some and go to bed. Then he'd want her to go with him on business trips, like to Acapulco. You couldn't leave the maid with all those kids. Diego would say, Well, I'm inviting you, if you don't want to come that's it. And he'd go off and all she'd think of was the secretaries in their skimpy bikinis. She was a thirty-two-year-old woman with five kids.

In the old system some of her friends complained that if you didn't go to a party with your husband the embassy would call up and chew you out. Nobody had ever called her. She'd never felt she had to do every little party and she hadn't. Diego was supportive. Some of the men had turned their wives into alcoholics. She had good common sense. She hadn't even needed the letter that came in 1971, or was it 1972, stating that wives were no longer part of their husbands' efficiency reports. *Mrs. Asencio is very cooperative with her husband, entertains well, is an asset to her husband.*

When Diego was assigned to Bogotá, her niece had told her that if she was going for Diego's sake, she should do something for her own sake while she was there. She had started painting lessons. Everybody in her class knew her only as "Nancy La Cubana." It was exciting to be incognito. It was also safer. Besides, a lot of the glamour of the foreign service was gone anyway, the ambassador as king, the ambassador's wife as queen. It suited her.

The stewardess was saying that they were getting ready to land in Bogotá. Nancy pulled out the roller skates her daughter had given her in Florida. A few people stared. First she put on the red socks, then the blue and yellow skates. She had a little trouble tying them. Now the thing to do would be to wait until everybody got out.

The stewardess couldn't believe her eyes. A voluminous, grinning middle-aged lady wearing a cape was skating down the aisle.

"Uh, maybe I can help?"

"Nope. Manage myself."

Nancy got to the door fine. She could see Diego staring incredulously at her, at the bottom of the ramp. One step. Another step. Whoops . . . missed that one. "No thanks," Nancy started to giggle. "No help needed."

3

"Do you see the guy sitting there staring at his crotch?" Dick Weeks cupped his hand over his mouth and leaned toward the Peace Corps director, Richard Baca. "He's checking to see if the hair he put in his zipper this morning is still there. If it's not, then someone's been in his fly. That's one of our CIA agents."

Baca let out a belly laugh, gratefully. Humor was at a premium at 10 a.m. every Friday. It was Howdy Doody country meeting time. Hi there, boys and girls . . .

There were about a dozen people seated around a rectangular table in the conference room. The conference room was just on the other side of the bullet-proof glass door with the cipher lock that led into the ambassador's and DCM's office area. Baca marveled at the room's lack of character. It was a wonder how government-issue wood furniture always looked like brown plastic. Shit. Maybe it was. The walls were cream, the no-plush rug rusty green. Beige curtained windows lined one wall, and black-and-white photographs of former ambassadors lined the opposite wall. The ex-ambassadors looked as if they were staring out the window. Nice that someone had opened the curtains for them.

Baca glanced around the table as the troops jabbered and waited for the arrival of the ambassador. He'd formed a few opinions in six months.

All embassies were divided into two parts. The insiders and the outsiders. Baca did not by any means consider himself an embassy expert, just an observer, but it didn't take much to notice the resentment that flowed constantly between the two groups. The insiders were the foreign service types who made friends with the movers and shakers of Colombia's oligarchy. The outsiders were the social program people, from government agencies other than the State Department. The twain rarely joined. The foreign service officers held that embassy involvement in social programs was interventionism, and interventionism was not taken kindly by the host-government people they were trying to communicate with. Something like that. Baca couldn't really find a right or wrong to it, but if an embassy is "the way governments talk to each other"—Asencio's definition—then it made some sense. He did wonder, and he knew he didn't wonder alone, how Diego figured that his drug program wasn't interventionism. He was sure Asencio had an answer for that. He had an answer for everything.

Baca himself was an outsider. As director of the Peace Corps he was semi-autonomous. It was the first defense against the danger of the host country's accusing corpsmen of being CIA agents. There wasn't any last defense. Suspicion was rampant. The Peace Corps was headquartered in a house a few miles north of the embassy, in a well-to-do, but not ostentatious, residential section of Bogotá.

Baca knew some of the people around the conference table. Others, he just knew of. Dick Weeks, of the crotch line, had a reputation for being one of the best officers in the embassy. He was the budget and fiscal man. An FSO4 at age forty-eight, he wasn't going to make ambassador. But he seemed to enjoy his work. He'd left a farm in New Hampshire to see the world and in twenty years he'd been to thirteen posts, most of them unpronounceable. What could you say about a man whose greatest joy was buying "the first embassy computer system in the southern hemisphere," and *then* telling the State Department that he'd done it?

Weeks was sitting next to his boss, Frank Ravndal. Somebody had to. Ravndal was third-generation foreign service. His grandfather had been a consul, his father an ambassador. Frank was the embassy's administration officer, and he was old enough to know that he wasn't going to follow in his father's footsteps. Now Frank just wanted to be a DCM. Baca had to admit that Ravndal had as nasty a job as his generally nasty disposition. The embassy in Bogotá was middle-sized: there were about 115 Americans and more than 200 Colombians. Almost all the professional and personal logistics, at least in the case of the Americans, was Frank's responsibility—the houses they lived in, the typewriters they typed on, the couches they sat on, the cars they drove around in, the school their kids went to. "Morale" was considered a problem, and many people traced the problem to Ravndal's attitude. Frank thought the junior officer generation of the foreign service was a bunch of spoiled, "coddled" brats and he told them so. Often. They had dubbed him, in turn, "Ratso" Ravndal. "In the old days . . ." was Frank's favorite intro, and he himself had transferred his affections from the State Department to the golf course years ago.

Frank's job was not made any easier by his general services officer, Ellis Glynn. GSO is supposed to share the administrative load with the admin officer. Glynn had ten Colombian staffers and he spoke no Spanish. His line was that English "was spoken but not understood" in his office, and that problems with cars and household goods that arrived months late from the States were not his fault. What they had in GSO was a failure to communicate. Glynn was retiring after his stint in Bogotá.

Chuck Boles sat next to Glynn, looking glum.

That was his natural demeanor. Baca liked Boles and he felt sorry for him. At age thirty-nine Boles looked sixty-two. He was the embassy's security officer. The embassy compound and all the people and papers in it were his responsibility. He was an ex-marine who saw communist terrorists around every corner. Boles liked to hang around the Israeli embassy guys whenever he could, because he figured they were the crackerjacks of the terrorist business. Boles chain-smoked for his nerves and ate Gelusil for his ulcers. He had been the security officer in Afghanistan when Ambassador Adolph Dubbs had been kidnapped and killed. He'd "lost one," is how it was put. There were the obvious black jokes around the embassy, about how safe everyone felt in the hands of a man with Boles's record, but no one told them to his face. Any reference to his "friend," "Spike" Dubbs, brought tears to Chuck's eyes.

The military men sat together. Baca didn't really know them. There was the defense attaché and the air attaché. And there was Colonel Carl Wittenberg, who headed an American Service contingent, called the "Milgroup," that worked directly with the Colombian military in the Ministry of Defense building. Baca smiled, remembering Dick Weeks's line about the embassy military types. He called them "dumb, gutless imbeciles who are all a waste of budget money." That certainly was one view.

There was a whole series of agency people: the agricultural attaché, the mapmaker guy, the head of the United States International Communications Agency, and a guy from the Federal Highway Agency. This was the kind of proliferation that drove Frank Ravndal nuts. Foreign service officers were the minority in the embassy population.

The consul general, Ken Keller, was a nice guy, and married to a Colombian.

Dave Burnett sat next to John McIntyre. Must have been the last seat John could find. Burnett headed Bogotá's Drug Enforcement Agency office, and McIntyre was the State Department's narc coordinator. To say there was no love lost between them was an understatement. McIntyre considered the DEA agents "cowboys." Burnett smoked a pipe and wore three-piece suits, but he'd never finished college and McIntyre's attitude hit him where it hurt. Their enmity was cemented by a bureaucratic fight between the DEA and State for control of the narc turf.

George Thigpen was a nice old man with six kids who was the economics/commercial counselor. He ran what could be best described as a "distracted" department. Baca had never heard George finish a sentence.

Next to Thigpen was Neil Billig, from A.I.D. The Agency for International Development had cut its budget so low for Colombia that a few years earlier they were invited to leave, effective mid-1980. Billig was into "pick and shovel" roads and the plight of the farmers. He knew that, for the embassy crowd, a "field" trip meant traveling to the Carulla super-market, and he had no illusions about the future of any A.I.D. programs once the agency was gone. Neil Billig held a different view of the FARC guerrilla group from the embassy "insiders." He had been in Nicaragua when the Sandinistas "weren't worth much either." The embassy did not appreciate his view. A.I.D. only had a couple of months left in Bogotá, and Neil was trying to get the econ section to look at the status of Colombia's social programs. "It will only take a minute," Neil would say. He was bending Thigpen's ear right now. George looked dis-tracted.

Dr. Miller, the medical officer, arrived and took a seat. He would be worth a few remarks about Bogotá's Andean altitude. Forget the FARC. Thin air was the enemy.

Frank Crigler came in. Baca and Crigler were friends, as were their wives. It was a small embassy scandal that a DCM would socialize with a lowly Peace Corps director. That had been Baca's first glimpse into how the inside-outside thing really worked.

And next to Crigler was John Simms, political counselor. They hated each other. Simms considered Frank Crigler a young upstart who had the job Simms should have gotten and Frank, Baca knew, considered Simms one of the worst political officers he'd ever seen. According to Frank, Simms got only what information came to him. Passive, instead of active. Frank had told Baca that Simms's reports were drab and dreary, and Baca had noticed that Simms's lips were always just an inch from Asencio's ass.

The ambassador arrived. Asencio considered the country team meeting a chance to "cross-fertilize." It was also a way for him to try to keep control over all the agency people who didn't work in the embassy proper. Asencio was good at creating a sort of us-against-them attitude—all of his boys in the field against all of their bosses in Washington. When that didn't work Asencio played the State Department off against whatever agency was challenging his authority. The old my-daddy-in-Washington-is-bigger-than-your-daddy-in-Washington approach. Diego understood power and how to use it. Baca thought he was impressive. Crigler too, in a different way. Crigler's talent was as a nuts-and-bolts man. He was not the politician Diego was. As DCM, he was supposed to keep the embassy staff's gears greased, while Diego maneuvered the Colombians.

Baca had talked to Crigler about maybe joining the foreign service. All you had to do was get shit-faced every night and make deals. You lived as if you had money though you didn't. He could do that.

The meeting was coming to order. Asencio would start with either a dirty joke or a science-fiction scenario.

"I've got it," Asencio began. "I've got an idea that goes beyond 1984. In a completely totalitarian society how would you handle absolute control—that at the same time would allow you to solve some of society's problems? Nobody would be happy. But everybody would be docile.

"What you do is eliminate the orgasm. . . ."

Phil Ferris ran up the three flights of stairs between the consular and political section. He placed himself directly in front of the small window in the door, and rang the bell. Looking into a mirror that allowed her to see around the corner, one of the section's two secretaries could identify him and buzz him through the cipher-lock door. Admittance to the political section was by invitation only—at least until Monday, when Phil would make his career switch from consular to political. In preparation for his new job, he had been invited for a political briefing. Any time Friday afternoon, John Simms had said. On Monday, when he started working in the section, he would have the five-number code that would release the lock from the outside. No more standing at the window.

Ferris walked down the short corridor and into a large room where the two secretaries, both Americans, sat. No Colombians worked here because of all the classified cables. Smaller offices opened off three sides of the room. Both women were on the phone, so Ferris stole a glance at the famous Xerox room door. There *was* a Xerox machine behind the door. And across from the Xerox machine was another door. Gray. Unmarked. Or so Phil had been told. He would soon see it for himself. That was the front door of the CIA offices.

"Yes?" said an amused secretary who had caught him looking.

"Phil Ferris here to see Mr. Simms. For a political briefing. Knock it off, Patt."

"Go right in," sang Patt, grinning, pointing toward the door on the left with her thumb.

"You look like a hitchhiker."

"Going my way?" Patt laughed. "Or are you happily married?"

Two steps and he was in John Simms's office. Ferris knew Simms by reputation only. He was about to be his boss, thought Phil, but certainly not his role model.

"Sit down, Phil. Make yourself comfortable. I'm just going to sort of ramble through this. If you have questions, stop me any time.

"We consider Colombia a moderate government and a moderate society. There is a constitution and this constitution provides for a republican form of government with separate executive, legislative and judicial branches. It provides the right of universal suffrage and stipulates that the president is to be elected by direct popular vote for a four-year term and may not succeed himself. Turbay was elected in 1978. The president is authorized to appoint his own ministers. A vice-president or *designado* is elected by Congress every two years. Senators and representatives are elected by popular vote.

"All of this makes little difference. The president runs the country. It is a 'democracy' only by Latin American standards.

"Have you read a history of Colombia? Do you know about *la violencia*—the twenty-year war in the forties and fifties that was a struggle for power between the Liberals and Conservatives? They killed two hundred thousand of each other off."

"Yes."

"Well, the pact that ended *la violencia*," Simms continued, "created a 'National Front' government, with the president alternately Liberal and Conservative. That National Front agreement ended in 1978 with Turbay, who is a liberal. There are enough conservatives in office, however, that his administration is still de facto National Front. There is no opposition government in Colombia, although the Liberal party has two dissident groups—both of whom attack Turbay on human rights—not just torture, but social and economic injustices. They call him repressive and a closet conservative. Gnats on an elephant.

"Democracy in Colombia does mean that people are not afraid to talk. And there is a free press. Although that can be limited. If the government gets unhappy enough with any of the newspapers, they will threaten to stop their newsprint imports. Offensive radio programs will just be yanked off the air and television doesn't matter. It's mainly reruns of 'Starsky and Hutch.' On the whole, none of this is done very often."

"What about the Catholic Church in Colombia?" asked Phil. "Are they a political factor?"

"No, and I don't know why that is," said Simms. "The hierarchy is quite conservative and the clergy more liberal. But as an institution the Church is politically inactive. Back in '65, I think it was, there was a priest, Camilo Torres, who was quite charismatic. He was well educated, from a socially prominent family and seemed capable for a while of uniting the radical left factions against the National Front government. His efforts were fruitless, however, and four months after joining a guerrilla group in the mountains, he was killed in a skirmish with an army patrol."

That seemed like a good reason for the Church to get out of politics, Phil thought.

"The army is obviously provokable. But, as Latin

American societies go, they are civilist. There was only one military coup in Colombia and it was short-lived. Army prestige is low at the moment because they spend so much of their time fighting other Colombians—the guerrillas, and now the drug traffickers."

Simms stopped and looked at Ferris.

"Do you know about the state of siege?"

"Vaguely," Phil answered.

"Under a state of siege," Simms droned, "the government has broad powers to arrest and detain people to preserve public order. Curfews can be imposed, demonstrations banned, the sale of liquor stopped. Under the state of siege, those accused of certain crimes can be held up to ninety days in jail without a trial. Quite frankly, under a state of siege all existing laws can be suspended. The state of siege is declared in the case of war or internal disturbances. Colombia has been under such a state on and off for the last thirty years. We are under one now. It's the foot in the door for human rights activists.

"Which brings us to the guerrilla groups."

Ferris watched Simms's mouth move.

"The rural guerrillas are the FARC, the Colombian Revolutionary Armed Forces, which is pro-Moscow and is supplied through the Communist party, which the Communist party denies; the EPL, the Popular Liberation Army, which is Peking-oriented but only gets moral support from China—and since Colombia will probably soon recognize the People's Republic of China, that moral support may disintegrate; and the ELN, the Army of National Liberation, which has been weakened by internal rifts. Originally the ELN received money and supplies from Havana and espoused the views of Castro and Ché Guevara. But Havana has turned its attention to the FARC now. The urban guerrillas are the

M-19, thought to be composed of professional people, and the Workers Self-Defense Movement, MAO, which at one time claimed responsibility for the bombing of the Marine House last spring. Their targets are 'fascism,' the 'oligarchy' and 'American Imperialism.' Among all five groups their membership is only in the thousands. There's not much indication of popular support. They are more a remnant of the past, the *violencia* type thing, than a portent of the future. The rural groups are irritants, and have been controlled fairly easily by sporadic encounters with army patrols. The urban groups are terrorists and, through kidnappings and assassinations, have created a much more substantial threat. However, since so many of the M-19s have been rounded up since the arsenal robbery, their present status is doubtful. The MAO hasn't been heard from in months.

"After Managua," Simms stopped for emphasis, "a cable came down from Washington that said 'No more surprises.' No more Irans, no more Nicaraguas. Our job is not to get into a 'who lost Colombia?' situation."

"Well then," Ferris asked "why are you so sanguine about the guerrillas?"

Simms smiled. There was a hint of condescension. "Our desk officer in Washington, Eileen Heaphy, says it best. She has annual policy reports dating back to the early sixties. The first reaction is 'The government is falling, the government is falling.' And then the blasé sets in. Eileen calls it her 'fun drawer.' There is a great deal of discontent in Colombia, that's true. The rampant crime rate in the cities is more of a manifestation of it than the guerrilla activity. But the discontent is unfocused. And there is no Khomeini out there. If the guerrilla groups could ever unite—that would be one thing. There have been attempts, all failures. And I suppose there's a possibility of what is called 'Uruguayization' where the army overreacts, repression is charged, and then the guerrilla groups start attracting large membership. More repression follows and etcetera. What happened in Uruguay in the sixties was that eventually the army just took over the country in the name of internal security.

"The other spot to watch is Labor. There are four national federations. One is openly Moscow-communist. One is communist-infiltrated. Thirty percent of organized labor is independent of the federations, and tends to be Mao-Trotsky communist. In September of 1977 there was a civil strike in Bogotá, Cali and Medellín. The army poured into the streets, killed forty people and rounded up thousands. Nothing like that has happened since. Again, no leader has emerged.

"I'm sorry," Simms said. "I've gone on too long. It's almost five o'clock and time to go home. Let me just quickly wrap up.

"The embassy's country plan, briefly," he sped on, "is to help preserve and improve Colombia's democracy and pro-U.S. feelings. The poor are not our job. Nor the economic section's.

"Our links with Colombia are that we are their biggest licit and illicit market—mainly coffee, marijuana and cocaine. And cut flowers. They love to visit Disney World and stay as illegal aliens. And the Colombian Government loves to see them go. Unemployment is high here. Most of the spillover slips into Venezuela, where there are jobs. If Venezuela ever kicks these people back to Colombia, that might create a tinder box. We also lobby Colombia to vote with us in the United Nations. There's been real pressure since the signing of the Mid-East treaty to get the Colombians to side with us and Egypt against the rest of the Arab world. Colombia prefers to abstain. They don't care about Egypt and ordinarily I doubt it makes a difference. There's a psychological U.S. dependency rooted in their history that I suspect the Colombian Government would like to break off. The country can be called, by the way, neither developed or undeveloped. The cities are highly industrialized. The countryside is without electricity.

"The summation of our foreign policy is democracy, narcotics, Quita Sueño and commerce. We've run through the democracy area. Narcotics, well, you've heard the ambassador's line. Drugs are dangerous to Colombia because they foment corruption, which foments revolution, and besides they cheapen the culture. Fifty percent of Ambassador Asencio's time is spent on drugs. Quita Sueño is a territorial treaty issue. It is a group of guano cays that the U.S. is relinquishing all rights to. Know what guano is? Birdshit. We've been trying to get the Senate to ratify the treaty since 1972. We'll talk about that later. The embassy is not really involved except as a target of Colombia's displeasure at the delay. It's a point of tension here, but it's Washington's problem. The commercial foreign policy is a question of tariffs and airline routes and fuel prices. That sort of thing. And then there's human rights. I personally am against selective butting in, but Heaphy, our desk officer, used to work in State's Bureau of Human Rights. She's gung ho on the subject. And so is our DCM, Crigler. Washington only pays attention to two things in Colombia: drugs—because Ambassador Asencio has taken an instruction and turned it into a policy—and human rights, because of Heaphy, and of course our president, Jimmy Carter.

"We can go into more of that later when you start writing the congressional report. The report is a pain in the ass. It's useless because it's unclassified. We write it mainly from a file of Colombian newspaper clips. We don't want to upset the Colombians so that they aren't speaking to us anymore. This year, because of the M-19 roundup, we know there have been more human rights violations than usual. It'll be difficult. The embassy is the man in the middle. Even with nothing of importance in it, the report is always too soft for Washington and too tough for Colombia. It would be intolerable without Ambassador Asencio. He keeps Washington at bay.

"We'll talk more on Monday after you've run through the clip file. Let's get out of here."

John McIntyre, the embassy's narc coordinator, was on the phone when the bugle blew. Three seconds later he was standing red-faced and furious in front of the bugler.

"McIntyre," said customs agent Clay Allison, "welcome to the five o'clock Friday afternoon happy hour in the customs cave!"

"Do you know that I was on the phone when that goddamned instrument went off?" screamed McIntyre.

"No lie," Clay said.

"And do you know that it was a minister of the Colombian Government I was talking to? He could hear the bugle! He asked me what that noise was!" McIntyre realized he was sputtering. God, he hated these goddamn cowboys.

"Call him back and tell him that it was a Czech cavalry bugle." Clay was having a good time.

"I absolutely forbid any bugle blowing or drinking in this office," said McIntyre.

"Come here," Clay said, putting his arm around McIntyre's shoulders. "Now do you see this plaque on the wall? Read it out loud, John."

McIntyre read the top line: "Institute for Abnormal Behavioral Study."

"Keep reading," Clay said benevolently.

"In recognition," McIntyre read, "of the abbreviated period it has taken U.S. Customs adviser, Harry M. Allison, a.k.a. 'Tio Clai,' to create a muddled vast abyss and total chaos among Foreign Service Office personn—"

"Now we in customs," said Clay, "do not recognize the authority of the State Department to order us to do or not to do anything and if you come into this office again I will throw you out the window."

McIntyre whirled and stormed back down the hall.

Allison and his customs partner, Bobby Herrera, doubled up with laughter, faced south and toasted the embassy, just visible two blocks away.

All of the narcotics staff—two customs agents, a dozen DEA agents and two State Department "coordinators"—worked out of the top two floors of the twenty-story UGI office building. The building was more dangerous than the job. The architecture was an engineer's nightmare. Built from a central core, the corners of the building were supported by a suspension system. As you walked from the center of the building to any of its four corners you walked downhill some five inches. In order to keep drawers from falling open, desks had to be put up on blocks. One of the DEA agents had tried to move a file cabinet once and was told he needed a building engineer to approve it. If he didn't place the file cabinet directly over a steel beam, the thing would fall nineteen floors to the ground.

The "cowboys" had started arriving for the happy hour and Clay was regaling them with the McIntyre encounter.

"Watch your step," yelled Clay, "don't get near the windows or you'll tip the building over. What would McIntyre say!

"Hey Bobby, remember the protocol bit last month?" Clay didn't wait for an answer; he had a captive audience. They'd all heard the story before, but it was good enough to be worth a repeat. "Well see, we're at this luncheon at Crigler's house. Diego was there. I don't remember what the occasion was but Bobby had to leave for a two o'clock meeting. So, Christ, when it came time he got up and left. When he got back to the UGI building McIntyre came storming in here and said, 'How could you do something like that? Just getting up and leaving?' You're supposed to whisper"—Clay dropped his voice to a whisper—"to the host that you have to leave, who then whispers to the ambassador. Jesus! Fuck that! So McIntyre hands this protocol manual to Bobby and says, 'Read this!' Bobby ripped the cover off, crumpled it up and ate it. We thought McIntyre was going to have a coronary right there!"

Somebody's voice emerged from the laughter. "Yeah, but what did Asencio think about Bobby leaving the luncheon?"

"Diego?" said Clay. "He said he hadn't noticed and couldn't care less about the protocol. But would we quit picking on McIntyre?"

"Awwwwww . . ." came a whole chorus.

"Let's get out of here," Clay said, putting the whiskey away. "Let's go get Tom Aldana and take him down to the whorehouse."

Gales of laughter greeted that suggestion. Aldana, one of the DEA dozen, had recently gotten himself rolled by a prostitute. He said he was "working a tip." Tom had lost his gun and badge. The boss, Dave Burnett, had covered for him with DEA in Washington but Tom's wife had told the story to everyone.

Emily Roth did not feel great. There were mountains as far as the eye could see outside her apartment window. In between her and the mountains was half of the city of Bogotá. She'd been in Colombia for almost two weeks and she wasn't so sure anymore that this was going to be such a great tour. Emily was having trouble adjusting to the country and to the embassy. That wasn't like her, and she just couldn't put her finger on what was wrong.

She looked around her apartment. She was on the twenty-third floor of a modern high-rise building on Carrera Séptima, one of Bogotá's main thoroughfares. The embassy's FLO office—Family Liaison Office—had found her the apartment. Jeannie Kuhlman was a sharp lady. Emily had never had to deal with papers or real estate agents. It was a small, two-bedroom place, very nice, with spectacular views of the city to the north and west. The apartment represented all of the things she loved about the foreign service. Her housing allowance as a single FSS8 was $7,100 a year, which just covered the rent. She had a $400 drapery allowance, and because the apartment was small, she had been able to buy very beautiful white lace curtains. A woman came and cleaned once a week for 250 pesos, which, at the going rate of about forty-four pesos to a dollar, was about six dollars. Emily had been left some furniture by the Colombian who had sublet the apartment, and she had asked for the rest of what she needed—a bedroom set, a dining-room set, a living-room couch and two chairs—from the GSO warehouse. She had asked for a green couch and two gold chairs. She'd gotten a brown couch and two magenta chairs. The GSO people said that's all they had unless she wanted to wait. She didn't want to wait. She had switched the landlord's and GSO's stuff around and the apartment now looked quite nice.

Emily looked out the window and watched dusk fall over the city. And then she looked down at the pizza she'd brought up from the pizza parlor downstairs. Maybe that's what was wrong. From the twenty-third floor Colombia was all right. Pretty, even. Up close things began to fall apart. The pizza, for instance—cheese and mushrooms—looked and smelled all right. But when you picked up a slice, the cheese broke up into small viscous chunks and took the mushrooms with it. Whatever you managed to get into your mouth before it fell into your lap was sort of tasteless. Bogotá looked like a copy of the United States—high rises, suburbs, shopping malls—and yet it wasn't. The telephones looked the same as in the U.S., but they didn't always work. Street lights were red and green but nobody paid attention to them. It was disorienting. That must be part of the problem.

And the fact that Emily was home alone on a Friday night, she knew, was another part of the problem. But she had always attacked problems in her life before. Now she was listless and vaguely depressed. She wasn't sleeping. Her stomach was always upset. Dr. Miller said it was the altitude.

Emily got up and went into her bedroom to get her diary. Maybe that would hold some clues to her unnatural lack of enthusiasm.

She stopped in the bathroom on the way back to the living room to get a bottle of Mylanta. She sipped straight from the bottle and started to read the diary aloud.

JUNE 29. I had a lovely day, and I'm very happy to be in Bogotá. I was picked up yesterday at the airport and put in lovely temporary quarters near the embassy. I'm so content. Today the two front-office secretaries, Ingrid and Alva, took me out for the day. We went to Ingrid's for a drink and then out to lunch. I had chicken and rice. We had sangria and then I went back to Ingrid's apartment. Ingrid is the ambassador's secretary and she lives on the tenth floor of a high rise that overlooks the bullring in downtown Bogotá. We saw an amateur bullfight, as the high season is in December. I enjoyed it. Ingrid is nice. We stopped on the way home at the Marine House. It's beautiful. I know I'm going to thoroughly enjoy Bogotá.

Sarcasm had crept into Emily's voice on the last line. That wasn't like her.

JUNE 30. Several people phoned. Tomorrow my boss, George Thigpen, is taking me to lunch and sightseeing. Had another nice day. The weather was nice. I saw the embassy—very modern. I also saw the commissary. It's minute. You have to buy almost everything locally, and lots of things are a bit more expensive. But you can get almost everything. Supermarkets are lovely. So is Unicentro, which is a brand-new mall, complete with a Sears store. I bought a Colombian doll to add to my world collection. Bogotá is a very cosmopolitan city. I dreamt last night that I was going to marry Paul again. But that I didn't love him. Why am I dreaming about my ex?

JULY 1. I had a lovely day with the Thigpens. They picked me up at 11:30 and took me to see their house. We had a drink and some nibbles. Beautiful house, six kids. Then we went to a roadside restaurant in a nearby village, to the salt cathedral—an underground cavernous church that gave me the chills—and back to the house for a drink at home. It was very nice of them and I certainly appreciated it. Tomorrow, it's work.

JULY 4. Two days at work and I'm frustrated and disgusted. And I received a violation. The marines here love to rifle through in-boxes of Americans who work near Colombians. One of them found some classified paper in mine, unprotected—I don't know where I was—and reported it. The econ section is very disorganized. Will I ever get through the debris? My boss is a nice guy, but not very organized. I'm supposed to develop in three months a system "whereby the section will operate in a more organized, efficient fashion." In six months I'm supposed to develop a "new efficient workable filing system" and I'm supposed "to contribute to the maintenance of high morale in the section between the nationals and the Americans by cooperating, sharing the workload, creating a happier, more open atmosphere—one that will promote communication and good relations between our two countries." So far it's been traumatic and tearful. I can't wait to be adjusted. It's really turning out to be difficult. Hope it gets easier. The people are very nice, though, and that's helped. I have a date with the Colombian guy I met on the plane Friday night.

JULY 6. Thank God it's Friday! Canceled the date. "Pepe" was asking too many questions about where I worked in the embassy. He wanted to know whether I was a secretary in the narcotics or visa sections. Didn't sound as if he loved me for myself. Nuts to that. Getting a handle on why I'm having trouble with the job. The paperwork in Bogotá is overwhelming. The government loves papers. I heard from a Jewish guy in the embassy today that I should contact this rabbi because there are a lot of nice people in the Bogotá Jewish community. Still feeling trapped in my office, though, there's always classified stuff out—they classify the coffee reports in this country—and the marines hover around my door. They must get points for each violation they get on a foreign service secretary . . . Just called the rabbi . . . he invited me to a singles meeting next week. I'm going. The only way to skin a cat is to get right in there. I'm a real foreign service type.

Emily smiled at what she'd written. She did consider herself a trouper. Somewhere in the last couple weeks she'd lost it.

JULY 7. Cocktail party tonight at the new DCM's house. Crigler is a very nice guy. Very, very shy. He's a music major and is going to play Sky Masterson in the American Society of Bogotá's theater group production of *Guys and Dolls*. He asked me to come and try out for a part.

JULY 8. I slept terribly because of the wine I had, and then found out I had flea bites. Ugh. Welcome to the foreign service. I took my first bus. That must be where I picked the fleas up. Bogotá has some lovely areas. Bob Pastorino, the commercial officer, was in today. He was out all last week because of his mother's death. He's very nice and an ally. He's at least human. I can talk to him.

Emily skipped through some entries and then started reading again.

JULY 12. Went to the rabbi's singles meeting last night. Oh my God, am I brave. A couple people spoke English but most spoke Spanish. It was torture. Mine's just not that fluent yet. And then some guy stood up and delivered a lecture—on ecology! In Spanish! I nearly died. It was like what the hell am I doing here? No more.

Emily skipped again.

JULY 14. Believe it or not, one of the guys at the singles thing called. He's a Colombian and he asked me if I wanted to go to the Unicorn *mañana*. The Unicorn is supposed to be a wonderful disco. I said yes.

JULY 15. I'm all dressed and ready to go. First time I've felt good in days. Work is getting better. Pastorino is a young guy. A soul mate.

JULY 16. The Colombian never showed. I called Jeannie Kuhlman, I was so upset. She asked me, "Well, what exactly did he say?" I told her that he said "*Voy llamarle mañana*"; that's "I'll call you tomorrow," isn't it? She just laughed and laughed. *Mañana* in Colombia doesn't mean the same as "tomorrow" does in English. It just means sometime in the future. . . .

Emily closed the diary and put it away. She'd gotten so low that yesterday she'd gone to get her cards read. The lady had told her that she was bright, pure of heart, liked at work, afraid to be hurt and going through many changes. She said that Emily would get a promotion in two months and would meet a new man soon. Someone would propose in December. She'd marry and have three children. A boy first and then two girls. She told Emily that she would be very happy. Right now, she'd said, she had not gotten over a past love. Emily wondered whether she meant her ex, or the Greek.

Maybe Bogotá was a good thing. She had gone into the foreign service expecting everything—romance, excitement and travel. And she'd gotten it in Greece. Colombia was the other side of the coin. All posts weren't going to be like Greece. Maybe now her expectations would be more realistic.

It was only about 9:30 but Emily was tired. She was always tired here. She got up and moved toward the bedroom, although she knew a good night's sleep was not a realistic expectation.

4

"HEY LISTEN, TOP," Asencio said to the marine standing in front of his desk, "would you tell your boys at the front door—uh, Post One—to take it easy? I hear they're getting a little nasty to embassy visitors."

"Well, Mr. Ambassador," answered Master Gunnery Sergeant Frank Wherly, "since this Teheran thing . . . you know you called them all in and told them, 'Nobody takes my embassy. . . .' "

"Then I overdid it."

"Yeah," smiled Top, "maybe so. You sure it's the visitors complaining? And not your FSOs?"

Asencio looked at Top. He was a little bald guy who loved his job as mother, father, chaplain, career counselor and you-name-it to his marines. Twenty-three guys had passed through Bogotá in the last twelve months.

"Listen," Top was saying, "I'll tell the guys to lay off but you know I'm getting four or five complaints a week now from the FSOs that my marines didn't buzz open the front door fast enough for them."

"I know there's no love lost between State and the marines," said Asencio, "but handle it, hm?"

"All right," and Top turned to go. "One more thing then," he said turning back around, "that I think you should know. I'm sending one of my men back to the States. He said he was too intelligent to buzz open doors for people all day. Said the marines had sold him a bill of goods on the 'romance' of embassy duty. And what did we need an embassy here for anyway? Nobody cared. Said if I didn't get him out of here, he was going to kill somebody."

"Get him out fast," Asencio said, "before I think of an FSO I'd like to get rid of."

Top left, and Diego watched his cowboys start to filter in for the 9:30 narcotics meeting.

"Hey Diego," DEA head Dave Burnett yelled across the room, "how's the book?"

Asencio got up from his desk and walked over to the table at the other end of his office. "You mean the Murphy book on the New York City Police Department?"

"Yeah," said Burnett.

"The book's okay," Asencio answered, sitting down at the table with the others. "But I haven't learned a thing I can use down here.

"Listen, Dave," he said, "I made a trip to Leticia a few weeks ago while you were in Florida. I figured, if we were going to plan an operation down there to try and cut off the cocaine base coming up from Peru and Ecuador, I wanted to see what the area looked like."

"So how did it go?" Burnett was smiling. It must have been a small circus.

"Well I flew down with Turbay's chief of staff and a platoon of Colombian marines followed me wherever I went. We stayed at the Colombian naval barracks the first night. Rather primitive. The second night I stayed at Mike Tsalickis' hotel—you know, the monkey man?—which is slightly less primitive.

"Well, Tsalickis showed us around. You can see the community in about a half hour. I met the local officials and then the navy types took me up the Amazon in their gunboats to show me what it looked like, what we'd have to troll, the inlets. The goddamn gunboat ran aground and they blew one of the engines getting it off. I wound up having to send them some spare parts from Bogotá. When we finally got off the river, Tsalickis took us to this little island where he has these thousands and thousands of reproducing monkeys. He's waiting for Colombia's permission to ship them out to U.S. laboratories so he can become a millionaire overnight. Funny guy. Buggy damn place. We crossed the border so I could get some Brazilian beer and ran into a German tourist group. God, they were telling a great story. Tsalickis has these little Indian communities set up along the river. He takes care of them, tends to their illnesses, keeps the local hospital supplied. Well, he took these German tourists out to see the Indian villages and in the middle of an 'authentic' rain dance one of the Indians slipped and fell and underneath his grass skirt was a pair of jockey shorts. Sort of ruined the primitive atmosphere. The Germans were pissed."

Asencio had the whole table laughing.

"Listen," he added, "speaking of Turbay's chief of staff, he's going to be Colombia's ambassador to the Netherlands. Too bad. He's been a very eager guy on the narcotics program.

"So John, what's up?"

"The usual," answered drug coordinator John McIntyre. "The lists of arrests and seizures from the army and the attorney general's office is up for last month but everybody's running out of money. The maintenance contract on the AG's airplanes has run out and birds are building nests in the cockpits. The army's got three out of four helicopters down. The radar we got them, the army says, never worked. Last year's few million dollars has long been spent. They want to know where the sixteen million is for this year."

"I think we're going to get it," Asencio answered. "How many congressmen have we had down here to 'look at the situation'? Rosenthal, Wolfe and Childs. We've flown them all over the Guajira so they could see the clandestine airstrips. They seemed impressed. And how many trips have I made to testify in front of Congress? You know, I told them we're working on a shoestring down here. We ask Colombia to cooperate, and then we don't. The army troops don't have any gas for the trucks. The helicopters and planes are down between maintenance contracts. It's a game. The Colombians seize six times as much cocaine as the enforcement boys in the U.S. If we're spending a billion dollars a year in the States it's absurd to argue over sixteen million for Colombia. The priorities are wrong. Tell everybody we're working on the sixteen million. Anything we can do to get that stuff back up in the air?"

"I'll work on it," said McIntyre without conviction.

"You know we're going to have problems spending the sixteen million when we get it," said Clay Allison. "Who gets what, why, the army, the air force. And the Department of State wants Colombian customs to run it. . . ."

"I know," said Asencio.

"Uh," interrupted Frank Crigler, "why don't we forget a shopping list for the sixteen million dollars and explore our rationale for the drug program? Let's get it on paper. The Colombians have started using the first shopping list we got them—the helicopters, the radio equipment and such—for things other than drugs. Which was not the deal."

Asencio ignored his DCM. "We'll worry about the sixteen million dollars when the check is in the mail."

"We wouldn't need any sixteen million if we quit this interdiction shit," said Burnett, "and destroyed the marijuana at the source."

"Oh come on, Dave," said Asencio. "We still have the Percy Amendment, remember? Paraquat is a no-no since Mexico. Turbay would let us spray anyway, he says, but if something happens, he'll say Asencio made me do it. I love the guy but . . ."

"Well," said Burnett, "the army is getting itchy.

They were supposed to be in the drug interdiction business for just a few months. It's been almost a year. They've got terrible corruption problems."

"But that first commander up in Barranquilla wasn't prosecuting the officers who were dealing," said Asencio. "They've put in a new guy, right? I know the army in drugs isn't good business, but we need their bodies. So tough shit."

"More good news," said Burnett. "The marijuana bosses in Barranquilla are getting into Quaaludes. All five families. The chemicals are coming in from Germany. The pills are being pressed in Barranquilla. Quaaludes are easier to handle than marijuana and much more profitable."

"Terrific," said Asencio.

"Hey," said Clay, "your econ counselor, George Thigpen, called me this morning. He had a five-drink lunch last Friday with the customs general. The general asked Thigpen for American captains for his gunboats; his people are corrupt. Well, for one thing, that's close to being against the Mansfield Amendment, isn't it? For another, anything that went wrong would be blamed on the American captains. Jesus, Diego, do you know what Thigpen told him? *'Sure!'* I told Thigpen absolutely not! George is nuts!"

Asencio sighed at the thought of Thigpen. "All right. Let's get out of this gracefully. Send a cable to Washington requesting the captains and then phone Washington and tell them to be sure and answer no."

"Diego," said Burnett. "Remember the army patrol that caught a nineteen-truck convoy carrying 198 tons of marijuana up on the coast?"

"Uh-oh," said Asencio.

"And remember that Julio Nasser-David himself, head of one of the five families, was sitting in one of the trucks?" Burnett continued.

"Tell me," Asencio said.

"The judge in Santa Marta released Nasser-David and his trucks," Burnett delivered with great drama, "for lack of evidence."

"Shit," was all Asencio said. "How are the prices?"

"They're still climbing," said McIntyre. "Marijuana prices are still holding at triple since the army went in."

"Well, *that's* something," said Asencio. "We have made a difference."

"I don't know, Diego." Burnett fidgeted. "The traffickers are just moving their operations a little farther south to the Llanos. That's guerrilla territory. We may be inadvertently forcing the drugs-for-guns stuff."

"Says you." Asencio stood up, ending the meeting. "I'm not convinced that's happening."

Burnett waited until they had all filed out of Asencio's office, through the glass door and down the corridor to the elevators before he turned to the Milgroup chief, Colonel Wittenberg.

"Well, Carl," said Burnett, "where was the sound of your voice in there?"

"To tell you the truth," said Wittenberg, "the Colombian military is fascinated with all the communications equipment they've been confiscating from the drug boys. Real sophisticated stuff. And they've taken over almost eighty downed planes. Some Cessna 310s, a DC-7, lots of Piper Aztecs. It's like an instant air force. Besides, the Colombians are making all this money. Nobody's getting hurt. It's like the prohibition era in the States. Those were great days. . . ."

Nancy Asencio sat in the circle of chairs with the rest of the embassy wives who belonged on the board of the U.S. Government Association, which used to be called the U.S. Women's Association, and of which the ambassador's wife was the honorary president.

"How was Florida, Nancy?" asked Bettie Crigler, who was the hostess and wife of Frank Crigler, the DCM. Bettie was tall, slim, with short black hair and terse wry humor.

"Oh, it was really great," Nancy answered ruefully. "Wish I were back there."

"Don't we all," Bettie said, and got up to tend to a new arrival.

Nancy found the DCM's house lovely and relaxing. It was one of a handful of homes leased by the embassy. Everything was done in shades of beige and white and the large living room they were sitting in faced out onto a lush garden. Gardens were wonderfully easy things in Bogotá's eternal spring-like weather.

Every wife, except for Nancy, had brought a dish of food for luncheon afterwards, and Bettie was serving white wine, tea and coffee.

The last to arrive was the real president, Hadia Roberts, wife of Don, who was number two in the political section. Hadia had joined the club because there was such a morale problem among the wives, such negativity about Colombia. As their husbands moved from post to post dealing mainly with different American colleagues and various models of U.S. made typewriters, it was the wives who were left to deal with the local culture. In Colombia the sense of isolation that could cause was particularly acute because there was no compound living. Few of the American families had American neighbors. Pakistani-born Hadia enjoyed the challenge of a different language, different customs, and different vegetables in the supermarket. But she knew she was part of a minority. Most of the wives in Bogotá had retreated into a shell of bitter silence. Hadia felt something like the U.S. Government Association could be essential connective tissue. Today she was passing the presidency to a new arrival—somebody who had been dragooned into taking the job. Could only have been a new arrival, thought Hadia, unacquainted yet with Bogotá—or the embassy wives.

"So let's start," Hadia said. "June?"

"Nothing to say," picked up June, wife of David Burnett. June looked Hadia's exact opposite, blond, all-American. "I sent the minutes out from the last meeting. That's it."

"Michele?"

"Our next field trip should be to the Almacén Porcelana on Quince," answered Michele Harrison, whose husband, Jerry, worked in the consulate. "They said they would show us their porcelain factory, and they give a ten percent discount to embassy people. Oh, and the reaction to the last trip—to the Galería Cano—was really pretty good."

"The Galería," interrupted Nancy, "will lend us a film they have about how they make their jewelry. The pre-Columbian artifacts they copy and all that. We can see it in the residence basement anytime you want. They said it was about ten minutes long."

"Thanks, Nancy," Hadia said, "I feel the board makes too many of these activity decisions, but the membership in general is apathetic. How many members have we got?"

"A hundred and four," somebody called out.

"And we're only getting twenty-nine to thirty-five attendance at the meetings," Hadia said. "There are always new people coming into town. Let's get to work on the wives. When you hear somebody complaining about Colombia, bring her here. It takes other people to help. Most husbands are too tired. People tend to discover the bad things about a place when they're on their own."

"Oh, do you know," said the incoming president, Harriet Digby, "I have a nice story about Colombia.

A taxi driver stranded me at a wrong address the other day and I went and rang a doorbell and asked to use the phone. This very nice Colombian lady let me right in and then asked me where I was going and drove me there."

Murmurs of surprise greeted that story.

"I've met the taxi driver," cracked Bettie.

"Social services?" Hadia asked.

"A couple of us visited the orphanage I told you about last time," said Sandy Witter, whose husband, Bruce, worked in security with Chuck Boles. "There are about thirty-five children. The kids are bright and the place seems well organized. They need some washing machines. There's still some dues money left."

"Sounds okay," said Bettie, "but give them the machines—not the cash."

"Two more things," continued Sandy. "Those deaf people with the stone floors need rugs. We should look into that. And we're sponsoring two children at twenty-five hundred pesos a child a year at the Jardín, the kindergarten Nancy's involved in."

"Speaking of money," Hadia added, "we've been asked to do a bake sale to help buy sports equipment for the marines."

"Isn't foreign service life exotic?" said Michele.

"Bake sales remind me of lunch," said Bettie, "let's eat."

The women formed a line at the buffet table.

"Michele," asked Sandy, "how's your maid—isn't this the third one?"

"Yes, it's the third," answered Michele. "The first one was whining and insulting, the second one burned eucalyptus leaves on the stove burners— said she liked the smell. That was okay until I got pregnant and she started leaving brambles under our bed. That's some sort of voodoo and it's not nice—brambles—if you know what I mean."

"Jesus," said Sandy, "I'm not complaining about mine anymore."

"Did you hear," said Hadia, "about Iris and Manny's maid?"

"So who are Iris and Manny?" someone asked from the back of the line.

"Manny Arenes is a communicator—a fifth-floor guy," answered Hadia. "Their maid started telling everybody that Iris's youngest child was really her baby and that she was the Virgin Mary and had given a virgin birth."

"Oh my God," somebody said.

"She started bringing seedy strangers to the house," said Hadia, "and saying they were her boyfriends and introducing Iris and Manny as her parents. Manny put her in a sanitorium for a few days—but it cost a hundred dollars a day. He had to let her out. Security moved them into one of the embassy apartments, right Sandy? She's called Manny at work to try and find out where they're living."

The clucking of tongues momentarily drowned out the clinking of silverware.

"I have another maid story," Michele said. "One of the USICA junior officers, a new arrival, came home late one night and found her bathroom flooded, the sink faucet still leaking like mad. There was a note from the maid saying she didn't want to 'bother' the woman at work. It had happened at three in the afternoon! Water was just pouring out of the faucet. The maid called and said, '*No mi culpa, no mi culpa!*' Isn't that typical? But the best part was that the girl tried to call the embassy for the name of a twenty-four-hour plumber. Well of course it was ten o'clock at night and she got the marine on duty at Post One. He treated her like she was nuts—what twenty-four-hour plumber? And then she asked for somebody's home phone—a friend to come over and help her. Do you know what the marine said to her? 'Sorry, embassy personnel's home phones are classified!' "

"They are, you know," said Bettie.

"Sure, but she needed help!" said Michele. "That's a typical marine putdown. Nuts to the bake sale."

"What happened?" asked Hadia.

"She fixed it herself, finally."

"Wow!" said Sandy. "How long have we been together—two hours now—and nobody's mentioned security problems. No robberies? No Colombian strangers at the door asking where your husband works? No poisoned cats?"

"Oh there's plenty of strange stuff around," said Hadia, "but what's the use of talking about it? Your husband's boss doesn't care about neighborhood harassment. He's saving the embassy from the communists."

"I know," said Sandy, whose resentment of Chuck Boles was shared by many, including her husband.

"Really," said June, "the security 'problems' are easy except when it comes to the kids."

The groans stopped June. Because of a high kidnap rate in Colombia, embassy wives were advised not to let their children out of the house or yard unless they were accompanied by a parent. Stir-crazy kids and crazed mothers were nobody's favorite topic of conversation.

"Carla," June Burnett said to another DEA wife, "that's a new emerald ring you're wearing, isn't it?"

"Yes," said Carla, "Tom bought it for me on his last trip to Barranquilla."

"He's been making a lot of trips up there lately," said June.

"What can you do?" said Carla. "You know how it is. I trust him."

"Well, it's like my grandmother always said,"

Nancy announced brightly. "It's not like soap. It doesn't wear out."

An hour later Bettie was sipping tea with the last to leave, Hadia.

"I'd like to see us do more Colombian things— weaving, art," Bettie was saying. "I assume that's why we're in the foreign service and are abroad. We can do exercise class in the States—no offense to Nancy's exercise thing in her basement. I like her, but she's a little unorganized."

Hadia said nothing.

"This is such a loose embassy," Bettie added. "Frank keeps crabbing. He's so frustrated. Junk comes up to his desk, not written in English. I mean I'm not against affirmative action in the foreign service, but blacks and women who aren't qualified shouldn't be given the jobs. I don't like women myself and I'm not much of a club person.

"And the junior officers here—I mean there isn't any protocol left! They didn't know they were supposed to arrive early at an American-hosted party. Now if they don't, Frank tells them about it the next day."

Hadia couldn't believe the DCM's wife could be so indiscreet. She hadn't seen that much of Bettie—she and Frank were sort of new. Hadia was stunned.

Bettie didn't notice. "I love the foreign service. Where else would I have the time to weave and make jewelry? In the States, without the maids, I'd be cleaning toilets and cooking meals."

Mike Kuhlman sat behind the wheel of the car and waited. Next to him was a Colombian agent from the attorney general's office, a sharp guy, DEA-trained. Inside the house across the street was a second AG agent making a cocaine buy. It was, Mike noted, a very nice section of town.

"How long has he been in there?" asked Mike.

"Ten minutes."

"Too long. I wonder what's up."

"Wait, there he is."

"That's not the signal he's supposed to give when the stuff's put out." Mike touched his ankle to check for the .38. "What the fuck is he doing?"

"He's going back in the house."

"Listen," Mike said, "maybe he misunderstood my Spanish. He was supposed to come out and take off his jacket when the stuff was out. He came out jacketless, and now he's going back in. Check it out."

Mike watched the AG guy run around the back of the house, gun drawn.

"Fuck," he said to the dashboard.

And then he heard ten rounds go off.

"Jesus, time to get outta here!"

Mike went as far as a church on the next corner. He parked the car, got out and stood around with a few old ladies and a priest who had come out of the church to see what the noise was.

Finally Mike spotted one of the agents coming out of the house. He was standing on the curb looking around for the car. Mike strolled down the block as casually as he could.

"What's going on?"

"There weren't any drugs. Just a guy and his family watching TV in the living room."

"Shit. Then what were all the shots for?"

"A Doberman. There was a Doberman waiting when I got round back."

"Ten shots for a Doberman?"

"Yeah, I plugged him good."

Ferris wasn't dreaming. The phone was ringing. He rolled over and picked it up.

"Hello?"

"Phil?"

"Yes."

"Listen, Phil. This is Jim Welch. The marine at Post One just called. I know I'm duty-man, but it's the kid from Grosse Pointe. They've picked him up again and this time he resisted arrest."

"Fuck," said Phil. "What time is it?"

"Two o'clock."

"What am I supposed to do at two o'clock in the morning?"

"The kid wants you to come to the police station."

"Where is he?"

"He's in the one downtown, behind the Hilton Hotel."

"All right."

There was no way he was taking his car into that neighborhood, even in the daylight. Phil drove as far as the embassy parking lot and took a cab the rest of the way.

"Wait here," he said to the cabbie. "No wait. No money."

"Can't wait long."

Phil looked around before he got out onto the street. A Peace Corps volunteer had gotten beaten up somewhere around here—after living and working in the neighborhood for months. Young guys hung around smoking God knew what in dark doorways. Dogs sniffed through the garbage in the streets. There must be some movie this scene reminded him of. The blocks behind the Hilton were the place to come to for small drug deals. He wondered if that's what the Grosse Pointe kid was doing here. He usually stuck to the nicer neighborhoods in the north part of Bogotá.

The police station was as run-down as the rest of the buildings. Two steps from the cab and Phil was inside.

The kid was sitting right by the door handcuffed to a bench. He looked filthy, but he was all right.

"I want to go home," he said to Phil.

"No you don't. You just want out of here."

"No. I want to go home."

"Look, there's nothing I can do until the morning."

"It is the morning."

"It's fuckin' three o'clock! I don't know why I came. Let's just run through things here. You are twenty-three going on sixteen. You have run away from home. You are the most irresponsible human being I ever met. You checked into a nice *residencia* last month flashing a BankAmericard. You then got a Colombian kid to steal food for you from the *residencia* dining room. You stole pictures off the wall and some other guest's short-wave radio. You then tied up the night watchman and started to leave with your luggage. The hotel called the police and also called the embassy. They put you in jail. You hired some sleazy Colombian lawyer who told you it would cost you five hundred bucks to get out. You gave him Daddy's home phone in Grosse Pointe and he tried to charge Daddy ten thousand dollars. You escaped one night."

"I want to go home."

"And here you are back. Were you dealing drugs?"

"No."

"But you resisted arrest."

"Yes."

"There's nothing I can do now. Let me make some phone calls. I'll be back later this morning. Will you please not deal with the Colombian lawyer anymore? He's ripping you off."

"But I have to get out of here."

"I'll be back."

The cab was still outside. There ought to be an intelligence test in order to get a passport, Phil thought, as he climbed in the back seat.

If he could just get the kid on a plane and out of

the country. I'm going to come back here, Phil said to himself, and he'll be gone.

At 8 A.M., Phil was back. The kid was gone. The police said "some lawyer" had come for him "just five minutes ago."

5

"I DIDN'T GET the cable approved, Diego," said Eileen Heaphy.

"Good," was all Asencio said. Heaphy was his country desk officer in Washington. State Department desk officers functioned as central coordinating points for day-to-day affairs between State Main and the embassies and consulates in their assigned country. Asencio didn't care that Eileen was a woman—although the best gossip at the Department of State was done at the urinals and he knew he was losing out. He did care that she used to be staff assistant in the department's Bureau of Human Rights. She was a "believer"—a decided minority at State. That he could have done without.

"I'm not going to mention any names," Eileen was saying into the phone, "but someone who is very pro-human rights here wouldn't sign off on my cable. He said Eileen, you have to learn to be more circumspect. You write a cable that says 'reftel your report number such and such, please comment.' You just do a reftel, refer to some past cable—preferably one you didn't write—and you say please comment. Don't use the words 'human rights.' "

"Are you going to buck it to Veckey?" asked Asencio.

Veckey was assistant secretary.

"I think I could, but he got me this job to start with and I don't want to blow it early on. So I'm just going to send a letter. I wanted you to know why you're getting a letter instead of a cable. I haven't changed my mind and I hope you answer some of the questions in my letter in your human rights report." And Heaphy hung up.

"A letter," Eileen muttered to herself. Everyone knew what a letter meant. It's not a cable. It's not registered in the bureaucracy so you ignore it. That's just what Asencio would do with it, too.

As Eileen understood it, there were two ways of looking at human rights within the bureaucracy. There are the people who look at it as Jimmy Carter's little game, and it's a body count. Like the body counts in Vietnam. How many tortured this year, versus last year? Do we write a better report this year? Everything focused on the report to Congress, rather than the reason for the policy.

Then you have those, and Heaphy included herself, who feel that the policy was a major development because it wasn't a body count but a way to move the United States from the old attitude: supporting conservative right-wing regimes because they said they were anti-communist, even though they did things that were just as bad as any communist regime. It was kind of shameful to be associated with the leftists, but not with the right wingers— though they used the same tactics as the leftists— because they were anti-communist. The human rights policy gave a way to balance that approach, Eileen felt, because it looked beyond how we label other governments—democratic, authoritarian or totalitarian—to how humanely they govern.

Heaphy would call Colombia a democracy. Does that mean they don't have human rights violations? It's like saying that the United States is a democracy so there was never a civil rights problem, there was never prejudice in the U.S. Who would believe that? No Colombian, thought Eileen wryly.

So she had looked at Colombia and said, Okay

there are problems here, especially the crackdown on the M-19 guerrillas since the arsenal robbery. Her attitude had been: Let's see what's really happening. We don't want to wake up some day and find that we have been saying wonderful things about this country and it's not true and it blows up in our faces. She had written a cable to the embassy asking questions like, "Who is being rounded up in this crackdown? Is it really guerrillas? Or is it labor people, peasant leaders, flaky people the government would rather get rid of?"

And the cable did not get approved. "Don't forget who you work for now," she was told. "You're not the Human Rights Bureau anymore." Asencio hadn't wanted her to send it either. He didn't want to hear about it.

If the Colombians have this wonderful democracy, Eileen had insisted, then what is this state of siege? People say, well, Colombia is a democracy "off and on," depending on the state of siege. Right in the *Area Handbook for Colombia* it says Colombia is increasingly dependent on the state of siege. In this book that's put out by the U.S. Government it says that the Colombian Government has increasingly depended on a state of siege. She wanted to know if it was true.

Here at State people said, "Why do you want to ask those questions? You're just trying to get the Human Rights Bureau's attention focused on Colombia—as if it were Chile or something." And Asencio just kept getting more and more nervous. "These are all my buddies you're talking about— they are all stopping the narcotics trade."

He's right, Eileen had to agree. But then what is the interest of the policy? It's not how many tortures this year versus last year, or how many tortures you have in Chile. But what kind of government is this? What is its future? How are we relating to it? What messages are we sending to them? If we are sending messages that we want to cooperate with their military, fine, a government traditionally has to, but let's also send another message. That we're not buying all this shit about everyone being "subversive" that they don't like. . . .

Heaphy was disappointed more than surprised at the reaction of her superiors at State. And she knew she had some things to learn about maneuvering effectively within the bureaucracy. So all right. She lost this skirmish. She would wait for the next one— the human rights report from Bogotá.

Eileen Heaphy loved her job. When the nuns at St. Joseph's College in Connecticut had kept asking her, "But don't you want to teach?" she had answered no, she wanted to work for the government. She wasn't even embarrassed to describe herself as one of those people who could stare at the Capitol in Washington and feel good inside.

Her first summer out of college she had taken the civil service exam, for lack of any better idea of how to start working for the government, and then she took the National Security Agency entry test because her girl friend's brother worked at NSA.

Eileen was an attractive thirty-four, and although government as a career had been her choice, her single social status was not. It had just happened. Within a year's time in Washington all of her friends had married and she was still going to Mass and asking God, "Why not me?"

For six years at NSA she was an intelligence analyst and kept track of Viet Cong battalions. She moved pins on a map and cracked that "All of the VC battalions were always named the Fifteenth Battalion, and that's why we lost the war."

At night she had been working for her master's degree in international relations at American University. She had switched her specialty to Latin

American affairs, telling NSA that when the Vietnam war was over there would be a glut of Asian specialists. NSA agreed and approved her Latin American redirection.

Eileen failed her first foreign service exam, passed the second, worked in the embassies in Costa Rica and Mexico City, and now she had been on the Colombian desk in Washington for just a few months.

There she was, she thought, in the Office of Andean Affairs, and she hadn't had an affair since she'd arrived.

Eileen picked up from her in-box the invitation to a big ball at the beautiful New Zealand embassy and threw it in her wastebasket. No date, no go.

Underneath the embassy invitation in the in-box sat Asencio's suggested draft for a letter from President Carter to President Turbay, thanking Colombia for its continuing anti-narcotics effort.

Eileen read the draft. She knew it would get rewritten and rewritten again as it traveled from her desk to the State Department's Bureau of Narcotics and then to the White House. Approvals and clearances. Welcome to the bureaucracy.

She would make the first edit. Picking up a pencil, she smiled broadly as she crossed out a paragraph that praised the Colombian army's "notable contribution."

She felt better as she turned toward her typewriter to redo the human rights cable as a letter.

Asencio sat at the head of the U-shaped table meditating on the fact that in the period of a twenty-minute car ride he had moved from human rights to hoof-and-mouth disease.

On the left side of the U sat all kinds of "under" and "assistant" secretaries to whomever and whatever in the U.S. Department of Agriculture. Some boys from the Sierra Club and the Cattleman's Association were there too, and the guy from Federal Highways.

On the right side sat the Colombian agriculture and cattle boys.

Asencio listened with one ear as Colombia's minister of agriculture rambled on in the best Castillian Spanish about how the United States enjoyed well-deserved prestige . . . how deeply grateful the Government of Colombia was for the United States' contribution toward the unity of the American continent . . . but of course the United States understood its duty toward weaker countries and this is why such a large group of representatives had come to Bogotá from Washington today. . . .

Deputy Under Assistant Secretary Bob Smith stood up and thanked the Colombian minister of agriculture for coming today likewise and, "Of course, what's good for Colombia is good for the United States . . . together as financial and technical partners . . ."

Asencio's mind wandered. The left side of the U was connected to the right side by a little white one-windowed hut in the back of a room where a Colombian woman sat doing simultaneous translations. Earphones were perched on nearly every head.

And of course underneath all the flowery, friendly rhetoric was the other link between the left and right side of the table: hundreds of thousands of aphthosa-infected cattle and the Pan-American Highway. Today an extension of an agreement made in 1973 between Colombia and the United States was being signed. The boys in the North would help the boys in the South cure their disease-ridden cattle—not because the United States cared that Colombia's cattle all have hoof-and-mouth, but because the construction of the Pan-American Highway was nearing completion near Colombia's Panamanian border, and if Colombia's cattle were still infected when the highway was ready to open, then hoof-and-mouth disease would slowly but surely work its way right up the highway through Central America and Mexico to undiseased U.S. cattle. Colombia didn't care about aphthosa either—the beef is still edible—but it desperately wanted the highway open, for the obvious economic advantages. Therefore, the United States and Colombia designed a program to eradicate the disease—well, at least in the areas bordering the highway.

And that, smiled Asencio, is the stuff of "foreign policy."

His turn to speak.

"I know I wasn't invited today, but I thought it was important to be here just to assure you all that I have made a personal commitment to President Turbay on the completion and opening of the Pan-American Highway . . . so important to both our countries. . . ."

"The Starr thing has begun to move," said Frank Crigler to Richard Baca. "A guy by the name of Jack Mitchell, who works for the columnist Jack Anderson, has had a face-to-face meeting with the intermediary, Villamil, in Mexico City. Ambassador Asencio has talked with Mitchell. Villamil asked for some 'pin money' for his 'couriers'—a couple thousand dollars—and he says the FARC is still insisting on a two-hundred-fifty-thousand-dollar ransom. Mitchell evidently told him Mrs. Jensen only had about eleven thousand and the U.S. Government was not paying. Villamil said he would pass that on to the FARC. Mitchell is back in the States waiting to hear. . . ."

Baca wondered, was it possible that the end was in sight? When he had arrived in Bogotá about seven months before, Richard Starr had already been a hostage for more than two years. Baca had been warned by Peace Corps Washington not to get as involved as his predecessor, who came close to breaking the rules. "Do what we tell you to do, no more." He had been given a number to call to check on a Christmas package for Starr from his mother. It was supposed to be the number of the nephew of Villamil, the intermediary, but Villamil himself got on the line. He said, "I have a couple of things for you," and Baca remembered thinking, Right: a bullet, a knife—I don't wanna go.

Villamil turned out to be very low key. He had given Baca two letters. One for the ambassador from the FARC. One from Richard for his mother. The one for the ambassador said if ransom wasn't paid in three months they would get rid of Richard. Starr's letter to his mother said, "I'm bored. Send me books and batteries for my radio and get me out of here." His letter went to the CIA. They said it was authentic.

The next thing that had happened was that Mama came to town. Mrs. Jensen and Baca had had lunch and she told him she felt she could trust him. Everyone else, she said, was doing her dirt. Baca told her it wouldn't be like it was with the Peace Corps director before him. He had been told to cool it. Mrs. Jensen had an appointment with Asencio the next day. Baca wasn't invited. He waited for her outside the ambassador's office. She came out in a good mood. That was a Friday. The following Monday Baca's phone had rung at 6:30 in the morning and it was Mrs. Jensen on the line saying, "How does it feel to have murdered my son? You've killed him! You've killed him!" and she hung up. On the front page of one of the morning newspapers was a story saying that Richard Starr had been seen hanging from a tree with a sign saying "CIA SPY" across his body. Baca called a staff meeting to see if they could find out if it was true and to discuss what to do about the other volunteers in the field. The DCM at the time, Ted Briggs, phoned to say that he had also received a "Murderer!" call from Mrs. Jen-sen. He said the embassy was working with the newspaper to verify the story. It was three or four days later that Asencio told Mama it was only third-hand hearsay. She was all bubbly. Baca had told her, "I don't want to shatter your mood, but I'm extremely offended by what you did. I didn't kidnap your son. I am not a murderer." She apologized pro-fusely and left town after about another week.

Baca had been cut out the next couple of months. He didn't know what happened. He did make a trip to Washington for some other reason and they told him at the Peace Corps office that Mrs. Jensen hated him.

One thing Baca knew was that Ted Briggs put together a $50,000 offer and the FARC rejected it. Diego, Briggs had told him, looked at the messenger and said, "If you don't want the fifty thousand then take out citizenship papers for Starr because we don't want him."

Ted Briggs's tour in Colombia came to a close without anything happening. He had told Baca that he thought they were getting lousy advice. Baca thought Briggs meant from Washington. At any rate Briggs went. Crigler arrived and started search-ing for other channels to the FARC besides Villamil, the composer. Mrs. Jensen sent a negotiator. Still, nothing happened. There was a rumor that Starr had been spotted working with the FARC actively on a raid. And then Jack Anderson's column appeared—"I'll meet anybody, anywhere. . . ." Die-go hit the ceiling. But it looked like something real was finally happening.

". . . and you are now on stand-by, Richard," Frank Crigler was saying. "Don't leave Bogotá for business or pleasure."

"How did the briefing with Simms go?" Political officer Don Roberts asked Phil Ferris. They were both in the back seat of one of the embassy's half-dozen chauffeured cars. "Chauffeur," as in ununiformed, unlettered Colombian, and "car" as in the embassy's sky-blue conspicuous station wagons. Phil hunched down almost embarrassed.

"That was fine," he answered. "It's the human rights newspaper-clippings 'file' that's unfathomable."

"Why that's everything *El Tiempo* and *El Espectador* have printed on the subject in the last year," laughed Roberts. "Plus a few remarks picked up at cocktail parties. Seriously, it's going to be a little more negative this year because of the army's M-19 roundup. More than five thousand people were arrested. You know there are human rights violations when civilians are saying, 'That's how you control terrorists. So what if nine innocent people are tortured?' "

"That's what Simms said," Phil replied.

"Well this trip should give you the flavor of the problem," said Roberts. "Besides the annual report, the embassy's other specific human rights mandate involves the tracking down of missing persons. Here's a letter from Senator Richard Luger's office. You will note that some staffer of Luger's spelled Colombia as in Columbia University. That should give you an idea of South America's importance in the scheme of things in Washington. Anyway, one of the senator's Indiana constituents wants to know about a university student named Christian von Walter Rodriguez who they believe is being detained by security forces that searched his parents' home without a warrant and then forced his younger brother to go with them to find him. There's not much to go on. But we will ask the general today. General Miguel Vega Uribe is the commander of Colombia's Brigade of Military Institutes—"

"What didn't Simms tell me?" Ferris changed the subject.

"Well," answered Roberts, "I don't suppose he went into his feelings about Crigler."

"No, he didn't," said Phil, "and I don't think I want to know the details. What I mean is, well, let me ask it this way. Do you like your job?"

"I did in the beginning. The housing in Bogotá is good, Spanish is easy, the climate is nice, the morale was good and the Colombians are friendly enough."

"You find the Colombians friendly?"

"Oh, they love to hate Americans," laughed Don, "but it's just a sport here."

Phil looked over at Don and he realized he didn't know him very well. Don had a reputation for being standoffish toward junior officers, but Phil found him friendly, and near brilliant. Don was an FSO5 who spoke thirteen languages. He was a graduate of Princeton and of a year in the Philippines with the Peace Corps. He worked on a state-wide Republican campaign—attorney general or something—in Minnesota before he came into the foreign service. Roberts called the outcome a "moral victory." His guy must have lost. He had worked in two posts, Pakistan and Turkey, before he'd come to Bogotá.

"And the job?" prompted Ferris again. "Bogotá's political section?"

"It's not particularly Bogotá's political section," said Roberts. "I'm thinking of another career."

Ferris was stunned. Or maybe he wasn't.

"Originally," Roberts continued, "I thought when things were wrong, they were quirks. But now a pattern is emerging. I just don't feel very patriotic. There's the official indifference—no response from Boles to eggs thrown at our front door. A year to get decent enough looking furniture to entertain Colombians with, which is part of my job. And, clearly, it takes years to be able to say anything in this system and be listened to. So many things are being botched. The biggest thing we have going between us and Colombia is drugs. We're supposed to stamp out a multi-billion-dollar trade with a sixteen-million-dollar program. We don't protect our own coasts, but we ask the Colombians to have their army patrol theirs. Even if five percent of the soldiers are corrupted by the easy narc money, we're talking about an army which took over the government in living memory. So on the one hand we preach human rights and democracy, and on the other hand we lead their army down a subversive road. And if you try to say something you're told, 'Shut up, you're just a five.' "

"You're talking about the whole foreign service system," said Ferris.

"I guess I am," answered Roberts. "The foreign service used to be a small elite corps. Now it's just another huge bureaucracy with the human rights people fighting the drug people fighting the whomever over the whatever. And out in the embassies we're all messenger boys. 'Tell the Minister of Defense' and then we paper back the answer. There's so much paperwork involved there's no time to mingle with Colombians, which is the guts of our job. Supposedly. And the kind of paperwork— I just received a cable this morning asking me what sizes of lumber are used to build Baptist churches in Bogotá. I forget who wanted to know."

"Jesus," said Ferris.

"And because of inflation," added Roberts, "I'm making the same money I was nine years ago. I know I'm not alone. There was an article in the *Foreign Service Journal* last month that said that more candidates refused appointments into the service than accepted. That was unheard of once. And the number of mid-level officers who are resigning is way up."

"We're here," announced Phil, a bit relieved. Roberts was depressing.

"Here" was an eight-floor, almost-all-glass building—more like a complex of buildings—which was the Colombian Ministry of Defense. Two soldiers stood by the door to go through briefcases and purses and to make sure whoever entered deposited his ID in exchange for a proper visitor's pass. Ferris noted that they missed checking a good third of the civilian people walking in.

Roberts and Ferris were accompanied to General Vega's waiting room by two armed officers. The large, bright room faced a large, bright courtyard planted with grass and decorated at four corners by old cannons. There was plenty of time to study the courtyard landscape. After three quarters of an hour they were finally led in.

Ferris had to stifle an involuntary gasp. Had this guy bought the Hollywood set from the *Viva Zapata* movie? The office was huge and dark. The general sat at his desk on a platform that was the size of half the room. Near his desk, a blue votive light flickered in front of an oil painting of the Blessed Virgin Mary.

Phil and Don walked halfway to the platform before the general looked up.

"Thank you for receiving me, General," began Roberts. "I have a name of a student here who someone has asked after in the States. Ordinarily I wouldn't bother you with something like this but it's an extraordinary time filled with extraordinary rumors."

"Yes," answered General Vega, "as you said, an extraordinary time. Desperate circumstances call for desperate measures. In the interest of preserving democracy, of course."

"You understand," said Roberts, "that human rights is a special concern of President Carter and the United States Congress."

"In Colombia," said the general, "the issue is often used by those who want to subvert democracy and who are themselves guilty of human rights abuse."

"There's talk in the Congress," Roberts ignored the predictable rhetoric and got to the point, "of cutting any further military aid to Colombia. You are the largest recipient of such aid in Latin America."

The general was unfazed. He'd heard that line before. "While exceptional security measures are justified by the present situation, I am not in favor of such measures on a permanent basis. . . ."

Phil found himself looking at a smiling General Vega and wondering if he was the kind of man who could apply electric shocks to somebody's penis.

Asencio wished he was back at the hoof-and-mouth meeting. Washington had just called. Another telephonic instruction. The FARC was sticking to their $250,000 demand for Richard Starr and it looked like Jack Anderson was going to get the money from somewhere. Asencio had just been told that Anderson's guy, Jack Mitchell, would be calling and the embassy should help him get the money through Colombian customs.

Goddammit, thought Asencio, enough of this "oral only" shit. He dashed off a cable that said that Washington's request was "a violation of Colombian and United States law."

Figure it'll take the cable about two or three hours to get to the proper desk in Washington. If he were lucky, it would take another two or three hours to get a phone line from D.C. to Bogotá. He could hear the conversation. "Why did you put this in a cable? What's the matter with you? Violations of law are not recorded on paper!"

"Fuck 'em," Asencio said out loud. His was not going to be the only ass on the line if something went wrong.

The place looked a little sleazy, but the mariachi band was wonderful. Emily Roth considered El Sombrero a "typical" Colombian nightclub and she felt very foreign servicey. The band was wearing neon-white jumpsuits with swinging white fringe and shiny gold studs. Ornately embroidered sombreros hung halfway down their backs.

Emily started to dance in her seat, moving her arms and shoulders with the beat. She loved Spanish music. These guys smiled better than they played, but they were too loud to hear in any detail anyway.

A photographer stopped by the table.

"Miguel," Emily squealed, "let's let him take our picture!"

Miguel obliged by leaning into Emily and mugging it.

Emily wondered briefly how sober she was but it didn't make any difference. She was having a great time. The party had actually started at the office. Her boss, George Thigpen, had decided to have a late Friday afternoon "pour"—for econ's "morale." George had provided the liquor, Emily had made a huge batch of popcorn.

Well, one thing had led to another, and Emily invited anyone who wanted to continue partying to come to her apartment. About six people showed up for tall glasses of homemade piña coladas with fresh pineapple and fresh coconut. Emily had put on a couple of records, moved some furniture out of the way and they'd danced.

The party, reduced to four, then went to dinner at a Chinese restaurant, stopped briefly at the "happy hour" at the Marine House where everybody was already smashed, and then had come "for one last drink" to El Sombrero.

Seated around the table with Emily and Miguel were two more Colombian embassy staffers. Miguel and Carlos worked for GSO and Ricardo worked in the economics section.

The best way to know a country, Emily decided, was to date a countryman. Miguel was unlike most Colombian men. He was tall and quite attractive. She wondered if he already had a girl friend or, oh God, a wife.

Emily felt kind of guilty about the Colombian staffers working in her section. She had received three security violations in less than two months for leaving classified material lying around on her desk for "anyone" to read. Emily thought she was being harassed by the marines and was helpless to do anything about it. She had asked Frank Ravndal in admin to move around the offices so the classified stuff would be more physically secure. What Ravndal had done was to put up a cipher-lock door, just like the controlled-access door upstairs in the political section. On one side of the door sat all the Americans. On the other side sat the Colombians. Their resentment was palpable and Emily, who was supposed to work on good relationships between the Americans and the nationals, felt responsible for the bad atmosphere.

"Listen," she began, taking a sip of her drink, "I just want to personally apologize to you again, Ricardo, for that horrible door."

"It's all right, Emily," Ricardo answered. "Frankly, I don't mind not handling money or classified. It's a responsiblity I don't want. The marines would be after me, too. Have they gotten you again?"

"Not since the door went up," Emily admitted.

"Then it was worth it," said Ricardo.

"Ricardo," asked Emily, "why are you working at the U.S. Embassy?"

"Well," Ricardo answered, "it gives you prestige. I feel better, more secure than my friends."

"Prestige?" Emily said. "I'm surprised."

"Oh, I get jokes from some people," laughed Ricardo. "They all think I'm rich because I work for the Americans."

"Are you paid American scale?" asked Emily.

"Oh no," Miguel answered. "We're paid Colombian salaries. For instance, your salary—a secretary's—is six thousand dollars a year here. Ricardo is the head of the nationals' employee committee in the embassy. He's gotten us regular raises and severance payments and advance payments—benefits you Americans get."

The mariachi band took a break and a jukebox came on—just as loudly.

"What's it like working for the Americans?" Emily asked. "I mean—for us."

"You're delightful," Miguel said, and Emily hoped he meant it personally.

"Seriously," she prodded.

"Well," said Miguel, "sometimes you seem to lean over backwards not to be 'ugly' Americans. You let us come in late, leave early, take long breaks in the cafeteria and long lunches. My favorite cosmetic was when the State Department changed references to us from 'locals' to 'nationals.' "

The whole table laughed. In fact, Emily suddenly noticed, the whole room was laughing and whistling. It was something on the jukebox. She could only make out an occasional *"Los Americanos . . ."*

"What's the song?" she asked.

"Uh." Miguel looked a little embarrassed. "It's something . . . a sort of funny folk song . . ."

"What are the words?" Emily said. "I can just make out *'Los Americanos.'* It's not complimentary, is it."

". . . if they know history it is not by reading it

but by seeing it in the American movies, with their grand scenarios and grand music in the superior style of . . . the Americans. . . ."

Carlos was doing the translating with the music.

". . . showing off a thousand colors, all but black, which they consider not to their liking . . . the Americans . . .

". . . when they get older they dress up as tourists and go out around the world . . . the Americans . . .

". . . the trip is organized with romance included, fee paid by . . . the Americans . . .

". . . with typical grossness they mix with the people and no one notices that they are . . . Americans . . ."

"I've got the gist of it," Emily said. "Do you guys feel that kind of resentment?"

"Frustration," said Ricardo, "is a better word for the embassy. We can't go to the fourth floor where the *internos* live—"

"*Internos?*" interrupted Emily.

"CIA," said Ricardo. "We can't talk to any Colombian on the minister level, an American officer must do that. And we must call the officers 'Mister.' Americans invite all or none of us 'nationals' to their parties. We're not individuals, and we're clearly not one of you. Carlos, tell her your story."

"I work on incoming shipments—household goods, cars," said Carlos. "Private people pay Colombian customs bribes to get their stuff out early. Not the embassy Americans. So they make you wait for weeks. Ten years ago if a guy came from the American embassy it was 'What do you want—anything.' Now it's 'Come back tomorrow.' I wouldn't say I'm good friends with the Americans. One of your CIA people called me an 'idiot' and 'stupid' and tried to get me fired because of a problem with his car shipment. I told him to go to hell. My boss, Ellis Glynn, said, 'Respect him. He's an American.' Well, I'm a Colombian. I deserve respect."

"Carlos doesn't have the worst story," Ricardo said. "Miguel does."

"Really," objected Miguel, "I'd rather not tell that one."

"C'mon," Ricardo said. "It's unbelievable."

"Well," said Miguel. "I started seeing a junior officer in another section. I'd rather not tell you her name. She's still working in the embassy. Evidently an American officer is not supposed to date a Colombian staffer. If, that is, the American is a woman and the Colombian a man. An American man can date or sleep with what he wants, I've noticed. Anyway, people in the embassy started avoiding her, not speaking to her. It was horrible. But the worst thing was the Marine Ball. She asked me to come with her as her date. There was this whole room of big, round tables set for dinner. We sat down at one of the tables and nobody, not one other couple, joined us. We ate all alone. She cried that night. I thought it was best we not see each other anymore. But she was stubborn. And then a letter was written to the ambassador. The letter was unsigned, but it said that the American girl and I were a scandal to the whole embassy. Whoever wrote it questioned her judgment and her morals. I was using her as a ticket to the States, they said. Everybody knew about the letter. We were finally called into the DCM's office. It was Mr. Briggs at the time. Both of us thought I would be fired and she would be transferred. Instead Mr. Briggs said that our personal lives were none of his or any letter writer's business and he simply wanted us to know how he felt."

"Are you still seeing her?" asked Emily.

"Uh," Miguel hesitated. "No. Things got better as far as treatment from other people was concerned, but she got very serious. She thought she wanted to marry me, uh, I told her I would just hurt her. I mean I loved her. I love women. I could never be faithful to one. . . ."

Ricardo and Carlos started to laugh. Emily poured a shot of vodka and the mariachi band came back and blasted away any further conversation.

The tables in the room were jammed up one against the other and Emily felt a sort of jostling at her back. The mariachis were playing, one guy was singing and all of a sudden Emily was on her way to the floor. Miguel tried to haul her up by the armpits. There was fighting at the table behind them, two men were shoving each other.

Miguel got her up on the chair, finally, and there was a noise like a firecracker.

"Are you all right?" the people at the table in front of them asked Emily.

"Yes, no problem." She was sort of embarrassed; the whole thing had been so clumsy. She looked over at Miguel. He was watching the table behind them. She reached down under her chair to retrieve her shoes. She'd slipped them off earlier, they were so uncomfortable. She put the shoes on the table.

The second time Emily heard the noise she knew what it was. They were shooting at each other! The band was still playing when somebody grabbed her arm and pulled her away from the table.

"Get out of here! Run!" yelled Miguel. She picked up her shoes, people had started screaming.

Emily was moved by the rest of the hysterical crowd out of the door, down the steps and out onto the street. Ricardo was next to her. "What about the bill?" she asked him. "We didn't pay the bill. . . ."

6

As soon as he walked in, Asencio knew that somebody on today's meeting list had pissed off one of the marines. The secure room was freezing, which meant that instead of turning on the heat forty-five minutes before, as he was supposed to, whichever marine it was had waited until the last minute. Asencio glanced at the marine checking off people's names as they entered.

There was absolutely no expression on the bastard's face.

Every Monday the daily staff meeting took place in the secure room. Asencio wondered mildly how "secure" it was. The room was an interesting piece of engineering. Situated on the fifth floor, somewhere between the embassy's communications area and the CIA's communications area, it was really a room within a room, a suspended Plexiglas bubble surrounded by some sort of insulation. It was dominated by a large conference table and dozens of No Smoking signs.

Asencio sat down and lit his pipe. A sigh of relief swept round the table and within three minutes the No Smoking signs were obscured by smoke.

"Mike," began Asencio, "there was a piece on the Washington wireless this morning about an increase in industrial imports in the U.S. because of lower tariffs. Can you get that placed in *El Tiempo* or *El Espectador*? I think it would be useful for us."

"I'll try," said Mike Kristula, public affairs officer

of the embassy, and chief of Bogotá's very large Communications Agency contingent. "Sometimes the newspapers print the articles we send them, sometimes they don't. We did get that USICA-produced propaganda short about Colombia's war on drugs into two Bogotá movie theaters. We also got excellent use of our 'Russia in Afghanistan' tape. It ran eight different times on TV news programs in Cali.

"Don't forget about that address you promised to deliver to USICA's North-South Conference next week."

"Tell whoever writes my speech not to gush," Asencio said. "I am against the basic principle that in the past we in the North have been nasty to them in the South, selling our technology expensive and buying their raw resources cheap, and that now we owe them. I think that's a prescription for disaster. That's my position, and the government's too. Washington just covers it up with bullshit.

"Oh, and Mike, I meant to mention something to you before about this—stop me if I did. Is USICA doing any work at all in the universities? I know there was a decision made before our time by Washington and Bogotá that we pull out of the campuses because they were dangerous places—especially National University, where they'd shoot at you. I think that decision was a bad mistake. Don't you think the situation has changed sufficiently so that it makes sense to go back?"

"Sure," said Mike, "why not?"

"So talk to your boys in Washington," Asencio said, "and I'll talk to mine. Frank?"

"I've enticed the new protocol guy in the foreign office to lunch by offering him a visa for his son to study English in the United States," admin officer Frank Ravndal responded. "I'm hoping we can get some new rules from him so we can cut the time our people's cars spend sitting on the Colombian coast. We'll see.

"I think we have a deal on a Tudor-style house just a couple of blocks away from here off National Park. If Washington accepts the one-million-dollar price then we'll buy it and put all the secret types— the DEA and State's narcs—in the more secure embassy building and move USICA or econ/commercial to the house."

Asencio glanced over at Mike Kristula. He had gone pale. Mike felt that if USICA were moved out of the embassy the agency would lose much of its clout. Asencio thought, in fact, that it would be smarter to move the business boys out, but he hadn't told Kristula yet. He loved to kid Mike about all the things he could use USICA's half-floor for. Kristula was so much fun to tease. He always got so upset, just as he was now.

"And speaking of the secret types," Ravndal continued, "Secret Service wants a permanent staff in the embassy. Goddammit, every government agency wants its own foreign service. We are fractionalizing diplomacy.

"The Government of Colombia owes us fifty thousand dollars in local tax reimbursements. They haven't bothered paying us back now for two years. I'm getting nowhere with the Foreign Ministry or the Ministry of Finance. Can you help?"

"I'm seeing the Minister of Finance at a party, I think, later this week," Asencio said. "I'll mention it to him there. Better this is handled informally."

"Just one more thing," Ravndal said. "I've fired a Colombian who was working in the visa section. He was running a travel agency for his relatives and I . . . "

"That's your bailiwick," Asencio cut him off. "Ken?"

"I've got a whole passel of Americans in the

States," said Ken Keller, the consul general, "who want their seized aircraft back. They all, of course, deny any knowledge that their planes were involved in any drug running."

"Tell 'em to get a lawyer," Asencio answered. "You know we've got a real crossfire problem here. Two American planes were shot down over the Guajira Peninsula last week. Now that's after Colombia announced that that would be a restricted air zone because of all of the Guajira's clandestine landing strips. Washington sent down a cable saying, 'Is this attack on American citizens a trend?' Do you believe that? Well, I ignored the cable. So Heaphy's boss in Andean Affairs, Dick Barnabey, sent another cable and then phoned to tell me to answer it. I answered it. I reminded the boys in Washington that Colombia was only doing what we asked them to. Stopping narcotics traffic. And then I asked them if they were in the habit of having sex and then shoving the whore out of bed.

"Frank cleaned my cable up," Asencio added amid the laughter.

"Frank?" Asencio turned to Frank Crigler, his DCM.

"Nothing to report," Crigler answered. "Except, do we know anything more about the Wycliff business?"

The Wycliff School was some sort of Bible-translating operation that sat right in the middle of FARC territory. Asencio was not really sure exactly what they did or why they chose to remain there. But he did know there were 300 Americans at the school and *El Tiempo* had reported a rumor that the FARC was planning to raid the place. He'd asked a few of his boys to check the rumor out.

He looked at the CIA station chief, who shook his head and said, "We know it hasn't been attacked yet. That's all we know at the moment."

Of course, that's all the CIA knew at the moment. The CIA was a shadow of what it once was, thought Asencio. They were his favorite rivals in the old days. Who got more stuff, better stuff. It was a young political officer's favorite game. Now they were eminently scoopable. The agency had cut back so much and was so demoralized that the amount of domestic—Colombian—intelligence they developed was rather limited. Their focus now was the iron-curtain types in Bogotá's other embassies, which Asencio thought was wrong, but the feeling seemed to be that what the KGB was up to was more important than following some half-assed Colombian left-wing outfit. How could those people threaten the U.S. realm?

"Colonel?"

"Same thing from my people, Diego," Colonel Carl Wittenberg answered. "It hasn't been attacked yet. The army officers at the Ministry of Defense say they'll ask their patrols out there to keep a close watch.

"Diego," added Wittenberg, "I'm pretty sure the air force has decided to buy their new fighters from France. Is there anything you can do?"

"Nope. Not legally anyway," answered Asencio. "Don't you know that ambassadors are prohibited from going in and making sales pitches on military equipment? I was cautioned that my desire for Colombia to have fast patrol craft for their navy so that they could pursue drug runners was getting dangerously close to violating the meaning of the law. But of course that's not it. We have this holier-than-thou arms policy. The theory is that undeveloped societies should employ their money in developing their society. Perfectly correct. Good theory. But when we won't sell them advanced fighters they go to the French. The French don't have any problems like that. They'd be happy to sell them all the

Mirages they want. So this 'good theory' has affected an area where we used to have absolute control—the military equipment that people were buying and using and so forth. We were training them. We had links with the military establishments up and down the board that no longer exist. Well, I don't have to tell *you* that, Carl. And all because of an ideological principle that sounds like it makes a lot of sense, but doesn't."

And to himself Asencio added that it reminded him of the whole CIA thing. The they've-done-wrong-so-let's-do-them-in attitude. Now we've done them in and we realize that maybe it was a good thing to have them around.

"And speaking of the French," Asencio said aloud, "our favorite nemesis, how we doing on the TV contract, Bob?"

Robert Pastorino was the embassy's commercial officer. He was young and brash, but Asencio liked him. He was good at his work. Drug trafficking had raised a lot of money for Colombia. The country's foreign exchange reserves had tripled three times in the last five years. And now Colombia was into "infrastructure" improvements—highways, airports, hydroelectric dams, telecommunication stations and a new color television system. Asencio saw no reason why American companies shouldn't get some of these contracts. Sagging balance of trade and all that. After all, what was the harm in having his econ/commercial people help Colombia spend the drug money? American companies liked the billion-dollar contracts in the Middle East more than the million-dollar contracts in Colombia. So Pastorino had some trouble getting the American business boys' attention. And of course, bribery. The Americans were prohibited; Asencio couldn't remember the exact title of *that* particular congressional mandate. Bribery was a way of life in Colombia's business world. The Germans bribed, and the French.

Of course the French. France had beaten his boys out on the TV camera contract. But the U.S. was still in the running for the rest of the system.

"Well, you heard about the fiasco at the communications committee hearing," began Pastorino. "The French had transformer problems and their picture went out all over the city in bright green."

"That's great," Asencio laughed.

"And," Pastorino continued, "the U.S. Department of Commerce really did a number for me. They called RCA and got a tape of Olivia Newton-John riding along a beach on horseback. She looked nude. So when our turn came in front of the committee they saw this beautiful blonde . . . la-de-da. I gave a copy of the Newton-John tape to each of the senators on the committee so they could go home and play it forever on their Betamaxes.

"You know, Diego, we have a couple of senators in our pocket and we've got a friend on the experts' advisory committee to keep us informed, so to speak. Mike has given us three USICA grants for the 'right' people to come to the States and 'study' our color TV system.

"But the *pièce de résistance*"—Pastorino butchered the French expression—"will be the cocktail party at my house, which is next week, just before the committee votes, of course.

"The only other thing I want to bring up," added Pastorino, "is that the vice-president of international affairs for Ford is going to request a visit with you soon. He's coming all the way from Detroit."

"Any idea what it's about?" asked Asencio.

"Well," said Pastorino. "They've been talking to Thigpen about pulling out of any Colombian investment."

"I'm not surprised," said Asencio. "You know they came dashing in here like Pavlovian dogs after General Motors. They asked me what I thought of their trying to open a couple of plants. GM is here.

Renault is here. How many cars can the market absorb? I said, Come on in if you think you can make money. And they went ahead. So have they come to their senses?"

"Uh," Pastorino said. "Word has it that they're going to say publicly that the reason they're pulling out is corruption and drugs."

"They can't say that." Asencio was furious. "Next Monday I'm delivering a letter to Turbay from Carter congratulating Colombia on a good drug-fighting year. When's this VP coming?"

"If you'll see him," answered Pastorino, "later this week."

"Tell him I'll see him," said Asencio. "They're not going to cover up a bad investment of their own with this Colombia-is-a-bad-and-dangerous-place shit. John?"

"More good news," said John Simms, "from the political front. I've gotten two phone calls this morning already—one from the Senate and one from the Foreign Ministry—about . . . "

"Oh, let me guess," interrupted Asencio. "Quita Sueño?"

"Right," answered Simms. "Well, you know as well as I that the U.S. Senate's delay of ratification of the treaty has left the door open for Nicaragua to claim the islands again. They say the treaty suggests that the U.S. thinks Quita Sueño belongs to Colombia."

"Delay? Delay?" mimicked Asencio. "So it's only been since 1972 that that treaty has been in front of the esteemed United States Senate Foreign Relations Committee."

"So first it was Somoza's friends who held it up," continued Simms, "and now the Sandinistas are trying to make it a Caribbean basin issue."

"And we don't want to offend the Sandinistas," said Asencio. "They're our enemies. So let's offend

Colombia. They're our friends. And in the best State Department tradition, the boys in Washington are hiding while we sit down here getting rocks thrown at us from both sides.

"Frank," Asencio said to Crigler, "write me a cable to send this afternoon reminding Washington that a fresh Nicaraguan claim has raised a storm of protest here. And remind them that we needn't have been sitting in the middle of this mess if the treaty relinquishing U.S. claims had been signed long ago. And then ask them what the hell is going on with the ratification? What am I supposed to tell Colombia? Take out my ruffles and put in your flourishes.

"Speaking of Washington," continued Asencio, "here is a story you'll all enjoy. I got a phone call from Dick Celeste, head of the Peace Corps. He says he wants to beef up the number of volunteers in Colombia. He wants to send down more bodies so he can keep his budget line in D.C. I asked him if he ever heard of a kid called Richard Starr? I mean a foreign service officer is paid to take risks. A Peace Corps volunteer is not. What do I want with more people running around here with a quarter-million-dollar price tag on their heads? And do you know what the guy said? He said, 'You shouldn't let some guerrilla group scare the Peace Corps out of the country.'"

Clay Allison glanced nonchalantly around the airport. He'd just flown in from Washington with an aviation adviser in tow. Both of them stood in the customs line waiting for the adviser's bags to be checked. The guy had a lot of baggage. Clay knew Bogotá customs wouldn't bother with the belongings of a U.S. aviation adviser traveling with a sort of dumb-looking U.S. Customs agent.

They didn't.

"You got everything?" Clay asked loudly, slapping his companion on the back. Keeping his smile fixed, Clay muttered, "Then let's get the fuck outta here."

Starr's $250,000 ransom money was past Colombian customs.

The sunshine committee meeting had done nothing but make Jerry Harrison even more angry. Harrison was a junior officer who worked in the American Services section of the consulate in the job Phil Ferris had recently left. Successful at pinpointing morale problems, the sunshine committee, a group of about a dozen embassy staffers, had been unsuccessful at solving them. Jerry was tired of being brushed off constantly by surly Ellis Glynn and snotty Ratso Ravndal.

Well. They weren't going to ignore *him* anymore.

Harrison sat down at his typewriter.

Dear Mr. Ambassador:
    As you are aware, much of the frustration of mission employees is focused on the Administration Section and, in particular, on the General Services Office. Some of the problems are in fact due to the Department of State or to the Colombian bureaucracy, but many are due wholly to the inability or unwillingness of the GSO employees to do their jobs. I have not addressed this problem before, feeling that it is commonly enough discussed, but I now feel that I must speak out because of my situation. I refer to three of my experiences.

Jerry wrote about the ten and one-half months it took GSO to import his car from the States and the two weeks his household effects sat, ignored, at the airport, while GSO employees tried to find the bill of lading. But the straw that broke the camel's back was the layette shipment:

My wife began soliciting a layette shipment in GSO five months ago. We still don't have it. In Personnel, no one knew how to initiate the layette shipment, nor how to find out—until my wife suggested that the file of someone who had gotten a layette in the past be consulted.

A telegram announcing the shipment was received three weeks ago. A GSO employee assured us that all was making regular progress. More than a week later, the GS office decided, perhaps because I was asking where my shipment was, that the shipment had gone astray. At this writing, two working days have elapsed since, and there is no reason to think that GSO has made any progress in finding it. I found it myself, in one hour, with two phone calls to Braniff.

Conclusions: I conclude from these experiences and from those of my fellow officers that the GSO employees do not know how to do their jobs or are unwilling to do them; that the GSO employees can be relied upon to say that things are going well even when they know they are not; that the GSO employees try to obscure the procedures so that progress can't be verified or measured; that the GSO officer does not properly supervise his employees in spite of being aware of the problems.

I would bear the current problem with the patience with which I have borne the other problems but for my current crisis: in five weeks, my wife will have a baby that it has taken five months to prepare for to the extent of getting the layette shipped. Now the GS office is mishandling the affair. I do not have five more months to repeat the process. I do not believe that I have the sincere cooperation of the GS office. I am plenty mad.

                              Sincerely,
                              Jerome Harrison

cc: Mr. Ravndal
    Mr. Glynn

Harrison ripped the letter out of his typewriter and signed it. He knew the ambassador wouldn't react personally. He had heard that Asencio's last post, Caracas, where he'd been DCM, had had just as shitty morale as Bogotá. Asencio didn't seem to care about anything that didn't advance his career. But by sending the letter to the ambassador he knew Ravndal would have to react.

He felt better.

"What is this shit, Emil?" Asencio asked economics officer Emil Castro.

"It's my long-awaited report on the economic impact on Colombia of the narcotics trade," Castro answered.

"It wasn't worth the wait," Asencio said flatly.

"Meaning what?" Emil asked.

"You know damn well 'meaning what,' " and Asencio picked up the cable and started reading snippets out loud to its author.

" . . . 'for the last five years, Colombia has been a major supplier of illicit drugs to the U.S. To date, Colombian narcotics traffickers have put little of their huge illicit gains into legitimate business activities in Colombia; rather they have contented themselves with the purchase of luxury housing and cars, urban real estate and recently with rural real estate—especially along the north coast . . . '

"But here's where it gets good," said Asencio sarcastically.

" . . . 'the over nine-fold increase in Colombia's foreign exchange reserves over the last five years, mainly resulting from increased coffee exports, is also partially'—partially?—'attributable to the illegal export of narcotics. . . . Contrary to the positive macro-economic impact of the narcotics trade, it has had very negative social and political effects. While narcotics traffickers are not now an important factor in the Colombian economy . . . '

" 'Not now an important factor,' " Asencio repeated, " 'positive macro-economic impact'—I won't go into the fact that that seems contradictory. Crigler has told me often that he thinks you can't write."

Emil blushed. "You can see that's just the summary section of the cable. I explain it in detail, point by point, beginning in the next paragraph."

"Right," Asencio said. "So you do." And he continued reading aloud.

" . . . 'in general, Colombian officials maintain that drug income is of marginal importance to the Colombian economy. They are proud of Colombia's excellent economic performance in recent years . . . and they do not want this growth to be attributed in any way to what has occurred in the narcotics trade. Their official line is that little drug money is converted into pesos and therefore the effect on the domestic economy is minimal. . . . '

"Which government are you working for, Emil?" Asencio asked. "Theirs or ours?"

"You mean 'theirs or yours,' " Emil shot back. "It's your economic 'theories' my report contradicts."

"Ve-ry good," Asencio said, smiling. "There's a section here that says all mafioso attempts to take over legitimate Colombian companies have been turned back, and you estimate in this chart that six to seven hundred million dollars was the amount of narcotics income that entered the Colombian economy last year—which you say was only 15.3 to 17.8 percent of the total money supply in the country. Allow me to read aloud my favorite part: . . . 'coffee is number one. A major misconception, apparently held by some reporters, is that the narcotics trade is more important to the Colombian economy than is coffee. For decades, coffee has been the motor of the Colombian economy—this is still the case today. Eight hundred thousand Colombians work on coffee farms of one size or another . . . a

May 1979 study on the drug trade done by Colombia's National Association of Financial Institutions estimated this force at forty thousand workers. . . . Regarding foreign exchange earnings, narcotics is a distinct second in importance to coffee. . . . It is apparent that a large portion of income to Colombians from the narcotics trade is kept outside Colombia or is used in the flourishing Colombian black-market dollar economy. . . . '

"In sum," Asencio looked up, "drug money isn't making any serious difference to the Colombian economy and what difference it's making at all is good."

"That's right," said Emil. "Money is money."

"That's wrong," said Asencio. "I just got through testifying in Washington to the Congress of the United States that drug money is endangering the stability of the whole Colombian economy. Ergo, the Congress of the United States should give Colombia sixteen million dollars to clean it all up. You got it? Your report is just the opposite of what I told those guys."

"There aren't any figures to support your claim," said Emil.

"Jesus Christ, Castro!" Asencio stood up and leaned over his desk. "You expect the drug dealers to open their books for you? You economists—if you can't measure it, it doesn't exist, is that it?"

"Maybe it just doesn't exist," Emil answered. He was not going to be bullied.

"If you can't touch it, feel it, smell it," said Asencio, "it's not there. Maybe it's just that *you* can't touch it, feel it or smell it. It's there."

"I'm the economist," said Emil.

"And I'm the ambassador."

"I take it you're not going to send my report to Washington," Emil said, returning Asencio's stare.

"You take it right."

"What if I use the dissent channel?" asked Emil.

"Use it. Which of us do you think they'll believe? The economist or the ambassador?"

"If you feel that way," Emil asked, "then why not just send it now?"

"Because this thing is not leaving this building before my sixteen million leaves Washington. I will not take a chance of jeopardizing the whole drug program with a report I don't happen to believe is accurate. G'bye, Emil."

"G'bye, Emil," Castro repeated in a sing-song after he got back to his office. Goddamn ambassador was using the drug program to keep himself important in Washington, and using the big bad drug monster in Colombia to scare the government into protecting the ruling oligarchy. Those were Asencio's buddies, the people he knew, the people he worked with.

How could anyone "ruin" this economy? It was run by the elite for the elite. Bavaria had 80 percent of the beer market. One man bottled every soft drink in the country except Coke. Banco Colombia controlled over 40 percent of that sector. Telecom and Ecopetrol were government monopolies. They all got together and set the prices for beer and oil and you name it. And if the prices were too high, and they always were—what else were monopolies for?—then the government subsidized the high prices so that people wouldn't riot in the streets. The GOC paid 60 cents of an 80-cent bus fare. There were subsidies for coffee, rice and milk—staples of the populace. The government released figures that put the inflation rate at 29 percent and companies signed wage hikes worth 33 percent. People felt as if they were better off.

Emil wasn't sure how much longer the economy could go on like this. Probably as long as the coffee market stayed good and Venezuela employed the hundreds of thousands of illegal alien Colombians who couldn't find work in their own country. Controls had led to such corruption in the marketplace. Enough maybe to force a right-wing takeover, which would be followed by the left. Coup after coup.

Ah, but that's not important, Emil my man. Not to Washington, and therefore not to Asencio. This is Vietnam with a daily body count to prove the U.S. was "winning" the war. Only here we counted burned bales of marijuana, and seized kilos of cocaine and two *traficantes* captured here and five *traficantes* captured there. Goddamn drug people and the drug-crazy ambassador.

This was the worst embassy he'd ever worked in.

"Hey Dave!" Mike Kuhlman yelled, just as the dart left Burnett's hand. "Have you heard we're winning the war against drugs?"

"Kuhlman!" Dave stood looking at the dart board. "Don't yell at me when my arm's poised like that. I missed my bull's-eye by more than two inches."

"Why, Dave," Mike said, squinting toward the dart board, "that's how you shoot, too."

"So who says we're winning the war?" asked Burnett.

"Who else?" Kuhlman answered.

"Yeah, but Diego always tells the Colombians that to make them feel good—and to keep them working at it," Burnett said. "Here, have a dart."

Kuhlman moved up close to the board.

"Get back here!" laughed Burnett.

"You don't think he's begun to believe his own shit, Mike, do you?"

Mike moved back. "I love the guy. We all love the guy. Life here was impossible before him. But he puts great stock in stuff like the tripling of the marijuana prices—"

"I know," Burnett said as he watched Kuhlman's dart land one inch closer to the bull's-eye than his. "Last year the army seized thirty-six hundred tons of marijuana. That's less than ten percent—"

"Right," interrupted Mike, "and then Diego says—'Sure, but we've moved the traffickers south.' "

"Right," said Burnett, flinging another dart. "It's supposed to be proof that the army patrols on the coast are effective. Bull's-eye!"

"Oh they're effective," said Kuhlman. "They've effectively shifted the traffic to the army's fourth brigade, whose priority is terrorism."

"So that's what I told Diego the other day at the narc meeting," answered Burnett. "I said we had pushed the mafiosos into guerrilla territory and that drug money was being traded for guns. The guerrillas were 'taxing' the traffickers. He said, 'I don't believe that.' "

"He's wrong," stated John Bosworth, walking into the room. It was his dart room in the back of his bar, and he liked the fact that the DEA agents came to unwind at The Den.

"There are Cuban arms coming in through the north coast," said Bosworth. "You know, you guys don't need an embassy here. You just need a small group of people to work the Americans who live here. Christ, I have more access to what's going on in one hour at my bar than those foreign service 'elite' can pick up at fifty of their cocktail parties. Here today, gone tomorrow. That's what embassy people are."

John Bosworth had been in Colombia just long enough to forget how long he'd been in Colombia. He was in his late forties or early fifties—it didn't matter. He would have liked to be described as a character out of a Graham Greene novel. A sort of seedily romantic expatriate.

"Forget the violence and the rudeness and the traffic," he would say about Bogotá, "you can live better for less here." He had married a Colombian woman, had four kids, "and never changed a diaper." He liked the maids, the chauffeurs and his sunny five-bedroom house in the fashionable El Chico section of northern Bogotá. He paid the liquor inspector a kickback, cheated on his income tax and dealt heavily in black market U.S. dollars.

"Hey Mike," asked Bosworth, "did that cocaine deal for a hundred fifty kilos go down in La Paz?"

"Never heard another word from the CI," said Kuhlman. "I knew that whole thing was too good to be true."

"Here," Burnett said to Kuhlman, "gimme three darts. Best two?"

"You're on."

"This drug interdiction thing is just a game," said Kuhlman. "We need to spray."

"Uh-uh-uh," answered Burnett, staring at the dart board. "Ask Diego about that. He'll tell you drug interdiction is—

"Cheaper—" First dart.

"Safer—" Second dart.

" . . . and—what he won't tell you—more politically wise." Third dart.

"Politically wise?" Mike asked, incredulous. "What do you have there, Forty points?"

"Forty-five."

"What's politically wise about corrupting the army?" asked Kuhlman, stepping up to the throw line. "What did you tell me this morning, Clay?"

From out of an unlit corner came Clay Allison's melancholy five-vodka voice: "It's so bad junior officers are cutting their own deals now, and selling the stuff they seize."

"It's a ridiculous situation," agreed Burnett. "They're given a great choice. The drugger says, 'Here, take this suitcase of pesos—or we'll kill you!' "

Mike threw his three darts. "You know the army is using the equipment we bought for them and spreading it around for other things."

"That knowledge is so common," said Burnett. "Hah! You only got thirty-five—that Frank Crigler's heard about it."

A sodden groan came from Clay's corner.

"Yeah," laughed Burnett, "he's still looking for a 'rationale' for Asencio's drug program. So's Asencio," added Burnett. "Must have been a couple of months back he and I were sitting in this crummy little hotel room up on the coast, in Santa Marta, just talking and drinking—"

"Never heard of whoring?" slurred Clay. "Good place for whoring. . . . "

"Half the Colombian army was surrounding the hotel," Burnett went on, "to protect the American ambassador."

"From whores?" Clay asked.

"Anyway," Burnett started to laugh, "Asencio had had quite a few—"

"Whores?"

"Drinks." Burnett was doubled over now. "And he turned to me and he said, 'Dave, why don't we make some kind of agreement with the cocaine dealers or with the marijuana dealers and tell them we won't do anything to them if they'll wipe out each other.' "

Mike Kuhlman missed the dart board altogether on that one.

"Meanwhile, while Diego is running around saying the war is being won," said Burnett, "McIntyre, our esteemed State Department narcotics coordinator, is telling reporters that really, the risks are not that great and the odds are in the traffickers' favor."

"Goddammit!" said Clay. "The man is right for once!"

"Do you know what I heard about McIntyre?" said Kuhlman. "My wife, Jeannie, told me. She heard it from one of the secretaries over at the embassy. McIntyre takes all these little side trips around the country, you know, tourist stuff. That's fine, but a lot of the time he goes by himself and brings back these pictures—John in the square, John in front of the cathedral—that he took of himself with a timer, I guess."

"Weird," Clay said. "Old bachelor's weird."

"Well, you know," said Burnett, "McIntyre's been in the foreign service for seventeen years—places like Lisbon, Costa Rica, Madrid—he's never worked drugs before. I don't know why they put him in this job."

"Neither does he," Clay started to cackle. "The prince and the cowboys . . . "

"Any contracts out on you guys?" asked Bosworth.

"Nope, not that I know of," said Burnett.

"And doesn't that tell a story," Kuhlman cracked. "That's how ineffective we are. Why bother getting us out of the way when we're not in the way? Christ, I haven't had one bull's-eye all night."

"Remember those two guys about a year and a half back, Dave?" said Bosworth. "There was a half-million-peso contract on them, and then they got ambushed outside of Medellín and killed some guys and the contract went up to two million apiece. They had to drive back to Bogotá, the Medellín airport was so wired."

"Yeah," said Burnett, "I got both of them out of the country the next day."

"Anybody drunk enough yet," asked Bosworth, "to tell me if there really is a narc file on President Turbay that you can't use because Diego cut this 'drug war' deal with him?"

"John," Clay sang out. "I'm drunk."

"Good," said Bosworth. "Well?"

"We don't know if Turbay is involved," Clay said.

"Bullshit," said Bosworth and left the room.

7

Richard Baca stared at the phone by his bed. This was more like senior prom time than James Bond.

"Ring, goddammit!"

Where was Richard Starr? The FARC had had their $250,000 since Thursday. Since Thursday, Baca had been in this hot, dusty, brown hotel room in hot, dusty, brown Neiva, waiting. Jack Mitchell and an ex-cop he'd brought, named Jake, were in a hotel down the street, waiting. Starr was supposed to be delivered to them, today, Sunday, and they were supposed to call Baca. Christ, he hoped there wasn't going to be a fuck-up.

Frank Crigler and he had spent a lot of time talking about the exchange and how to do it. First they were going to have Starr just go to Mitchell's hotel room and knock on the door. But that meant the FARC would know where they were. Not great. Then they were going to park a car in Neiva's square and have Starr dropped off there. But no one was really sure what he looked like. In the end, the composer had called the shots. Starr would be brought out of the jungle by the FARC to the composer's *finca*. The composer would deliver Starr to Neiva's police station, where he would be questioned by an army general. The general would then deliver Starr to Mitchell's hotel room. Baca wasn't sure Mitchell knew about the general. He did not want Starr interrogated by the Colombian military. But it was the composer's way of squaring himself with the government. Dick Celeste, the head of the Peace Corps, had sent a cable asking that Starr's questioning be as humanely brief as possible, but the embassy wanted the military in on it to keep to a minimum any harm in the relationship between the two countries. The embassy also wanted no one anywhere near the FARC. Baca couldn't have agreed more.

Celeste had sent a lot of cables to his country director that treated the State Department like an adversary. Now that it looked as though Starr was coming home, Washington Peace Corps wanted the limelight. Baca decided to ignore them. Besides, Frank Crigler was getting a lot of cables of his own. Do whatever you can, said State Main, to keep Starr away from the Colombian Government, without, of course, violating Colombian law. Frank Crigler had looked at Richard Baca the day he'd got that one and said, "What do I do with this?" Baca had told him it's cover-your-ass time, and we're one blanket short. Write a cable back, Richard had suggested, with specific questions. Get it on paper. Frank had said he couldn't do that, so Baca had written the cable and Crigler had signed off on it.

Number One Rule in the foreign service, Baca was learning, was Don't fuck up. If you're ambitious, be cautious. Don't fuck up. Baca knew that Frank had a reputation for being a cold cutthroat when it came to his career, but Crigler had put his ass on the line more than once for Starr. Asencio would not have backed him up. Frank knew that. The ambassador had passed the buck, literally. Jack Mitchell, Jake the ex-cop, and Frank had talked at the ambassador's residence Wednesday afternoon, but the ambassador wouldn't touch the money. Frank kept the duffel bag overnight in his house.

Fuck it, smiled Baca, the embassy had broken all kinds of laws on this one.

Baca, and a doctor the Peace Corps had sent from Washington, drove down to Neiva Wednesday night from Bogotá. Five hours in the car had been a life-time with the good doctor. He had this one story about an archeological dig for Aramco in Saudi Arabia that never quit.

Jack and Jake flew in Thursday morning and Baca sent the doctor over to check in on them. He was afraid he might be recognized by some wandering Peace Corps volunteer and their cover would be blown.

The rest of Thursday he spent flat on his back with a book on his belly, just as he spent his days in the office. Meals and showers were done in shifts. This particular hotel had discovered neither room service nor air conditioning. The phone was never left unattended.

At 8:30 on Thursday night Jack and Jake called a meeting to say that they had delivered the money to the composer. They had been told Starr would be released in twenty-four to seventy-two hours. The composer had suggested it might be Sunday night.

Friday morning Baca and the doctor had driven back to Bogotá. All they were doing there was eating and peeing—and beginning to look like drug dealers, with Baca's big, red station wagon parked in a town half its size.

They drove back Saturday morning for more eating and peeing—and reading and reading. The book wasn't any good, but it beat the hell out of talking to the doctor.

Jack and Jake were antsy and bored and . . .

There was the phone!

"Hello?" Baca practically yelled.

"Monday night," Jake said, and hung up.

Asencio had never seen John Simms so upset.

"Crigler says I don't stick my neck out far enough in my reports," Simms was saying, "but I've never seen him take an unpopular position."

"Uh . . . John . . ." was all Asencio got out before Simms rushed on.

"I *have* seen him do some naive reporting. Last September, after the anniversary of the violent 1977 civil strike turned out to be so quiet, Crigler called the labor minister and sent up a one-source report, one source, that said there was no demonstration because the people were happy with their government. Happy with their government! There was a soldier on every corner that day! Of course it was in the interest of the labor minister to say what he said. But you don't pass that kind of self-serving tape-recording reporting on to Washington!"

"You're right, John," said Asencio.

"Crigler says that the political section's summary report of the week's events is 'trivial,' " Simms was almost yelling. "He wants 'spot' reporting. He wants the analytical long-range reports in 'on time.' But every day he bothers me with his little memos: 'When are you doing this report?' 'When are you doing that report?' When he leaves me alone! That's when.

"Goddammit, Diego," Simms said sadly as he dropped into the chair in front of Asencio's desk, "I've been in this country twice as long as he has. I've got good contacts. I've got seniority in age and rank. I'm fifty-five. He's forty-five. I'm an FSO2. He's an FSO3. I just can't take his high-and-mighty attitude anymore. I want you to know I've put in a request to curtail. I don't want to do the third year of my tour here with Crigler as DCM. He won't let me run my own section."

"Run your own section, John," said Asencio. "I'll talk to Frank."

Asencio gave Simms time to clear the glass door before he buzzed Crigler. God forbid their paths should cross.

"Have a seat, Frank," Asencio said and started to light his pipe.

"Was that Simms I saw leaving?" asked Crigler.

"Yes," answered Asencio between puffs.

"Is that what this is about?"

"Yes."

"Diego," Crigler began, "the reports out of the political section—and the economic section, for that matter—are lifeless, boring rehashes of newspaper clips. Simms knows a lot of people, granted, but he doesn't have the kind of relationships with his people where one of them might call up and say, Hey, this is going on, I thought you should know—which is what is supposed to be in those reports."

"Simms is understaffed," said Asencio. "He's one man short."

"I know he works hard," agreed Crigler, "and as far as I'm concerned he's two men short. I think Don Roberts is lazy. Maybe it's just that Simms isn't sharp."

"I understand that you want a different style of reporting from him," said Asencio, "not just the 'Joe hit Moe' stuff. But don't forget Simms is from the days when they wanted political reporters to go heavy on biography. Now they don't, but John is still writing who's sleeping with whom or what so-and-so eats for breakfast. I know he's not a street man, Roberts either, but Simms is good in people's offices. He's not stellar, maybe, but he's adequate."

"But Diego," objected Crigler, "I had to stop the weekly summary. It was useless. I asked Simms and Roberts to do short, terse, spot cables, daily, at least analyzing the clips, instead of just regurgitating them. Quick, grease-the-mill stuff for Washington. Well, I'm not getting anything from them, and now Washington says there's not enough paper coming from the political section. Simms and I are just going round and round with each other."

"I have a suggestion," Asencio said quietly. "I told John that he could run his own section. He doesn't know how to do what you want him to do. Razzle-dazzle is not his style. And he resents your pressure. So, Frank, do it yourself.

"I remember an embassy where I was DCM," Asencio continued, "and the consul general was an absolute disaster. In effect, I became the consul general. The administration officer had retired years before, but he was still in place, so I became the admin officer. I was doing my job and their jobs in order to accomplish the things that had to be accomplished. You do that. You compensate. I've been in situations where political sections have been weak and I was the DCM. I wrote reports. You try to use the material you have. You point your people in the right direction. You inspire them, you kick them in the butt, but if you still don't get their best from them—or if their best is not good enough—then you step into the gap. That's part of what a DCM does, Frank."

"Simms will be offended by that," said Crigler.

"Tough," Asencio answered. "My view is that I am here or there, wherever, to do a specific job and I am going to do it with or without the people around me. Now I want them to help me, but if they are incapable of doing so, or don't produce, I am still going to do the job."

"All right, Diego," Crigler sighed and stood up.

As he turned to leave he stopped, as if he had remembered something.

"Speaking of admin officers," and he handed Asencio a memorandum. "I don't think I'll wait while you read this gem. Let me know what you want to do about it, if anything."

Asencio started reading.

To: The Ambassador
   Through: Mr. F. Crigler, DCM
   From: Frank M. Ravndal

Subject: Mr. Harrison's Complaints about the Administration Section
I have attached statements from GSO and Personnel clarifying what happened.

"Dear God," Asencio said out loud. He'd read that Harrison letter, given it to Crigler and forgotten about it. Ravndal had actually answered it. Well, thought Asencio, what did Ravndal have to say? He started reading again.

I don't want to suggest that we are infallible, but I do think it is manifestly unfair of Harrison to lay the blame for his troubles (and those of other employees) to "the inability or unwillingness of the GSO employees to do their jobs." I think it is disgraceful that the alleged shortcomings of GSO personnel are "commonly enough discussed" by members of this mission. This is the kind of griping that causes bad morale for everybody and divides us among ourselves. We didn't have much of that sort of thing before last summer: before then people griped about the inefficiency of the various Colombian agencies, or the airlines, or the ports, etc., but didn't suggest the admin section wasn't doing its best to cope with a lousy situation. Maybe it's high time we got some public moral support from top management to correct this backbiting syndrome. . . .

So that's why Crigler wanted him to read it, Asencio said to himself. "Top management." Sounded like goddamn IBM. Asencio flipped to the next page. Jesus, it was a whole list of shit—"August 28/78, typed car import permit . . . August 29/78, import permit submitted to foreign office . . ."Asencio moved down the page. "Nov. 22/78, copy of import permit sent to customs for tax exemption . . . Dec. 18/78, approved tax exemption received from customs . . ." the list went on until "March 30/79, car arrived Bogotá and delivered to Mr. Harrison."

There was another, similar page devoted to the air freight and layette shipment delays.

> In conclusion, I reject Harrison's contentions. I do admit that our GSO employees have sometimes given overly optimistic clearance time estimates to people awaiting the arrival of their vehicles, and I have cautioned them against doing that. I hope the new chart on the wall in GSO will help people to understand that the procedures are many and time-consuming. The GSO does not get awards for delaying clearance; I'm surprised that people would think we are deliberately making things bad. FYI—my vehicle took four and one half months to clear after my arrival, and my wife rode buses and taxis during that time while I car-pooled, and I swear we never took it out on the GSO.

Asencio sat and stared at the memorandum. The role of an embassy, he always said, was to keep governments talking to each other. That's all. In an embassy of a hundred and some Americans, his cutting edge—the guys who were there for specific foreign policy reasons, not just to ship in household effects or send messages—was actually rather thin. Most of the people in the embassy were not there to conduct foreign policy. Asencio would compare it to the military; the number of guys at the front line shooting at the enemy, as opposed to support personnel, was limited.

The embassy's "support" infrastructure was a problem. He knew that no one knew that better than Frank Ravndal. The staff types were generally considered not to have to relate to the society they were living in. Asencio felt that was a bad mistake. It made them unhappy—the fact that they were in a foreign venue and couldn't swing in it. The secretaries didn't meet boys. They couldn't go out and get laid. They couldn't go anywhere by themselves. It was hard, and they kept falling back on the services of the embassy. Jerry Harrison obviously hadn't yet acquired the expertise to be able to be comfortable in a foreign society. And he'd had some training for it. A secretary may or may not get language or some kind of cultural training. There was usually a great deal of pressure to assign them rapidly to fill gaps where there was a shortage. Also, secretaries were usually hired from, for want of a better term, the heartland. They are not cultural relativists. They are not recruited as foreign service types. They are recruited as secretaries. They've never seen a foreigner before. They are given this glamour bit about white-tie balls. To dump these girls into a society where they can't really talk to people is a problem. Some of them rose above that and did well. Learned the language. Liked messing around with foreigners. Liked seeing strange societies. But the run of the mill found it difficult. The communicators on the fifth floor weren't recruited for foreign service either; they were recruited because they knew how to work those little machines.

Added to the Department of State support system was the growing number of other sorts of agencies who had acquired a kind of foreign service interest, and have assigned people abroad. What they did was take people out of their ordinary channels, give them a two-week course, and send them overseas. The military included. There were always, of course, marvelous exceptions. Asencio remembered the military attaché in Brasilia. That guy was the best military attaché he'd ever seen anywhere. Even now, the thought of him made Asencio smile. He had been trained by the army as a specialist in Brazilian matters. He could speak Portuguese, most unusual for a military man. He had known all the Brazilians since they were second lieutenants. He was an unusual fellow. What you usually found was a guy who, after he'd killed his bag limit in Vietnam, got a job in an embassy as a reward. Or they sent someone they didn't know what else to do with.

At any rate, all these agency types complicated the administration of an embassy. They didn't have their own support staffs. You had to wipe their noses continually. They couldn't do it themselves, because they couldn't talk to anybody. They didn't understand what the cultural imperatives were in their society. All they understood was that they were uncomfortable. They had to lean on somebody. The lightning rod was the general services officer and the administrative officer. And of course, Asencio had noted over the years, while they were busy bothering admin and GSO, they weren't doing their jobs all that well.

Asencio leaned back in his chair and lit his pipe. Instinctively he looked toward the window and, of course, was met by the usual sight—a wall full of gold brocade drapes which were never open, day or night. Security. There were the classified materials on his desk that someone with a long lens could photograph from the high rise across the street. And there was his bulky body that would make such an easy target for a sniper. And, according to his security officer, Chuck Boles, he was a target in high demand. Rumors of trouble were almost daily fare. Boles had "heard" reports the other day about "trouble" brewing. Asencio couldn't even remember the details. The thing was, if you followed every security prescription, the embassy would come to a grinding halt. You wouldn't be able to do any work at all. You wouldn't be able to do any writing. You wouldn't be able to talk to anybody on the telephone or in person. It would be a perfectly secure embassy, but it wouldn't have any reason for being here.

Asencio made a face at the drapes, got up and

walked out onto his porch. The "porch" was a narrow, unfinished concrete room, next door to his office. It overlooked the inside of the embassy "L." He leaned on the waist-high parapet and found himself at eye level with the American flag, which was slowly descending.

He was only vaguely aware of the din of rush-hour traffic. The marine and the flag seemed to move in a pool of silence.

That's what the foreign service was about. Showing the flag. Not missing layettes.

When he joined the service, back in the good old days, you arrived and they said, Nice to meet you, lots of luck, here's your first assignment. Then you met your boss and he said, Okay, get to work. Nobody held your hand. Nobody showed you anything. Nobody let you cry on his shoulder. You took care of it. It was harder, maybe, but it was better for you. Asencio wouldn't have considered for a second going to the admin officer and saying, Where are my household goods, you dirty bastard? Why aren't they here? It just wouldn't have occurred to him that that was something to do.

Asencio wondered whether Jerry Harrison wasn't more a reflection of the United States than he was of the foreign service. This whole "me-generation" stuff. People who want to be taken care of. What was happening in the foreign service was a conflict between the two worlds. Frank Ravndal obviously belonged to Asencio's time. When some snotnose kid comes in and says, "I wasn't able to clean my living room because my vacuum cleaner broke and what are you going to do about it Mr. admin officer?" Ravndal's impulse would be to reach for the guy's lapels and shake him.

Now poor Frank had to write memoranda.

What about the wives? Asencio wondered. Maybe they made the difference. The old two-for-the-price-of-one he'd always thought was a crock; but wives could be effective in setting a tone for an embassy. Not anymore. There were a lot of wives now who didn't know what to do. They aren't part of the team any longer and yet they haven't adjusted to being something separate either in these societies. He'd tried at other embassies to do something for them. He'd set up a club. Nobody came. He'd scheduled a picnic. Nobody came. He'd set up briefing sessions but unless they were made compulsory, maybe four or five would come. The rest would stay home and bitch that they didn't have anything to do. He'd finally given up.

Or maybe the difference was that it was harder to get into the foreign service when he entered. He knew that there were a lot of old-time types running around now saying affirmative action had destroyed the foreign service. But he was the result, sort of, of affirmative action. Georgetown University's School of Foreign Service, where he'd gotten his degree, was founded to "infiltrate" the Harvard-Princeton club at the Department of State. Good old Father Walsh thought the East Coast types were too soft on communism. It had never dawned on Asencio to be wary of WASPs in the foreign service. He had found them no better than anybody else, and they seemed to view him, with his name and religion, as some kind of exotic.

The marine and the flag were gone.

There was no question that the concept of an embassy needed to be changed. The question was, how?

Asencio looked at the opera-scenery sky. Loud, dramatic oranges and pinks blazed behind the sharply silhouetted mountains that surrounded the city. The windows of the office buildings around the embassy reflected the bright sky colors.

It was quite beautiful.

The British embassy was in one of those buildings. They had a terrible diplomatic service. The Brazilians were very very good. Surprisingly good. They had a tradition. Every Brazilian FSO you'd meet had a daddy or a granddaddy who was an ambassador. And they were usually wealthy. They didn't have to rely on their salary. They also had a damn good training institute.

Pound for pound, Asencio thought, the United States did well. We have it all over the French. The Russians are awful. They are terribly stiff and high-handed, sloppy, obtrusive, obnoxious. The Germans have a good foreign service, but it's small.

Asencio had as little to do with the other embassies in Bogotá as he could. He went to their "national" days and he went to arrival and farewell parties, but he found most of his diplomatic colleagues in Colombia a bunch of clunkheads. There were plenty of Colombians to make friends with. Why should he make friends with the Austrians? He knew it was an untraditional view, but he figured if his colleagues wanted to see him, let them take *him* to lunch. Or they could see him at the embassy. Why should he spend his time going to their cocktail parties? Particularly since they were usually stupid, and hardly anyone ever went except other diplomats.

Now you get a bunch of Colombian politicians together and immediately you get a round robin on who struck John. Who's doing what to whom? What did this meeting mean? What was he really saying in that speech? What is so-and-so doing? What are his ambitions? Is he really going to be a candidate for X? You pick up stuff you don't read in the newspapers. It was intelligence gathering.

As far as Asencio was concerned, he worked for the best diplomatic service in the world, warts and all, and he was very happy. He was doing what he liked to do, something that had meaning for him. It wasn't just a job, a way to earn some money. It was a career. It was a calling.

Uh-oh, there was Boles coming out into the parking lot. He better leave his porch or Chuck would spend all of the rest of the week chewing him out.

Asencio went back into his office, past his desk and on toward the couch. He sat down, lit his pipe again and put his feet up on the coffee table.

Money. He'd never had much. In two years he'd be eligible for early retirement. He wondered what he'd be worth in the private sector. But could he be happy in the private sector? Where else but in the foreign service could you get such a mix of people and issues?

Take President Julio César Turbay. "Julius Caesar," the embassy boys called him. He and Turbay had a good relationship. Asencio saw him a couple of times a month and talked to him a lot more than that by phone. One of the more unusual facets of Colombia was that you could reach for the phone, say this is the American ambassador, and talk to the president. Turbay was a nice guy. Square, fleshy face. Square, fleshy body. An intelligent man and an accomplished politician who happened to have a wooden delivery. He spoke in a nasal monotone. Asencio smiled, remembering a television interview in which he'd been asked about dancing and his first date; it was some kind of attempt to humanize Turbay. It had put everybody to sleep. The other lovable thing about Turbay was that he was unlike most of the pols in Bogotá. He was the son of a Lebanese immigrant, had no university degree, and had terrible taste in tailors and bow ties.

Asencio felt that his job was important. He wasn't ambassador to the Court of St. James, but the fact that the United States was perceived as not giving

Colombia much weight made his job—trying to get across that we did have some interests—more important than ever. Colombia was not Camp Swampy, after all.

Drugs were very important. They were the only thing besides coffee that Colombia was linked with in the popular mind, and Colombia was getting a bum rap. He'd made them do something about it and had affected the country's image in the United States. The drug program wasn't effective across the board yet. Colombia had directly intervened in the trafficking and had helped refurbish its image of itself, but the rehabilitation effort, getting the farmers not to grow any more marijuana, had not been totally successful.

The point was, we were winning. Jamaica and the Bahamas were going to be the new suppliers. Of course there was corruption. That was to be expected. What kind of corruption must there be in the U.S. if the Colombian boys were seizing more drugs?

Turbay had been as good as his word. On his inauguration day, Julio had turned to Treasury Secretary Mike Blumenthal, representing President Carter, and said, "The first thing we're gonna do is shoot the traffickers out of the sky!" And Asencio had said, "No, no!"

Asencio started to laugh remembering the scene. Turbay had said to him, "Don't you want me to stop them? I'll shoot them out of the sky!" He had answered "Don't shoot them, just stop them." Turbay had turned to Blumenthal again and said, "Send me an antiaircraft gun and we'll shoot them."

He hadn't gotten Turbay any antiaircraft gun, but he had gotten some helicopters and radio equipment and some money for fuel. And now he was going to get his sixteen million dollars. Congress had finally approved it. Already the fights had begun on how it was to be spent. The Department of State wanted Colombian customs to have it, to turn over the whole interdiction effort to them. Ridiculous. They were the most corrupt department in the country. The army wanted all kinds of new toys. The Colombian Government wanted to get the army out of drugs and replace them with a national 600-man police force. Asencio wanted radar for the air force and patrol boats for the navy. Malthea Falco, the State Department narcotics bureau chief, said, No boats—they'll use them for other things. Bullshit. Everything he'd bought them was used for narcotics. Of course, patrol boats have to be out there doing other things. It's absurd to think they won't be. But they'll also be patrolling for narcotics traffickers. Falco's argument was too pristine to make any sense. Peter Bensinger, over at DEA in Washington, hated the State Department altogether. And then there was the White House narc. Poor Eileen Heaphy would call twice a day sometimes, asking him how to handle one or the other of the Washington types. He told her the best thing to do was what he did—duck.

Asencio had to admit he was tired of being a policeman. It wasn't the guys here. They were top-notch. It was dealing with all those prima donnas in Washington.

He remembered once coming up with a brilliant idea on how to handle his narc section, with its built-in organization problem. Neither McIntyre, nor any other State Department coordinator, for that matter, had authority over the DEA types. Asencio had suggested bringing in a U.S. attorney who had task-force experience. He would be neither State Department nor DEA. Sounds good, Malthea Falco said, but Bensinger will never buy it. She agreed to try it out on Bensinger if her buddy Dr.

Peter Bourne, the narc at the White House, would also agree. Asencio had called Bourne. Bourne agreed, and Asencio had flown up to Washington to meet with all three of them. His mistake was that he had mentioned the plan to Dave Burnett and Burnett had evidently warned his boss. Bensinger, a very clever fellow, started the meeting by saying that's just the greatest idea he'd ever heard and Malthea said, hey, wait a minute, and started bad-mouthing the plan. Then so did Bourne—just because Bensinger had said he liked it. It was the most hilarious meeting Asencio had ever had.

Asencio considered his diplomatic style non-interventionist. He didn't mind horsing around with drugs, but he did mind supporting one faction against another. It was none of his business. Political intervention was out of order. Asencio didn't think the U.S. ought to overthrow societies, whether they were left or right. It was a nasty business, terribly dangerous because you don't know what you are going to get, and in any case the United States did it badly. As the ambassador, he felt he was required to maintain contacts, which didn't imply approval or support. You have relations with the government that's there. Of all the Latin American regimes, Colombia was certainly among the most liberal and democratic. Income distribution was a problem. Asencio didn't consider improving the living conditions of a society interventionism. It was good for everybody. Good for business, good for Colombian relations, good for the image of the U.S. But the United States didn't have an economic development program anymore, and the Alliance for Progress was dead. Economic aid, he realized, was terribly easy to attack. Why in the hell should we support foreigners?

One of the reasons, thought Asencio wryly, was that otherwise they would end up in Miami in tent cities. He felt that the United States was getting deeper and deeper into a protectionist mentality. Sadly, we are, in the end, a parochial society.

Asencio's pipe had long gone out. It was late. Time to go home. He had a nice quiet evening to look forward to for once. No parties. No dinners. Maybe he'd put a few "Star Trek" tapes on the Betamax.

Asencio knew his science-fiction addiction was a bit of an embassy joke, but he considered science fiction a didactic tool. Just the thing a developing society needed. It was a way of teaching people to think long term. The ordinary Colombian didn't think past next week. The government only got as far as next year.

"Come to think of it," Asencio said out loud, "that might be a good way to get our foot in the university doors again, where those professors are feeding their kids a lot of raw meat about the U.S.A."

Asencio picked himself up off the couch and marched down the hall toward the elevators. Maybe Kristula was still around.

Richard Baca's eyes shifted back and forth between his watch and the phone. Starr was supposed to be handed over between nine and ten o'clock tonight. Jake had worked out a code. At ten Baca was to call and ask Jake out for a drink. If he said, "Sure," that meant Starr was there with him and Jack Mitchell. If Jake said, "It's kind of late for me," that meant they would meet the next morning.

At 9:59, as Baca started to reach for the phone, it rang.

"Come over and have that drink," Jake said.

"Good," Baca answered and hung up. He and the doctor did the five-minute walk to Jack and Jake's hotel in two.

Baca was taken aback for a split second by

Starr's appearance. Almost all of the hair on his head was attached to his chin. The dazed eyes behind the granny glasses and the huge unkempt beard reminded Baca of Washington Irving's Rip Van Winkle. Starr was wearing a rumpled blue polo shirt, blue cotton pants and boots up to his knees. The parrot on his shoulder took off as Baca gave Starr a bear hug.

"Is this really it?" Starr asked the room. "Is it over?"

Jake had ordered a round of rum and Cokes. Starr picked his up and looked at it a long time. "First alcohol in three years," he said.

Baca stayed about an hour. A stunned Starr was slowly absorbing his surroundings. He seemed confused to hear English spoken and was clearly not used to a roomful of friendly faces.

When Jack Mitchell started to interview the poor bastard, Baca delivered a you-guys-are-really-compassionate crack and returned to his hotel room. He dialed Frank Crigler's home number. It was now after eleven o'clock.

"Frank?" Baca said. "It's done. We've got it."

"How does it look?" Crigler asked.

"Fine."

"Good job."

Crigler hung up and called the ambassador.

8

RICHARD BACA was again taken aback by Starr's appearance the next morning. Starr arrived for breakfast wearing a pair of Baca's jeans, carrying Baca's sister-in-law's suitcase full of underwear and socks—looking like nothing more than a kid who had been away a couple of weeks at camp.

All during the meal, "Charlie," their name for him in public, asked about the most ordinary events: the presidential primaries in Iowa and New Hampshire, the Super Bowl game. He asked Baca about what had happened to some of his former Peace Corps colleagues and he thanked Baca for the packages of books and batteries that he said had saved his sanity.

Starr explained that he had wanted algebra and trigonometry books because working out math problems helped pass the time and kept his brain active. For some reason the guerrillas were suspicious of the math books and only allowed him fiction. He had been moved around a lot, but managed to raise some pets—one of which, the parrot he named Solzhenitsyn to irritate his guards, he wanted to take home to the States.

The shortwave radio he had in his knapsack when he was captured had been his tie to freedom. He had listened whenever he could to Voice of America and BBC broadcasts, but had to ration himself because the guerrillas kept taking his extra batteries.

It was Richard Starr who delivered the best line of the morning. He said he would love to write about his experience but, "Who would buy a book with an exciting first chapter, an exciting last chapter, and three boring years in between?"

The rest of the day had gone according to plan. The general came with a couple of maps to try to pinpoint with Starr where he'd been held by the FARC. When he saw there was not going to be any interrogation session, Baca had driven to Neiva's airport to meet the chartered Lear jet arriving from Bogotá.

He sent the car back to pick up everybody at the hotel and went with the pilot to file the flight plan. It was illegal to fly from Neiva out of Colombia non-stop, and Ken Keller, the consul general, was supposed to have wired it with the Colombian Government. It was the last chance for a hitch.

Baca watched the car return and waited until everyone was in the plane before he told the driver to call Frank Crigler as soon as they had taken off.

They were minutes away from Walker Air Force Base in Panama before Baca felt the first wave of real relief.

His job in Neiva had been to prevent any hysterics, to change anybody's diapers if they shit in their pants—and to make sure that Starr wasn't a Patty Hearst. His job in Panama was to make sure that Starr talked as little to the press as possible, and that he didn't say something like, "Damn the U.S. I was sold out. Three years they let me rot in captivity." Baca was also supposed to remind Jack Anderson's guy, Jack Mitchell, of the deal he'd agreed to: not to write a word about the embassy's involvement in Starr's release.

Baca scanned the caravan waiting near the runway. He couldn't see a hint of any press.

Richard Starr was the first out of the plane. He ran toward his waiting mother and their embrace brought the first warm feelings toward Charlotte Jensen that Baca had felt in months.

"Oh God . . . my son . . . my son," she was saying. And then, with a hand on each of her son's shoulders, his mother leaned back to take a good look at what three years had wrought.

Baca watched her face fold into a frown.

"You need a haircut," she said.

The sunshine committee meeting was broken up by a bomb scare at four o'clock in the afternoon.

It was a pleasant surprise. Late afternoon bomb warnings were truly a bit of sunshine for the whole embassy. There was no point in waiting for the marines to finish their sweep of the building, so it meant "early to home," as Jerry Harrison would say.

The bomb scares were always false alarms. There had been one small thing that had gone off in the embassy parking lot a couple of months ago without even damaging a car. And, of course, there had been the bomb that exploded last year near the door of the Marine House, throwing one marine across the pool table in the front room. But, by and large, Jerry found bomb scares to be welcome, vicariously dangerous escapes from desk and phone.

This afternoon's interruption was particularly welcome. Every time the committee had steered anywhere near the problems with GSO and admin, Mrs. Frank Ravndal had whined: "Why is everyone always blaming everything on GSO?"

The bomb scare separated the wheat from the chaff. Marilyn Ravndal and the senior officers went home. Figuring good company and commissary liquor would transform the sunshine committee's deadlocked agenda from impotent conversation to potent commiseration, Jeannie Kuhlman, who unofficially chaired the committee, invited the rest to her house—almost all junior officers. It was one of the natural social splits in the embassy—the young separate from the old.

"All right, Jerry," Jeannie said, "what happened with the letter you wrote to the ambassador?"

"It got Ravndal's attention," said Jerry. "The layette was delivered soon thereafter and neither Ellis Glynn nor Frank Ravndal is speaking to me."

"Reason enough to write a letter," said Phil Ferris dryly.

"And," added Jerry, sipping a beer, "Ravndal sent me a Xerox of his letter to the ambassador. It was full of the usual junior-officers-aren't-what-they-used-to-be shit."

"Any reaction from Asencio?" asked Phil. "Did he see the letters?"

"There won't be any reaction from the ambassador," Jerry answered. "The inside of the embassy is Crigler's responsibility. I'm sure the letters were passed on to him—not exactly your port-in-the-storm kind of guy."

"Christ," said Phil, "do you remember the meeting Crigler had with us juniors after the embassy takeover in Teheran?"

Jerry Harrison started to smile. "Yeah," he said. "And we answered that we felt we weren't getting paid enough for that kind of duty. He blanched. I don't think he thinks junior officers are what they used to be either."

"Nothing is ever as good as the 'good old days,' " said Jeannie.

"A vintage line," Phil observed. "And there's another one. 'If you don't like your job, wait two years, it'll change.' That's the old State Department standard. If you don't like your present post the next one will be different. Well, what a waste of two years. The foreign service is just another way to make a living for me. I'm not necessarily looking at it as a career."

"Hear, hear," cheered Michele Harrison, as she walked into the room. "Your son let me in, Jeannie. Don't let me interrupt."

But in absolutely no time, Michele, with Jeannie's help, turned the conversation to the subject most dear to both hearts—the wives. "Women come to talk to me in the Family Liaison Office because they don't have any place else to go," said Jeannie. "They don't know what to do with their kids. And they don't know what to do with themselves."

"Have you ever heard Fran Pastorino run through her list of activities?" asked Michele. "Tennis, horseback riding, group trips to orchid farms and pottery factories. I hear she's taking classes in cake decorating! Jerry and I just joined one of the country clubs here—it's just a sports club really. But it's a chance to get away from a social life totally immersed in the embassy—no offense. There are some young couples from the Canadian and British embassies who belong."

"Yes, you two can afford that," said Jeannie. "But most of the families can't. The minimum membership in a Bogotá country club is something like sixty thousand pesos a year, with a ten thousand-peso initiation fee. That's more than fifteen hundred U.S. dollars."

"Present company aside," said Jerry, "I think more than a few wives here have taken up bitching as a full-time job."

"There's no doubt about that," agreed Jeannie, "but I think that can be avoided. You know those first days in a new country can be so traumatic the wife never recovers. She just isolates herself as a form of self-defense."

Jeannie refilled her gin and tonic and recalled her own first days. She, her husband, Mike, and their two young children were put into a three-bedroom suite in the Hilton Hotel when they arrived in Bogotá. It was wonderful. Jeannie had help interviewing for a maid because she couldn't speak Spanish then. And DEA friends helped her and Mike find a house. They moved in and, overnight, Jeannie was helpless. When the maid arrived Jeannie was so embarrassed that she couldn't speak to her in Spanish, she would sit in the bedroom all day writing letters and reading. She remembered being near tears one day trying to get somebody on the phone who could translate for her because a repairman couldn't understand what she wanted. They had no car for six months. Mike was on the road all the time. No language, no car, no Mike.

"And what happens," said Michele, "is that you come to hate the environment that has put you on the defensive."

"Right," said Jeannie. "First you hate Colombia, and then you hate Colombians."

"I considered myself a broad-minded person until I came here," Michele said. "They're such rude people. I still feel intimidated when one of those 'guards' comes up to me in Carulla's parking lot and says, 'Can I protect your car?' If you don't pay him some pesos, you'll come back with your groceries and find your windshield wipers gone. He means protect the car from himself!

"And the Colombians when they're being polite," added Michele, "are so absolutely insincere. They'll come up to you and give you this flood of hellos— '*cómo estás . . . qué hay . . . qué hubo . . . cómo te va . . . qué mas . . .* It's all strung into one sentence. They don't want any answers. I prefer them rude.

"You know what it really is," Michele continued, "We just aren't anything alike as people. They've screwed up their country with their 'patience' and their fatalism. They say they care about family here. Yet they let their children beg and steal on the streets. What they really mean is they care more about who they're related to than what it is they do for a living.

"Sorry to get so carried away," Michele said abruptly. "I was a person who never yelled until I moved to this country."

"I know what you mean," Jeannie said. "I elbow people in the bank and grocery lines with the best of them now." Jeannie remembered when a cab driver tried to charge her double because he could tell she was an American. Jeannie refused to pay him, so he locked the doors on her. She pulled out her trusty can of Mace and he still wouldn't unlock the doors. But Jeannie wouldn't pay him what he asked. Finally her next door neighbor—a wonderful Colombian lady, in fact—came home. Jeannie yelled at her to call the police. The cab driver let her out then. She never paid him anything.

"C'mon, Jerry," Michele said, "we've got to get ready for that party at the *residencia*. Crigler expects you to be stationed near the front entrance by seven o'clock. See you tonight, Phil?"

"I'll be there," Ferris answered.

When Jeannie got back to her living room, after seeing everyone to the front door, she found that Jim Welch had not budged off the couch. Nor, it suddenly occurred to her, had he said one word since he arrived.

"Jim?" asked Jeannie. "Is something wrong?"

"Sean wants to go back to the States," Jim said, his eyes filling with tears.

"Oh God, I'm sorry," Jeannie said and she sat down beside him. Jim Welch was a junior officer in USICA, the information agency, and Jeannie knew that his oldest son, sixteen-year-old Jimmy junior, had left three months after his arrival, refusing to make the adjustment from Houston to Bogotá. Sean was one year younger.

"Same reason?" asked Jeannie.

"Not really," Jim explained. "It's been a year now and he's adjusted to everything but the school. He's had it with Colegio Nueva Granada."

"Hasn't everybody," Jeannie said ruefully. The student body at Nueva Granada was fifty-one percent Colombian. The school's *bachillerato* program was more advanced than the U.S. K-12 equivalent, and there was a problem with marijuana. Jeannie had spent hours with the school's director, Phyllis Mullenax, trying to find answers to some of the problems. The Americans dressed in blue jeans. The Colombians dressed in cashmere and emeralds. There was no school identity, no school spirit.

"Have you ever talked with Ratso Ravndal about the school?" asked Jim.

"Many times," said Jeannie.

"And?"

"And . . . let's see if I can quote the last conversation directly: 'In 1978 Colegio Nueva Granada got a high rating as a quality school. Here we are two years later and it's the number one issue in the embassy. Why? Because there are a lot of new officers and there's been a big turnover at the school and these new kids are having academic problems. Probably because they're a bunch of dummies. There are a high proportion of senior officers' kids involved. It was the front shop fellows who started these school meetings. They'd sit around and say, Can you top this? So now it's become a morale problem. The State Department only pays two percent of the school's budget, but early this year we tried another school survey anyway. The response was so low it wasn't worth tabulating. People who complain like something to do. And you know something else? Lots of these kids are just little bigots.' "

"That's what he told you?" asked Jim, bug-eyed. "Well, Sean's not a 'little bigot.' I mean I don't think that . . . you know, I don't know. I listened to everything said here this afternoon and couldn't have agreed more. I used to think of myself as the traditional American liberal. But not since I came to Bogotá. I feel real hostility here. Maybe I have passed some of that on to Sean. I was wrong to bring my boys here. I joined the foreign service last year to escape. I was an assistant professor of English at the University of Houston who wasn't publishing enough to qualify for tenure. I had just gotten a divorce. At age thirty-five I wanted a change. And the foreign service has been like 'Mom.' Job security, housing, furniture, social life. Dr. Johnson had it wrong. Patriotism is not the last refuge of a scoundrel, it's the last refuge of a coward."

By eight o'clock Phil Ferris was on his fourth sherry. He could see the Asencios still greeting people by the front door. Phil thought the ambassador's grin had turned into a bit of a grimace. In fact, before the guests had started arriving, he'd overheard Asencio complaining to Mike Kristula that there were fifty too many people on the guest list and why hadn't Mike cut it as Asencio had requested?

"Hey Mike," said Phil, catching the embassy's USICA chief by the right elbow. "Why didn't you cut the guest list like the ambassador said?"

"Ferris," Kristula began.

"It's just a joke, just a joke!" Phil laughed. "This is hard work! Asencio is right. He says the first thing to go in the foreign service is the stomach. The second is the liver, and the third is the arches. Tell me who's here again?"

"The guests of honor," said Mike, "are some people from Florida, which is a 'sister state' of Colombia. You can't miss them. They are the ones with the suntans. Ever seen a *bogotano* with a sun-tan? Can't be done. Since this is a sister-state party I've just tried to get a good mix of Colombians who speak English and a crosscut of the American com-munity in Bogotá. And this party wouldn't have had to be so big but for the fact that the Asencios don't have enough of them."

"Why not?" asked Phil.

"You've heard him on the subject," answered Mike. "He considers parties work. He considers the stuff USICA does—the cultural affairs, the ballet companies, musicians and artists we bring from the States—as 'crap.' If it's not science fiction or drugs, he doesn't pay attention."

Ferris had heard Mike Kristula on the subject often enough too. He knew Kristula felt that the United States' real manipulation of Colombia was cultural. USICA placed a lot of Voice of America pro-grams on radio and television in Colombia because there was a real need to fill airtime here. And because their TV system was so primitive, in com-parison to the U.S., anybody who was anybody owned a Betamax or two. What they played on their Betamaxes were Spanish-dubbed American mo-vies.

"But you guys have a huge program here," said Phil, "complete with an auditorium in the embassy. Wasn't that Diego's idea?"

"No," Mike said. "That was an ambassador's before him—Pete Veckey. Veckey saw Colombia as a wide-open country, culturally. And he thought we should take advantage of it. USICA is here to project a certain image of the United States. I think we do more for relations with Colombia—we clean up after the rest of the embassy. 'And malt does more than Milton can to justify God's ways to man.' Housman. Now go mix. There are a lot of interesting people here."

Nancy Asencio was showing a handful of Floridian women around the residence. "Now straight back from the foyer is the formal dining room. The cut-glass chandelier and all the sterling silver was here when we came. I had the walls painted violet and put in the magenta rug. I think warm colors are important, don't you?"

"Ummm," murmured one of the Floridian ladies, whose ample bosom supported a "Hi, I'm Olive Johnson" tag. Mrs. Johnson exchanged a look of horror with a very tan Mrs. Judy Richards.

"There are really three wings," Nancy continued, "coming off the circular foyer. The dining room is one, with the kitchen behind it. Another is the den. And the third is right over here. . . . ."

"Oh this peach color is lovely," exclaimed a relieved Mrs. Johnson.

"This is the morning room," Nancy said. "We have a dramatic view of the city from here, as you can see."

"Oh, and look at that sky!" Mrs. Richards effused, stepping up to the full-length windows. "All that pink!"

"That's just pollution," Nancy remarked flatly.

"What it must be like to have a home like this," Mrs. Johnson said, turning toward her hostess. "I'm so jealous."

"Don't be," Nancy said. "It's not mine. It belongs to the United States Government."

"Oh dear," murmured Mrs. Johnson to Mrs. Richards. "Uh, Mrs. Asencio . . . I mean . . . your lifestyle. Isn't it better than you could afford in the States? I mean, isn't it sort of fun to live beyond your . . . what I mean to say is, isn't this kind of lifestyle an advantage?"

"It does have advantages," agreed Nancy, "we've lived in some very nice places. Our children are all bilingual and, we hope, bicultural. But it can be a fast-moving and lonely life at times. One beauty of the foreign service is the number of relationships you develop with people of all kinds. You find out things about yourself. I was pleased to find that I have tremendous humanity. . . ."

"Por favor, señoras?" asked a pretty young girl in a black dress and starched white apron as she offered a tray of sherry.

As everybody politely refused, Nancy said, "She came to us from the convent. The convent kicked her out. She didn't fit there. She doesn't fit here either. Too dull. . . ."

"So forget about love between our two countries," José Fernandez was telling Phil Ferris. José was a bristly older man who hosted what was considered one of the best television talk shows in Colombia. "You Americans are white, blond and you have good milk. We are a very poor, disorganized country with milk full of amoebas. Some hate is logical. Besides, you are not sent to make friends. You are sent here to watch. All your intelligence collecting and you never know exactly how to relate. You don't send your first-class people to Colombia. Your first-class people go to Paris and London.

"Oh, we Colombians like the material things of the United States. And we know all about them. We are educated by American publications and news organizations. The minister of public works studied at Harvard. But we distrust American politics. In matters of foreign policy, the U.S. plays poker, while the Russians play chess. Our 'Big Brother,' John F. Kennedy. Then LBJ and Nixon. From bad to worse. Soap opera images. Do you know whose image the poor hang in their house? Castro's! Maybe Castro is good. He finished the rich—that's enough for the poor."

"Castro doesn't promise democracy," Phil said.

"Democracy!" intoned Fernandez, who was clearly having a good time. "Democracy is a concept.

Abstract. Poverty is real. Six people run Colombia. They are clever men and very rich. We have only one hundred fifty years of history. Our laws are easy to avoid. We have too much bureaucracy. Two-thirds of our country is jungle. Forget about it. The rich help the poor because they are worth votes. I am not optimistic for the middle class. Colombia has a machine—like what was his name in Chicago?"

"Mayor Richard Daley," said Phil.

"Right," Fernandez said, grabbing another sherry off a passing tray. "That is the man. You mustn't be upset with us. You know we don't feel secure about the future of our country. In the United States you make your life better for your sons and family. You are sure about tomorrow. We live for today in Colombia. That is all that is ever guaranteed. So you see the feelings of envy and resentment. It is necessary to be anti-American to be 'in'. . . .

"Ah!" Fernandez said, pulling a younger, pudgier redhead into the group. "Speaking of leftist as fashionable. Here is my favorite 'communist'—Daniel Samper, the famous columnist of *El Tiempo*. He also owns stock in the paper and a lovely apartment. Daniel, what are you doing in this fray? I thought you only attended parties of less than eight?"

"It's all right," laughed Samper, "I brought my brother Ernesto for protection."

"This is Phil Ferris, a young officer of the embassy's political section," said Fernandez. "Do you think he is CIA?"

Phil blushed while Samper scrutinized him through his horn-rimmed glasses.

"Too tall."

"So, Daniel," said Fernandez, "I was telling Mr. Ferris about Colombian and U.S. relations. How would you describe them?"

"Briefly," Samper laughed. "First, there is the

goverment-to-government relationship. Second, there is the people-to-people relationship. Third, there is the analytical, intellectual community. In the first category, there are not many touchy issues now, especially if Turbay pulls the army out of the drug war. Turbay is pro-foreign investment and Colombia cooperated closely with the United States to keep Cuba out of the United Nations Security Council. In the second, there is more admiration for the U.S. dollar than the U.S. people. Colombians go to the United States to work. They send U.S. dollars back home to their families and return to Colombia themselves after four or five years. There are a thousand Colombian prostitutes earning a thousand dollars a month in Panama. They send home four hundred dollars a month. They think gringos are stupid. Third, the analytical, intellectual community in Colombia considers Americans to be a mix of naiveté and gracelessness. Americans are not intellectuals; they are conspicuous consumers. They do not think things, they have things."

"Which you are all crawling all over each other to get," Phil said flatly.

Samper laughed.

"Daniel, I'm surprised," said Fernandez. "Have you not one word to say about human rights? That's your favorite issue! The FARC versus the Colombian army. Jimmy Carter would have the FARC as the personification of human rights. Do they have wings? Are they angels? It's stupid!"

"Ah, the Colombian army," sighed Samper. "Our 'civilist,' anti-coup army. You would call our democracy 'precarious,' no, Pepe? We have a ruling class which is very able and doesn't like change. But the army has changed. The army is on stage as never before. The guerrilla groups are not important; the army is using them to seem important, to keep their state of siege. The military is all around our civil institutions: justice, defense, the executive branch. And because they have been given control of the emerald mines and the drug war they are now corrupt. If you compare Colombia to Argentina or Chile we are not bad, I agree. But we are not what we were even one year ago. Your government, Mr. Ferris, has great power in your human rights policy."

"Bah!" Fernandez said. "In El Salvador the people say the army is protecting them from their government. I can see that happening here."

"Do you believe Jeannie Kuhlman's twelve-year-old, David?" Marilyn Ravndal asked Michele Harrison. "He rides the buses by himself. He visits their maid's family in the slums in south Bogotá. He even got on some old dirty clothes, put some mud on his face and went out on Carrera Quince pretending he was a *gamini*! You know, those poor scruffy kids who sell contraband Marlboros and beg at cars stopped at the lights?"

"Have you met David?" asked Michele.

"No."

"He's really quite extraordinary. He's totally bilingual and totally curious about his surroundings. He says his American friends don't even have permission to go around the block, and so they sit and watch their Betamaxes all the time. He finds them boring, so he plays with Colombians."

"I've raised three children," sighed Marilyn, "and fifty thousand maids. Now I want some privacy. I've always made my calls and fulfilled my entertainment responsibilities, and I still do. But here I've not gotten involved in a blind school or a retarded school or a deaf-and-dumb school. Frank made me take up golf when the kids grew up and left. That was a hard stage. I would be miserable now without golf.

"—Did I tell you? I took the foreign service exam."

"Oh really," Michele answered, looking around for someone else to talk to. "What happened?"

"I flunked it," Marilyn laughed.

"There is something to be said for fascist societies," Diego Asencio was telling a group of American businessmen. "Lisbon was probably the most comfortable post I've ever had. We had beautiful housing. The beaches were just a few miles away. A very picturesque country with castles on the hill and medieval fishing villages. It was a pleasant, orderly, neat, clean place.

"Did I ever tell you my Lisbon riot story?" Asencio asked. Now *there* was a reason for parties, the ambassador thought. New audiences for old stories. The Lisbon riot story was one of his best—in a repertory of dozens. He had been relatively new in Portugal at the time. It must have been '67, '68, and the embassy was expecting a demonstration. Their information was that the demonstrators were going to bring a petition about the Vietnam war. The police wanted to divert the people from the arrival home of the president of Portugal from a trip to Africa. There was some linkage by the demonstrators between the Vietnam war and the Portuguese African war, so they said okay, let them fuss at the American embassy. The ambassador, whom Asencio considered a bit strange, decided that it was going to be business as usual. They would fly the flag and go about the usual things, no matter what. But as it got closer to demonstration time, the ambassador kept getting more and more nervous. Finally, he allowed most of the secretaries and staff to go.

There was this naval attaché who was a hilarious guy, absolutely insane. Rody was a very social type, very wealthy. He was given charge of the security of the embassy. On the day of the demonstration he arrived in full dress uniform with a sword. It kind of made everybody think. He went puttering around, placing people at different spots.

Eventually there was a staff meeting and the ambassador said, "Well, someone should be downstairs to receive the petition." Lisbon was a quiet spot then, where they sent people for R and R. So suddenly everybody had looked at Asencio. He said, "Well, all right," told Rody he would receive the petition and then went outside. The embassy was in the center of town, with all sorts of traffic and cars double parked—usually. Now there wasn't a soul in sight! There was absolute silence.

"And then I hear Rody locking the door and dropping the steel curtain, so I banged on the door and said, Rody, what the hell are you doing? He said, Bye, bye"—and Asencio waved his hand at the transfixed businessmen.

"And then I heard the chants as the kids marched down the avenue. Jesus Christ, I said to myself. Here they come with these banners and I said, Well, what the hell? So I'm waiting at the curb, you see, and they were within twenty-five feet of me, shouting and chanting, when the police arrived. They bounced out of these buses with dogs and truncheons and just rolled over the students as I stood there with my mouth open. They just mauled the hell out of them. And that's when this Fulbright kid I knew starts to scream, Help! I'm an American! I reached into the pile, grabbed him and yelled, He's one of ours. I told the kid to scram.

"The crowd eventually dispersed, and Rody let us back into the embassy. I had a few words with him like, Listen, you son of a bitch . . ."

The Colombian psychic had Nancy Asencio pinned against the wall while he stared deeply into her eyes and breathed heavily through his nose. "*La embajadora no está contenta . . . la embajadora está intranquila. . . .*"

"*Embajadora*?" said a young Colombian lady. "What country are you *embajadora* from?"

"The United States," said Nancy, peeling her eyes away from the psychic.

"Oh, *Dios mio!*" the lady screamed. "You're Nancy La Cubana!"

It was a woman from the art class that she had been attending incognito.

"Oh, please don't say anything back at the school," Nancy pleaded.

The lady was still wide-eyed when she walked away. Nancy looked at the psychic and said, "Damn." Now she would be back to being the ambassador's wife again. The jig was up. She grabbed a glass of sherry and went toward the food table.

"What is it you do here, Colonel?" asked the tall florid-faced Floridian wearing a "Hi, I'm Mr. Bud Johnson" tag.

"I head up what's called the Milgroup," explained Colonel Carl Wittenberg. "We work right in the Defense Ministry with the Colombian military—only foreign military allowed there since World War II. There's six of us including me. Two air force, two navy, and two army. We're not part of the embassy, strictly speaking. But we are part of what is called the country team.

"The main reason we're here, Mr. Johnson, is because of the security assistance program. We give direct aid, credit and long-term loans to Colombia to procure American military equipment and parts. We're here on the spot to help them choose that equipment and to help train them to operate and maintain it.

"Meet Colonel Diego Monsalve. He works at the helicopter base in Melgar, which is a couple hours down the mountain."

"How d'ya do," Mr. Johnson said.

"Colonel Monsalve," said Colonel Wittenberg, "has two primary missions: guerrillas and narcotics."

"My principal mission is guerrillas," corrected Colonel Monsalve. "We should not be in drugs. That is customs and police work."

"Well, it certainly is in the U.S. of A.," agreed Mr. Bud Johnson.

"Those bullet-proof seats in the new helicopters any help against the FARC?" Colonel Wittenberg asked Colonel Monsalve.

"It's better," Colonel Monsalve said, "but we lost another man last week you know. . . ."

"How are you doin' against those fellas?" asked Mr. Johnson. "The guerrillas, I mean."

"No better, no worse," said Colonel Monsalve.

"Ummm," murmured Bud Johnson as he started to scan the room for his wife, Olive.

"Hey Diego!" Stan Kleppe grabbed the ambassador by the arm. Kleppe was Exxon's man in Colombia, and one of the few American businessmen around Asencio considered worth his salt. "I hear Father Bean gave you a lecture at Mass last Sunday!"

"Was that for me, do you think?" laughed Asencio. "Weren't you sitting in the back there, you stinking-rich oilman?"

"I was out playing golf," answered Kleppe. "Did I tell you I took up the game of golf? The country club is the only safe place where I can get away from my bodyguards for a little walk and a little peace. I hate golf. You're changing the subject on me. I hear Father Bean talked about 'people living comfortably overseas in the midst of poverty, who sit back and let half-cocked Marxist philosophy fight the fight instead of changing government structures that treat people as throwaways.' "

"Oh, I agree entirely," said Asencio, "and if he

wants to change things through love, that's all right.

"Hey Stan what's going on with the Guajira coal project?"

"I'm going to recommend that we go ahead," answered Kleppe. "Not only do our studies show that the stuff is commercially viable, but there's enough of it to generate as much income as coffee for Colombia."

"Do you have the usual deal with Ecopetrol?" asked Asencio.

"Yes," answered Kleppe. "It's an association contract. We'll pay for all exploration costs. The mining of the coal and the building of the port and railroad, we split fifty-fifty with Colombia. They'll then take twenty percent off the top in royalties once we get started. And of course fifty-six percent in taxes. It'll take us twenty years to get our money back."

"How long is it before you get started?" asked Asencio. "Will you be in time to help me with my Guajira project?"

"I don't think so," Kleppe answered. "I don't think we'll be operational until 1985. Then we can hire three thousand to thirty-five hundred of your Indians away from the drug traffic."

"Have you had any trouble up there?" asked Asencio.

"Well, we've been drilling now for three years. We've only lost one truck. There's a detachment of twenty or thirty Colombian military protecting the camp."

"I was just curious," Asencio said. "Gene Grogan, you know, Cities Service, says there's been trouble between union leaders and the army up where he's drilling in the Magdalena valley. Saturday, the army detained three union leaders, communists, I gather. Sunday morning an army lieutenant and his driver were killed."

"No, nothing like that."

"Something else," Asencio added, "Grogan mentioned the fact that the French are paying money under the table for access to radar mineral maps. You know anything about that?"

"Well, Diego," answered Kleppe. "Don't you sometimes think we Americans are at a bit of a disadvantage with that Foreign Corrupt Practices Act?"

"That may be," Asencio said, "but you oil types are doing fine. They need your exploration money and technology. The manufacturing types, well, there really hasn't been any growth in foreign investment here since Colombia joined the Andean Pact eleven years ago. No American company wants a fifty-one/forty-nine percent deal. General Electric is still moving into a minority share. Sears sold out. They weren't making any profit."

"Uh, Diego," said Kleppe, "you forgot to mention they got their American vice-president kidnapped too."

"Yeah, but they only kept him three months and then released him. There wasn't even any ransom paid. And, Kleppe, that was way back in 1975."

"Things have seemed quieter lately," Kleppe agreed. "I'm thinking of dropping one of my two guard cars."

"God, the food's good, isn't it?" Jan Grogan remarked to Phyllis Mullenax. "Have you had any of that stuff wrapped in bacon?"

"I have tasted every single thing on this long, ladened table," laughed Phyllis. "I don't get invited to the residence much anymore. Ambassador Veckey's wife used to call me all the time to come over and drink sherry and talk shit. I don't know Nancy very well."

"Well," answered Jan, "don't feel special. The Asencios don't spend much time with the American community here. A few noses are out of joint."

"You know," Phyllis said, "I've lived in Colombia eighteen years. The embassy people used to be brilliant young men on their way up. They were better educated. Now they don't seem to be in touch with reality. They work with paper, not with people. I don't know how we can justify embassies much longer. They regard themselves as closer to God, a cut above the ordinary American overseas, but they don't even get to know the country. I mean, can embassy personnel ever *know* a Colombian? Can they talk about *close* Colombian friends? Forget foreign policy. They have trouble getting from day to day. Such a boring, inbred group. And their kids. The kids I see at Colegio Nueva Granada are hemmed in with all the security precautions, and thrown on their own resources too much by socially overcommitted parents. There is a lot of anger at their parents for bringing them here."

"My girls tell me the embassy kids are spoiled," said Jan. "What's the problem with drugs?"

"Marijuana, mostly," answered Phyllis. "It's so easy to get. The kids buy it at certain kiosks on the street. They know which ones. My Americans are smoking marijuana, and my Colombians are beating up queers in downtown Bogotá. Do you believe it?"

"*Cómo estás? . . . Qué hay? . . . Qué hubo? . . . Cómo te va? . . . Qué mas?*"

Michele Harrison just stared at the lady. She was a Colombian embassy staffer Jerry worked with in the American Services section. They had had her over for dinner several times. They had never been invited to her home. Typically Colombian, thought Michele, as she made a quick excuse and walked away.

"Mrs. Grogan!" Michele found a friendly face. "How are the prisons?"

"Prisons?" asked Phyllis.

"Well," answered Jan. "I just make a few visits, now and then, to American girls in prison. There are not that many really. The embassy people cut back their mail-and-money-from-home visits to once a month, so I asked to do a little filling in. Diego wrote a nice letter back reminding me that if I had trouble I was not protected by diplomatic immunity. I think the embassy feels these kids did something wrong so they let them sit there."

"That's not entirely fair," said Michele. "The American Services section is so understaffed."

"True, I guess," Jan answered. "You know I was telling Phyllis here that the Asencios don't spend much time with the American community in Bogotá. I know one reason. Nancy has come to a few of the American women's club meetings. She calls them 'kindergarten,' with their book-review groups and their gardening classes. They're worse than that. I went to those women and asked whether, as one of their charities, they would fund some holiday meals to the girls. You know, nothing is free in these prisons. They can't afford to buy the better canteen food—even lights are not free. Anyway, the club fought over giving food to 'prisoners' and they voted against it!"

"Jesus," said Phyllis.

"And that's not all," Jan went on. "Father Bean has a ministry with prostitutes. He runs a place downtown where they can keep their children and get a decent meal—and of course where he can try to talk them out of prostitution. I think the Peace Corps is helping him. Anyway, he's come to the American women's club several times for some money. 'We don't further prostitution' they told him."

"Maybe the book-review group could go over and read *The Scarlet Letter* to them," said Michele, and all three women started laughing.

It wasn't hard to pinpoint the laughter. Nancy could see Michele, Jan and Phyllis from across the room. That's what she needed, Nancy thought, a good laugh.

Jan saw her first. "Did you put away everthing you care about before your first guest arrived?"

"God," said Nancy, "do you do that too?"

"Anyone who entertains Colombians does that," Jan said.

"What do you mean?" Michele asked.

"Well," laughed Jan. "I'll never forget my first party. I lost not only ashtrays, but some of my sterling silverware. I mean they just picked up their spoons and forks and put them in their pockets! And ashes! If they're talking and drinking, and there's not an ashtray in sight, they just flip their cigarettes on the rugs! Before every party now, I roll up the good rugs, empty my tabletops of any kind of knickknacks and put out the stainless steel flatware!"

"Jesus!" said Michele. "That hasn't happened to me."

"It's happened here all right," answered Nancy. "I figured they were just looking for souvenirs. And I'm not sure it's just the Colombians."

"The fact is," said Jan, "if you're going to live in these countries you better not get hung up on material possessions. I mean Gene and I have a twenty-four-hour guard in one of those little metal huts on our front lawn—like a lot of people do, foreign and Colombian. But for what he's paid he'll look the other way, I'm sure. We have an alarm system on the windows, and there's a gun in the house. The girls and I are always chauffeur-driven. Gene has a Colombian bodyguard who follows him everywhere with a little briefcase. The 'little briefcase' is some kind of James Bond machine gun—all you have to do is press a button and it fires, without even opening the case. I don't know how I feel about it. I guess

I think it'll never be *my* husband that gets kidnapped. The old 'It'll never happen to me.' "

"Nancy," said Michele. "If I could ask you a question?"

"Sure."

"This is my husband's first post, so I'm a new foreign service wife. Something's been building that I really don't know how to relate to. I mean, people are so curious about what my husband does. Jerry only works in the consulate, I mean we're not talking about anything that sensitive, but I find myself always on guard, anyway. Am I overreacting?"

"Stay on guard," said Nancy. "It's something you'll learn to live with. Let me tell you a story.

"Diego was working in Mexico City in the early sixties. We lived right near the University of Mexico and I wanted to sign up for some classes. It was the first time he said no to me about something like that and I reluctantly, angrily, agreed. Those were the years when the university was almost under siege. Buses were being burned and there were Russian agitators on campus. This was a time when no one was allowed to speak to the Russians. If you did, you had to report what was said.

"Anyway, Diego's stepfather came to visit. He used to go to the park every day and take my kids. One day he came home and said, Why do you people think the Russians are so bad? They're nice people just like everybody else. Why, there's this perfectly nice man that comes to the park with his child. We talk every day. One afternoon my father-in-law brought this guy home! While they were talking, I ran to the phone and called Diego. He came right home and the guy started giving Diego the third degree. He wanted to know how much money Diego made. He noticed we had all these children. He was looking to bribe my husband! Turns out the embassy had his name as one of the campus agitators. I don't know whether my father-in-law ever believed it.

"I didn't want to know anything sensitive after that."

"Five years ago," Ferde Grofé, Jr., was telling Phil Ferris, "USICA hired me to do a film on drugs in Colombia. The idea was to show how effective the Colombian law enforcement people were. We were working with the F2, you know, the detectives. Anyhow, one day we get this call saying, We've got a hot tip on a plane passenger coming into Cali. Well we ran out to the airport and got the cameras running while dogs sniffed everybody as they got off the ramp. Which one, which one, we wondered, and we kept the cameras running. Finally we went into the baggage area to watch the luggage start coming in. The cameras were running when suddenly those dogs rip apart a beat-up piece of green luggage. Sure enough, it was loaded with bundles of grass. This little, poorly dressed guy is taken to the *comandante*'s office. They start to interrogate him. He doesn't say much, and finally some F2s pull aside the *comandante*. While they're huddled together the phone rings. The little guy picks it up and says, '*Comandante*'s *oficina*.' " Ferde laughed. "Get it? The whole thing was rigged!

"Next stop was Santa Marta, up on the coast. We asked to photograph growing marijuana. The F2 guy says, 'Are you kidding? You want to get killed?' "

Phil started to laugh.

"The third stop was Medellín. Nobody wanted to help us there. Finally a traffic cop offered to take us around. He picked us up at the airport in a brand new BMW! Now where does a traffic cop get enough money for a BMW? That's a forty-thousand-dollar car with all the Colombian tariffs on it! What does that guy make? Maybe two hundred pesos a month? We didn't get anything done there either."

"Have you seen the USICA film that's in the Bogotá theaters now?" asked Phil. "Same theme—Colombian drug enforcement. The audience I saw it with seemed to consider it a comedy. There was a lot of whistling and jeering going on."

". . . so the foreign minister had sent one of his relatives over for a visa." Asencio launched into another favorite story. "It was a complicated matter and the consul general didn't, presumably, treat her with the deference that Jaime, the foreign minister, thought he should. At that point they had changed the regulations on the shipment of diplomatic vehicles to Colombia. They were not permitting any more eight-cylinder cars, except for ambassadors'. Well we checked and we had eight on the way. So my admin boys went to see protocol and said, Well, we have these eight vehicles on the way. Can you make an exception? From now on we won't ship any more than six cylinders. Of course, they said, No, ship them right back. Well, the expense—and they were people's cars and all that sort of stuff. But protocol was adamant, so the admin boys came to me. That is one of the functions of an ambassador. And they said we have this morale and logistical problem. So I picked up the phone and called Jaime. Of course I was aware that they had mistreated one of his people, and I said, Hey Jaime, why don't you cut this shit out?

"You know, Jaime, I said, we have these eight vehicles and it would be terribly expensive and bad for morale to have to ship them back. And he said, Yeah, but your goddamn consul general doesn't treat my people correctly, so why the hell should I treat your people correctly? I said, All right, let's talk about it. I will send the consul general to your office with an abject apology and make him grovel, if you let in our eight vehicles. And he said, How about six? And I said, No, it's got to be all eight. So he said, All right, but from now on I want good service from that consul section. I said, You got it. It was a ridiculous thing. The consul general at that time was a little on the pedantic side and instead of giving her the red carpet, he was making Jaime's relative wait. That was number one. And instead of issuing the visa and explaining that it was terribly complicated—she had to do fifteen different things—instead of doing it and getting credit for handling a tough case, he blew it. So they got mad. It was just a matter of doing things with a little pizzazz to earn a little gratitude."

"Was the abject apology made?" someone asked.

"Oh, you better believe it. He really was abject. I shouldn't talk about the guy," Asencio said, lowering his voice. "He's one of the hostages in Teheran now. Poor bastard."

"Hey! Daniel!" Asencio spied his favorite *bête noire* nearby. "C'mere, Dan! Speaking of bastards . . . what was that column of horseshit you wrote a while back about Congress holding up the sixteen-million-dollar drug appropriation because of Colombian human rights violations?"

"That's ancient horseshit," Samper laughed.

"It was ancient horseshit when you wrote it too," said Asencio. "You got me a lot of flack around here with that.

"Now that column you wrote a couple weeks ago was terrific. The one about Colombia not adopting the good side of American culture—cornflakes, blue jeans and McDonald hamburgers."

Samper grinned over the rim of his glass of Scotch.

"Did you get the case of Kellogg's cornflakes I sent you?" asked Asencio.

"Yes," laughed Daniel. "On the day of the revolution I will take it into account."

It was past midnight and the much smaller party had shifted to the piano in the peach room, where

Frank Crigler had organized a sort of songfest. When he started singing, "Show me the way to go home . . ." Asencio, a bit annoyed that his good-looking, golden-voiced DCM had taken over the party, got up from the peach wing chair and pointed to the front door.

Phil Ferris gratefully accepted a ride from Mike Kristula. He climbed into the back seat. Mike and Mario, a Colombian neighbor of his, got in the front. The car was one of the embassy's sky-blue monsters, with a driver.

The ambassador's residence is in the foothills of the mountains that ring the city of Bogotá, so everyone spent the first few minutes of the drive stealing glimpses of the stunning night view of the city that appeared and disappeared as the car wound slowly downward. The driver had just gone about two miles north on Carrera Séptima, the boulevard at the base of the mountains, when Mike spotted the soldiers.

"Hey Mario! See them waving cars off the road? What are they doing?"

"Oh, they're probably checking for drugs and contraband. You have diplomatic license plates on the car, don't you? They won't stop us."

But as they approached the soldiers, one of them stepped off the shoulder of the boulevard and waved his rifle.

"Pull over," Mike said to the driver.

"Please, drive down a few yards," the soldier said in Spanish, leaning into the front seat of the car. "And show the F2 your identification."

The driver started to move slowly down the shoulder of the road when Mike yelled, "No! Don't stop! Keep driving!"

Mike turned around in his seat and said to Phil, "If you see any of them climb into a jeep with their machine guns and start following us, duck!"

Everybody turned around except the driver, who was busy breaking the speed limit. There were no soldiers following.

"Mike," Mario said, "why did you do that? What was the big deal?"

"A lot of assassinations have been set up just like that," said Mike. "Why would they be stopping an obvious, and obviously marked, diplomatic car to search for contraband?"

9

THE FIRST THING Eileen Heaphy saw when she walked into her office in the State Department was the slip of paper in the middle of her clean desk.

"On note to Government of Colombia from Carter," Heaphy read, "send condolences on deaths and damage caused by earthquake, do *not* imply money."

From the moment she'd opened her *Washington Post* that morning, Heaphy knew it was going to be a vintage State Department day. On page A23 was her favorite Latin American headline: PRESIDENT LOPEZ PORTILLO SAYS, "NO FRICTION BETWEEN MEXICO AND U.S." That was the first laugh of the day.

Eileen turned her windowsill gardenias around, plugged in the old, noisy percolator and opened the combination lock on her file cabinet "safe." She pulled her in-box out of the second drawer and her out-box and half-full burn bag out of the third drawer. The daily collection of burn bags had stopped last week. The General Services Administration had temporarily run out of replacements.

Heaphy sat down at her desk and looked over the day's schedule while the coffee water came to a boil. She had a late morning briefing with some Mobil Oil executives. She would tell them Colombia was a good, safe place to invest. And then, she knew, they would go talk to Chuck Boles in Bogotá, and the embassy security chief would tell them, "Any company that values their people won't send anybody to Colombia."

Lunch was with a professor from the Johns Hopkins School of Advanced International Studies. Eileen tried to keep track of specialists in Colombian affairs outside the Department of State.

Late afternoon, there was a regional briefing for South American military officers who had been attending the U.S. Army School of the Americas. Deputy Assistant Secretary Samuel Eaton was doing the briefing. Good. That meant the Colombian soldiers wouldn't be visiting her office, seeing her marijuana Colombian flag poster and telling her that the FARC guerrillas were teaching Colombian children about communism. That conversation always went in the same direction. Eileen would then ask, "Well, why don't you teach them democracy?" And they would say, "We have no money."

Heaphy could predict how Eaton's briefing would end. Some American military type from the army school would stand up and say, These guys tell us there's a Cuban-Soviet conspiracy in South America.

If it were true, how come U.S. Intelligence didn't have it? Which reminded her, as she glanced over at the inbox, of the pile of paperwork she had to move today. There was the Department of Defense intelligence report, always either mediocre or alarmist. But since it went up to Assistant Secretary of State Warren Christopher with the Bureau of Andean Affairs name on it, she'd better take a look at it.

Oh, and here was a letter from Senator Charles Mathias about a Colombian relative of one of his constituents who was having trouble getting a tourist visa to the United States. Eileen would have to call Lyn Curtain on that. He would yell about congressmen going after votes and she would say I know, Lyn, but take another look at this one. Visas were bad business in Latin America. Poor people registered the fact—how could they help it?—that

MARGUERITE MICHAELS   175

flashing bank account papers got them a visa. It all came down to having money. Not a great image to project, she thought.

A Virginia high school student wanted help on a research paper. A junior officer just arrived in Colombia needed one thousand pounds of lost household effects tracked down, and Ambassador Asencio wanted help in getting one of his kids to Bogotá for a visit.

There was a gruesome cable from the consulate in Barranquilla about a decomposed body of an American male found in some plane wreckage in the Guajira. Another drug-runner. The consul in Barranquilla wanted some dental charts sent from the States to verify identification of the remains.

But that would be a whole lot easier to deal with than the cable that lay beneath it in the in-box. For days Eileen had been shifting it to the bottom of the stack. Asencio wanted to know, once again, what the hell was going on with the Senate ratification of the Quita Sueño treaty. The islands in dispute weren't even above water most of the year. Asencio wanted a decision one way or the other. Don't we all, Heaphy thought. Quita Sueño had started before she came on the Colombia desk and she was sure it would still be festering when she left. Hundreds— thousands—of memos had been written. What to tell the Senate? What to tell the press? What to tell the press about what they'd told the Senate? Nicaragua's objection to the treaty had been the fly in the ointment from the beginning. Originally, the delay had been caused by friends of Nicaraguan President Anastasio Somoza on the Foreign Relations Committee. Since the Sandinistas had taken over in 1979, the delay was in the State Department. No one wanted to be responsible for "another Cuba." Let's not drive Nicaragua into the Soviets' arms. A decision was made not to make a decision. So many "option" memos she'd worked on had come back with accusations of clientism on her part. That was the favorite word at State Main. If you argued too much for the country you represented, the honchos upstairs accused you of "clientism," of "losing perspective." At the moment, the Latin American bureau was considering renouncing U.S. rights to the islands unilaterally and rejecting the idea of any treaty. After eight years, they were thinking of just throwing it out. Asencio will go crazy if he learns about *that* option. Colombia likewise.

There would be some interesting cables from Bogotá in a few days. Deputy Assistant Secretary William Bowdler was going to Colombia, and Asencio had set up a whole day of meetings for him with President Turbay, the foreign minister, and assorted other high government officials. Reports of those discussions would be important. When the U.S. wanted to move on some particular policy, those cables would provide the reference points. The U.S. could say, Ah, but on such and such a date President Turbay said such and such. You said . . . He said . . . —that's how foreign policy was made.

The last item in the box was a telephone message from a friend on the White House staff. He wanted to know if Eileen would like to come to the south lawn to see the presidential helicopter leave this afternoon for Camp David. Now here was a really cute, interesting guy she'd made plain she'd like to go out with. Who wanted to watch Jimmy Carter wave goodbye? What about an invitation to a state dinner?

Six marines in beige and blue semi-dress uniform stood at attention at the base of the flagpole while the tiny cassette player blasted out a tinny rendition of "The Star Spangled Banner."

Master Gunnery Sergeant Frank Wherly's eyes wandered from the flapping flag to the visa line. The Colombians were standing respectfully; the Americans sauntered by on their way to work, laughing and talking, paying no attention. Sergeant Wherly wished he had a grenade.

His eyes wandered back toward his men. Embassy duty was supposed to mean thirty glamorous months overseas. At the Marine Security Guard Battalion training school in Quantico, Virginia, soldiers were taught how to hold a cocktail glass in their left hand while shaking hands with their right, what all the spoons and forks were for at diplomatic dinners, what kind of bullets went in what kind of weapons. They were told to fire those weapons only if their lives were in great danger, or if ordered to fire by a senior officer present. The marines provided security inside the embassy compound. That was all. They protected embassy personnel and embassy classified documents only within the embassy compound. The host government was supposed to defend against any attack from outside the embassy grounds—which, of course, was what had gone wrong in Teheran.

There were twelve marines and three duty posts in Bogotá. Post One was the embassy's front door, which was guarded twenty-four hours a day. Post Two supported Post One when the embassy was open, giving any assistance necessary at the door, roving through the building periodically. Post Three was the DEA office in the UGI building. Ever since the last DEA director had been shot and killed by a crazed informer a few years back, a marine had controlled access to the drug agency's office.

Each duty was eight hours long, one man to a post, and Sergeant Wherly told his soldiers they had two choices in dealing with the boredom: get used to it or get over it.

Morale was a huge problem. The marines had

pooled some money together for a Betamax, and Sergeant Wherly asked each of them to write his congressman for a state flag. Twenty of them now lined the winding staircase that dominated the first floor of the Marine House. They had a team in the embassy's bowling league, and they played softball and basketball against Colombian high school teams but, by and large, his boys led a twilight-zone existence.

And they were boys. No married marine, unless he was assigned as commander, qualified for embassy guard duty. Loneliness, on and off the job, was a constant fact of life. The single embassy secretaries wouldn't look twice at a soldier, so the marines dated Colombian women. It amused Sergeant Wherly to know that his boys knew more about how the average Colombian lived than any of the ivory tower foreign officers. It did not amuse him that nine out of ten of the marines who had passed through Bogotá during his command had married Colombians. To marry a gringo was a big thing. It was a ticket to the United States, where nine out of ten of the women eventually divorced their marines. It was depressing, but each time he tried to counsel one of his boys against marrying a local lady, he was met with, "But she's different."

The anthem was over. Sergeant Wherly dismissed the marines and walked toward the back gate. As he turned to face the embassy, a glint of light from the roof caught his eye.

"Jesus. There was the other marine morale problem. Security chief Chuck Boles was standing on the roof of the embassy staring through his binoculars at God knew what. Boles always had these "gut feelings" that somebody was coming to take his embassy. It drove the marines nuts.

"Terrorism is big business," Boles liked to say. "The biggest worry is random violence, whether it is political or nonpolitical." But if you asked him a question about nonpolitical random violence, or harassment of embassy personnel, chances were Boles wasn't interested. He didn't have time for "poisoned pets." He was saving the world from communist terrorists. All terrorists were "communists."

Boles had never forgiven himself for what had happened in Afghanistan while he was security officer in the Kabul embassy. What wasn't clear to Sergeant Wherly was exactly what Boles had not forgiven himself for: that his charge, and friend, Ambassador Dubbs, had been kidnapped and killed; or that just the night before, Boles had finished a report to Washington saying there were no known terrorist groups in Afghanistan. Sergeant Wherly had grown weary of hearing about how much there was to learn from the Israelis, who "had the best anti-terrorist tactics in the world."

Considering the fact that Boles was the man who had to make the call to the Colombian police for help if the embassy were attacked, the marines would feel a whole sight more comfortable if Boles spent less time with the Israelis and more with his Spanish teacher.

Asencio got as far as the operator in Rome before he had trouble.

"Yes!" he yelled into the phone. "You heard me correctly! Teheran! I want the American embassy in Teheran! T-E-H-E-R-A-N! Put the call through!"

There were about a dozen people in the ambassador's office. Frank Crigler, John Simms, Don Roberts, the board of directors of the liberal youth group, the board of directors of the conservative youth group and a cousin of the Shah of Iran, who lived in Bogotá and spoke both Spanish and Farsi.

A cable had arrived the previous week. Washington thought it important that student activists in every society contact Teheran and talk to the students who were holding the American embassy. The cable had made Asencio tingle with delight.

Ninety percent of all cables were bullshit. Every little agency and every little subdivision in the State Department sent stuff that might be of interest to them, but was not really pertinent to anything—things like requests for surveys of the wood finishing industry in Colombia. Nonsense. And Asencio had learned that if you let them flood you with that kind of junk, they'd drown you.

In the case of the Teheran cable, someone in some meeting probably had said, Wouldn't it be a nice idea to have students all over the world get in touch with the radical students in Teheran? And without giving it any further thought—such as how many people spoke Farsi and how much it would cost—that someone had shot off a round-robin message to every U.S. embassy.

There were a couple ways to handle bullshit cables. The first was to send a cable right back saying, We are studying the proposal and trying to relate it to Bogotá, or wherever. You waited a few weeks before doing anything, and by that time Washington had forgotten.

Or, you could send a cable that said, This is stupid. Shove it up your . . . nose. The harpoon style, directly from the ambassador, singled out the idiot in Washington and, since that was bad for business and very embarrassing, it made people think a little more carefully before they sent the next piece of shit. But this Teheran cable was special, and Asencio was going to have some fun with it. Washington hadn't said how to do it, they had just said, Do it.

He had called in Crigler and the political section boys and said, Okay, what happens if we go to the youth party people and say, Please contact Teheran? His boys answered, They'll say sure, sure, and nothing would happen.

Well, Asencio then said, how do we make it happen? We are going to follow these goddamn instructions to the hilt. So he and his boys had decided to bring the youth types into the embassy and hand them the phone.

They were loving it. Asencio turned on the squawk box so everybody could hear.

The Colombian "students," with the Shah's cousin interpreting, were telling the Iranian "students" to be kind to the hostages and not to hurt them. There were stories that they were maltreating the Americans and that wasn't a good thing.

No, no, the Iranians answered. They were not harmed. They were not going to be killed.

And then the Iranians thanked the Colombians for calling. They said they felt sympathy with the Colombians because they too were victims of the Yankee imperialists.

The Colombians gazed uncomfortably at the ambassador of the Yankee imperialists.

Only Da Vinci could have done justice to the smile on Asencio's face.

"Red Chicken, Red Chicken, you there, Red Chicken?" crackled the airplane radio.

"Who the hell is that?" Dave Burnett asked his red-headed pilot.

"Are we far enough back, repeat, are we far enough back?"

Burnett yelled into his walkie-talkie: "Don't use the radio! They'll pick it up! Use your walkie-talkies! Do you understand? No radio!"

"Oh, right," came a much clearer voice. "Are we far enough back? Can you see us?"

Christ, thought Burnett, maybe it wasn't such a good idea to bring along the new walkie-talkies. The

Colombians hadn't used them before. Too late now.

"That's better," Burnett said. "We can't see you. You're far enough back.

"Jesus, God, let this one work," Burnett muttered to himself.

Operation Noventa had had the right feel about it from the beginning. The CI was an informant who'd worked with the DEA before. He was pretty reliable, and the amount of the cocaine buy, and the name of the seller, had been too big to pass up. Jaime Cordova wanted to get rid of 100 kilos of base. Cordova was the number two coke trafficker in the whole goddamn country. The operation was named after his *finca*, near Medellín, where the pickup was to take place.

They were maybe fifteen minutes away from Noventa's airstrip now. He and his pilot, in a Piper Cherokee, were all Jaime was expecting. The three Asencio-bought helicopters behind them, full of Colombian agents from customs and the attorney general's office, were the surprise.

Every effort had been made. Burnett had brought in an undercover agent from the States—someone Cordova's boys wouldn't know, and someone who would check out. And they had checked the shit out of him. The agent had met with Jaime's men several times to discuss when and where and how much.

The airstrip chosen had been the first piece of luck. It was the *finca*'s own, and meant there was a good chance Cordova himself would be nearby, overseeing the sale.

The DEA had already laid out $25,000 of the $100,000 asking price. That's how bad they wanted this one.

They'd photographed Noventa's strip from every angle and spent hours camouflaging the plane with unregistered tail numbers and a new set of colored stripes.

The deal, in the end, was simple. The Americans were supposed to arrive first. The plane with the traffickers would show up shortly after. Dollars and coke would be exchanged. The American plane would take off.

Their plan was also simple. They would wait for the traffickers to arrive first. Then Burnett's plane would simply dive over the strip, or do a touch-and-go, giving the helicopters following time to land and make the arrests.

They were now five minutes from the *finca*.

"Red Chicken here," Burnett said into the radio. "Is everything a go? We're coming in."

"Come on in," the radio crackled back. "Come on in."

"There they are," Burnett said to his pilot. "Jesus, there are three planes down there! What the hell is going on? Pull out of the dive! Pull out! Pull out!"

Into his radio Burnett said: "Sorry, bad approach. We're circling to try again. Repeat, we're circling to—"

"Get out! Get out!" the radio screamed. "The Colombian army is behind you!"

Jesus, thought Burnett, those dummies still think we're on their side!

"Get out! Go to Panama! Go to Panama! Get out!"

As Burnett watched from 3,000 feet in the air, one of the trafficker's airplanes successfully took off. The helicopters blocked the other two. Two of the copters landed while the third peeled off after the plane.

No way they're gonna catch that baby, Burnett thought. He wondered if Jaime was in it.

"Okay, Red Chicken," Burnett said, "that's all

I'm doing for the Mansfield Amendment. Let's get down there."

While the Colombian agents went to check out the *finca*, Burnett talked to the attorney the Colombians had brought with them. The first plane had the 100 kilos of base in it. The second plane had a bunch of middle-level traffickers whom nobody had ever heard of.

"We're going to have to let them go," said the attorney. "Nobody knows any of them and they don't have any drugs on them."

"Who was in the third plane?" asked Burnett.

"They say they don't know."

"Bull."

"Hey, Burnett!" came a shout from the side of the strip. One of the Colombian agents was waving him over.

"We've got him! We've got him!"

Jaime Cordova was in the *finca*, with fifteen guns, a huge cocaine kitchen and about 300 more kilos of base.

"Holy shit," said Burnett. That was more than any DEA agent in the whole United States had seized in the last two years.

Burnett smiled for the first time all day.

"What's the matter, Emily?" Miguel asked. The view from the bar on the twenty-third floor of the Tequendama Hotel was lovely at night, but Emily Roth's gaze was fixed somewhere beyond the city lights. "Thigpen is driving you crazy, isn't he?"

"Oh, it's not just George," Emily said, her reverie broken. "It's just . . . everything.

"Working in an embassy is like living in a small town. The tone is set by the ambassador, GSO and admin. In Bogotá, GSO and admin fight with everybody, and we never see the ambassador or the DCM on the third floor. There is such a caste system here, and the economic people are stepsons. There was such a different feeling about the embassy in Athens. Warmer. Closer. Admin would send me a note and say, What do you think, we're trying to improve morale. . . . You know. My morale is low here. There, it was high. Morale is something that's watched in every post. There are so many different problems when you're abroad that it's very easy to have a morale problem in an embassy. You're dealing with so many things you're not used to . . . you know . . . big flying bugs . . . something. I didn't have a morale problem in Greece. I loved it."

"I've worked in the American embassy for six years," said Miguel. "People come, and people go, and nothing really changes. The CIA drinks with the KGB. The ambassador's secretary is the most difficult person in the building because she keeps forgetting she's not the ambassador. The embassy's Colombian drivers buy whiskey by the case from the U.S. commissary and sell it for profit to their friends. And somebody is always selling 'tickets' for the front places in the visa line. This year the price is up to five hundred pesos.

"One thing has changed though. You know we Colombians put our highest class people in our embassies. Every year you send us more women and Negroes. How can they be effective officers? No Colombian government official is going to work with a woman or a black—especially a black. A *bogotano maid* won't work for a black! A Negro is an insult in Colombia."

"Miguel," said Emily, "you sound like some of the American FSOs. They think the foreign service has gone overboard with affirmative action, like when the State Department started a new FSR designation for minorities. The new FSR is somebody who didn't take the written entrance exam. Minorities were having trouble passing it.

"Anyway, why should we be sensitive to an

insensitive country? A country that lets its children walk the streets!"

"Ah, Emily," Miguel smiled, "you must understand something important about Colombia. You call the United States the land of unlimited opportunity, no? Colombia is the land of limited opportunity. Everything my neighbor has means there is that much less for me.

"Three hundred thousand children cannot go to school. There are no classrooms for them. Twenty-eight percent of those who get into grade schools graduate. Most of the high schools are run by the Catholic Church and are expensive. Maybe another sixty-five percent who can afford to go graduate. At the most, one percent of those students make it to university. The literacy rate is seventy-two percent in Colombia, but it is measured at age fifteen and above. Forty percent of the twenty-six million population is under fifteen.

"There is no Christ in Colombia, only suspicion of the archbishops and cardinals, who are richer than the oligarchy they support.

"Our liberals would be called conservatives in your country. The liberals and conservatives are really politically interchangeable and yet two hundred thousand of them murdered each other during *la violencia*. Not just murdered, mutilated. There was the 'tobacco cut,' where the penis was put in the mouth; there was the 'tie cut,' where the tongue was pulled out through a slit in the neck. Stomachs were sewn up with live chickens that killed as they tried to claw their way out.

"Most of Colombia's wealth is controlled by a tiny portion of our population. Between 1976 and 1978 our oligarchy got scared at the rising crime rate. They wanted a strong government that would give the army carte blanche. So President Turbay made a deal with the oligarchy. They helped elect him. He kept the state of siege in place for them."

"Why are you so resigned to all this?" asked Emily. "Isn't there some way to change it?"

"I thought so once," said Miguel. "For ten years I worked with Colombian leftist groups. First with the ideologues of Russian communism. But they were stupid and ambitious. Then with the ideologues of Chinese communism. The last thing I did was go up to the city of Cartagena to rob a bank some guy had already taken money from. The robbery was supposed to be a cover-up for the embezzlement. Everything got messed up, as usual. So I sold the gun they had given me and flew back to Bogotá. They put me through a 'self-criticism' session for selling the gun and spending the money on a plane ticket without permission. They were big on self-criticism sessions. I dropped the whole thing. That was the end of my leftist days. At some point I said to myself, What would these bumbling idiots be like running my country?"

10

"HELLO, MR. LI," Phil Ferris said into the phone. "What's up?" Chin Li was an odd little fellow Phil had met at a Korean embassy cocktail party more than a year ago. Their friendship, which Mr. Li initiated the day Phil had started working in the political section, consisted of two or three drinks two or three times a month. Phil enjoyed the verbal acrobatics of diplomatic brain-picking much more than the liquor. Everybody in town knew that Mr. Li was KCIA.

"I beg your pardon?" Phil said. "Oh, you mean the national day reception this afternoon at the Dominican Republic embassy? No, I'm not going."

Phil stared at the phone receiver in his hand. Mr. Li had said "good" and hung up.

"Well, we've heard from Washington on that call to Teheran," Asencio said, grinning.

"You reported that?" asked an incredulous junior officer whose turn it was this month to sit in on all the ambassador's staff meetings.

"Of course," answered Asencio. "You never lie to Uncle Sam. They'll get you if you lie. I reported it. Washington called and said, What the hell are you doing? I said, Following my instructions. They said, Those were informal, not formal. Hey listen, I told them, you asked me to get Colombian students in touch with the Teheran radicals. That's exactly what I did. I think someone in the Iran operations center wondered what we were up to."

Asencio waited for the laughter to die down before he turned to Bob Pastorino.

"How'd that cocktail party go, Bob? Did you convince the Colombians that American TV sets are better than the French?"

"Remember, Diego," said Pastorino, "what I told you about what we had planned? Zenith and RCA sent me some equipment and I set up a closed-circuit television system in almost every room of the house. It was fabulous. The Colombians stared at themselves drinking and laughing for hours. But then came the clincher. That senator we've had trouble with? He came late, with two beautiful girl friends. When he saw those television screens he cuddled for the cameras all night. First with one girl, then with the other. At twelve midnight I had to pack up the equipment to get him out of there."

"Lovely," Asencio laughed appreciatively. "And of course you're giving everybody the replay tape of themselves to keep."

"Of course," said Pastorino. "Listen Diego, you know the Colombians are already having trouble with the TV cameras they bought from the French. They're not going to be ready for delivery when promised, just as I predicted. Can't I do a press conference on how bad those cameras are?"

"No. You'll just embarrass the minister of communications. Forget the camera contract. We lost it. Let's just make sure we sell our sets and our telecommunications satellite. The political advantage in having American television beamed directly into Colombia is obvious."

"Bob," added Asencio, "when is Thigpen back in the country?"

"Next week."

"Good. I think I've worked out something he can sell to the Braniff airline boys. Braniff was prepared to cut Avianca out of the U.S. market unless they got the differential they wanted on the price of fuel here in Colombia. And they were going to do it this summer, which is a good season for Avianca. It would have caused a war between Colombia and the U.S. Well, I went to see the foreign minister and I said, I don't know your airline boys particularly well, but I know my airline boys and I know they're sons of bitches. They'd sell their grandmothers for two cents. I assume your boys are the same. He said, Absolutely. So I said, Why should we let them screw us up? Well, he and I got together and we've worked out a differential agreement. I'd like George's help selling it to Braniff.

"One more thing. The minister of agriculture wants to buy U.S. wheat outside of channels. I told him sure, in exchange for . . . Talk to O'Mara, would you, and see what goodies the Department of Agriculture might want to trade for the favor of looking the other way."

"Probably a better quality aphthosa vaccine," said Pastorino. "You sure you don't want to talk to him yourself?"

"If the Colombians can make a better hoof-and-mouth vaccine, I'm going to use it on O'Mara and, yes, I'm sure I don't want to talk to him myself.

"Frank," Asencio said, "I want to see you for a minute after the meeting."

"Right," answered Crigler. "Do you want to write the cable about Colombia's recognition of the People's Republic of China?"

"No. Just write a straight message about Turbay confirming the story that appeared yesterday in *El Tiempo*. Colombia is going to break with Taiwan and establish relations with the PRC. Turbay has already called in Ambassador Shen and given him the bad news. Turbay said that Colombia has been moving in that direction for some time. Washington knows all that. Colombia was ready to do it when

Carter announced that the U.S. had already made the move. Colombia waited so as not to look as if they were copying us. Don't put that in the cable. Turbay would be unhappy if I said that they did anything in relation to us.

"John," Asencio said to Simms, his political counselor, "did Roberts tell you about my scene with the delegation for International Indochina Refugees yesterday? What a riot. FYI for the rest of you, Washington has sent four different cables asking what Colombia is doing for the Asian boat people. Each time we've answered that Colombia is a poor country and they would be glad to consider specific cases, but certainly nothing en masse. Well, Washington insisted that this delegation come and talk to the Colombian boys anyway. They came—a bunch of higher State Department types on per diem for this special deal, retired ambassadors, that sort of thing. Roberts took them all around to the proper GOC types and then they asked if I would set up a meeting with the foreign minister. I said, You've got to be kidding. They said, no, this is serious business. They were sure they could convince Colombia to take some of these refugees. So I called Diego Uribe Vargas and asked him to receive these gentlemen, please, and be nice to them. He said, Sure, send them over. Well, they came back walking on air. They were making estimates of how many they could send in, and I said, Hey, wait a minute, did he say yes? Well, not quite. He told them he thought this was the greatest humanitarian gesture he had ever heard of. They said if he thinks it's such a great program he must mean Colombia is going to take some refugees. Well, I picked up the phone and said, Hey Diego, what did you tell these guys? He said, Well, you told me to be nice to them. I said, How many boat people are you going to take? He said, Are you out of your mind?"

Everybody around the table was laughing.

"So I told the delegation that Colombians have a very hard time saying no, but that's what Diego had said. He was just being polite."

"Did you see Daniel Samper's column this morning?" asked Crigler.

"He got hold of a copy of a government report that says that until Colombia can provide economic alternatives to the money being made in drug trafficking, the government invites unrest if they stop the drug trade altogether. Especially in the Guajira area where marijuana has become a way of life."

"Well," said Asencio, "when I was up in Washington last time, I went to the World Bank to see if I could interest them in making a Guajira development loan. The director of planning here says he doesn't have the money. They need to find water on the peninsula and get the Guajira Indians out of smuggling and into agriculture. They need money to dig wells and build dams. The area has enormous potential. We'll have to wait and see what the World Bank decides.

"In the meantime you will all be surprised to know that Eileen Heaphy has rejected our human rights report."

Everybody at the table groaned.

"Do you know," said John Simms, "that Eileen Heaphy told me she considers Managua and Teheran victories for human rights? Jesus! I asked her whether she'd ever heard of King Pyrrhus."

"She didn't buy our It's-all-over line, huh?" said Crigler.

"You bet she didn't," answered Asencio. "She said she's heard that one before and she doesn't care if Colombia rounded up five terrorists or five thousand terrorists. She wants to know if we're being told the damn truth and whether or not we understand what's really going on in this damn country. 'Are you so close to the security forces that you believe whatever they tell you? Or do you choose to believe whatever they tell you because of the army's help in the drug war?'

"I explained to Eileen," continued Asencio, "that the point, it seemed to us, was whether the human rights violations were part of a conscious policy of the government or the military or whether they were accidental. Everybody agrees there were human rights violations in the army's roundup of the M-19s but, I told her, we believe those violations were accidental. Colombia was faced with a problem—the robbery of an army arsenal—and they unleashed the army because that is their chief security force. In the process, a bunch of second lieutenants and sergeants were set loose and they racked up some people. I also pointed out that it was all over. The M-19s are decimated."

"This is ridiculous," muttered Simms. "Our butting in with some selective morality."

"I have no quarrel with the policy," said Asencio. "I don't think they should yank fingernails off people. And I have no problems about telling them so. But the report is a patronizing, condescending, paternalistic pain in the ass.

"Turbay has already called me in a rage saying, What's this I hear about a bad report? I'm tired of pleasing neither side.

"At any rate, Eileen said that what we'd written was not a report but an 'apologia' and it was not going to sail through the Human Rights Bureau. I told her to rewrite it herself. Any objections?"

Asencio looked around the silent table. "I didn't think so. We're well rid of it.

"That's it—I must now go drink rum and sing the national anthem of the Dominican Republic. Anybody know it?"

Frank Crigler waited, as requested, while the others filed out of Asencio's office.

"Frank," said Asencio. "You saw Chuck Krause's story in the *Washington Post* about how the U.S. Government was trying to cajole the Venezuelans into buying thirty thousand tons of aphthosa-infected beef from Colombia so that the Colombians wouldn't sell the stuff to the beefless Russians?"

"Yes."

"And you know of course what happened after the article was published? The deal is off."

"Yes."

"Good. Now I have just kicked O'Mara's butt all the way across my office because he couldn't keep his goddamn mouth shut. I am now going to kick your butt all the way across my office because keeping the staff in line is your responsibility. They're your people. You got it, Frank?"

Crigler stood in silence as Asencio stalked out of the room. Being number two was bullshit. Being number two meant no personal visibility in Washington. He felt like some kind of stand-in, waiting for his own chance to shine.

Instead of eating lunch, Phil Ferris watched an hour of two-week-old Walter Cronkite CBS Evening News tapes. As he walked out of USICA's underground auditorium into the bright sunlight, he passed Chuck Boles and his assistant, Bruce Witter, hustling one of the ambassador's bodyguards toward the embassy's front door. There was blood all over the guy's face. Must have taken quite a fall, Phil thought absently.

"Where in the fuck did *you* come from?"

Startled, Phil looked into the face of a furious marine. He was standing in the lobby, outside of the glass-enclosed Post One.

Jesus. He had a shotgun in his hand!

"Uh, I came from the USICA auditorium. I was watching some old newscasts. What's going on?"

"Were you alone? Is anybody else over there?"

"Yes, there are about fifteen people in the auditorium. What's going on?"

"Fuck."

Phil watched the marine run out the door.

"AK7, AK7, this is AK4. Do you read me?"

"This is AK7. I read you."

"Are there any demands yet?"

"Nothing yet. Not a thing."

"Who else is inside besides Asencio?"

"No one is sure here. Maybe the Israeli ambassador and the Austrian . . . and the Venezuelan. . . . Nobody knows."

"Is there any more shooting?"

"Sporadic. The police and the soldiers have moved back away from the Dominican embassy. They stuck Asencio in the front door to yell that request."

"Jesus. Who are they?"

"Don't know. Maybe the MAO guerrillas."

"Is Asencio all right?"

"Impossible to say for sure. He looked okay. But I'm two hundred yards away."

"There is a medvac plane ready in Panama."

"The police are asking for the marines to come help."

"Can't do that."

"AK4, AK4, this is AK10. Do you read me?"

"This is AK4. I read you. Where are you?"

"I'm at National University, right across the street from AK7 and the Dominican Republic embassy. There are no student demonstrations here. That's a negative. No trouble here."

"This is 21, repeat 21."

"This is AK4, 21. Get off the radio.

"Goddamn military wife," Chuck Boles muttered to himself. "AK7, AK7, this is AK4. I'm coming over. Stay put until I get there."

When John Simms came out of the Foreign Ministry the embassy car had disappeared. That's odd, Simms thought. How am I supposed to get back?

"Grogan!" Simms yelled. "Is that you?"

"John Simms!" Gene Grogan answered as he walked over. "What brings you here?"

"Nothing much. A meeting on the United Nations convention against the taking of hostages. Teheran fallout. Listen, my embassy driver has stranded me. Don't know what happened to him. Do you have a car? Can you drop me off?"

"Sure, car's right at the curb. Let's go."

"How are things at Cities Service?" Simms asked, climbing into the back seat. "Did you ever find out who blew that pipeline up north?"

"We'll never know if the explosion was accidental or not. But we're rebuilding the homes that were destroyed and we've taken care of all the hospital bills. I wish we could bring back the eleven people who were killed but it's been months now, and there's been no further trouble. Jesus, John, look at the embassy!"

Simms looked out the car window. "It looks almost like it's closed for the day or something," he said very slowly. "No . . . Look at the marines. They're everywhere. At the gates, on the roof. They're wearing flak jackets . . . carrying shotguns. Some of them just have jogging stuff on. This is not a drill. Something's wrong."

By the time Simms arrived at Frank Crigler's office, he had learned that the Dominican embassy had been seized mid-party by a group of well-armed guerrillas. Nobody knew who they were, what they wanted, or how many ambassadors they had hostage.

Simms waited while Crigler finished pleading with the defense minister, General Leyva, to please stop all firing at the Dominican embassy. If the Colombian army attacked, the hostages would be killed.

Even before he'd hung up the phone Crigler said to Simms: "What do you know?"

"No more than what the marines told me. I just got back from the Foreign Ministry. I had no . . ."

"John," barked Crigler, "call around to the different sections and find out if anyone else from the embassy went to that damn national day party. And then call around to all the other embassies and find out if their ambassadors are inside. Let's see if we can get some kind of list."

"Washington knows?" asked Simms.

"I've called with everything we know. They'll have an open phone line set up soon."

"Frank," said Simms, hesitantly. "Can I get a little help on the embassy phone calls?"

"Use your secretaries."

"Neither of them speaks Spanish."

"What happened out there, Chuck?" asked Sergeant Wherly. Boles was standing in the middle of his office, surrounded by crates of gas grenades.

"Our protective team was superb," Boles answered. "We were the only 'friendlies' who responded. Asencio was in the doorway of the embassy saying his goodbyes, so a bodyguard was walking across the front lawn to meet him when these guys in green jogging outfits came running at him, shooting. The bodyguard took a bullet in the groin but fired back. He took another bullet in the left arm, but he kept firing. He says he hit one of the guerrillas. He was reloading when they shot him in the head. It was two more of our men who provided enough cover fire to get him out of there.

"You know, you drink coffee and go shooting with these guys, but you never know about the local employees . . . whether they'll shoot at their own people. They were superb."

"What are all the grenades for?"

"If we're attacked, we're fighting . . . superb . . . he'll be all right. . . . Jesus, Top, you know it was just a year ago this month . . . Afghanistan . . . Dubbs . . . God, why me?"

Boles walked over to the wall and bowed his head against it. Sergeant Wherly couldn't see his face. He could hardly hear him.

"Washington just called. 'All right, Boles,' they said, 'what happened this time?' I can't believe it!" Boles yelled, banging his fists against the wall again and again. "I can't believe it! I can't believe it!"

The phones had finally quit ringing. Emily sat outside Frank Crigler's office writing a letter to her sister in Chicago. It was just after midnight. John Simms was talking quietly with Crigler. Chuck Boles had fallen asleep on the couch in his office down the hall. A few DEA agents and a few marines were patrolling the building.

Emily didn't know what to tell her sister about this day. It was just after lunch when word spread around the embassy that something had happened to Asencio. All curtains were ordered closed, and the Colombian employees were sent home. Most of the econ section had spent the afternoon around the radio, just like the rest of Bogotá, trying to find out what was going on.

At 5:30 everyone was allowed to leave, with warnings to park themselves, and their diplomatic-license-plated cars, indoors that night.

Frank Ravndal had called Emily just after 5:00 to ask if she would do some late duty in Frank Crigler's office. Answer the phones, run out and get some fried chicken for dinner, whatever was needed.

She'd been thrilled. Finally, there she was in the

middle of the action. Emily hoped the whole thing would be over by the weekend, though. Miguel had asked her to come with him to Cartagena. She did not want to be stuck here on crisis duty. Asencio better get out of there by Friday afternoon.

At 12:30 Frank Crigler called the ambassador's residence.

"Bettie? It's me. How's Nancy holding up?"

"She's made of sturdy stuff. She spent the whole evening on the phone with her children. She talked to all but one, I think. They had all sorts of wrong information, including the original reports that Diego had been shot."

"Hadn't the State Department called any of them?"

"Yes," Bettie said dryly. "That seems to have been the problem.

"Chuck Boles was by earlier, Frank. He said there were still no demands."

"No. But the shooting has stopped. We have a few people posted, watching . . . waiting."

"Well, don't worry about us here. Nancy has taken some Librium and stretched out on her bed. Maybe she'll sleep.

"Frank?"

"Yes?"

"They don't pay us enough for this."

11

"WASHINGTON'S ON THE LINE, McIntyre!" Richard Baca yelled across the room. "They want to know whether the army's going to attack the Dominican embassy! The White House heard some press report . . . check it out!"

"Check it out with who?" asked John McIntyre. "That's the fifth call on that rumor today!"

"Fuck. How do I know?" Baca said, unbuttoning his shirt so he could breathe. "Why in the hell are the windows closed and the curtains drawn? There's no air in here!"

"Chuck Boles's orders," said Jerry Harrison. "You wanna get shot by a guerrilla?"

"Open the windows," Baca barked. "I feel like we're the hostages instead of Asencio. And then run upstairs and check the cable traffic, Jerry."

"It's Washington again, McIntyre!" Baca yelled. "Goddamn open line. Pain in the ass. Some radio station is saying the hostages are going to be killed one by one if their demands aren't met—starting tonight! Check—"

"Check it out, I know," sighed McIntyre.

"Look," said Baca, "it figures if this is some kind of threat that they would have communicated it to the Colombian Government. Call the Foreign Ministry and then the Ministry of Defense."

"Any idea who I might ask for?" said McIntyre. "What kind of information system have these guys set up? Are they working shifts like us, or what?"

"Ask John Simms," said Baca. "And then call the

CIA on that army shit. Maybe they can make a few calls for us. They must have some friends in the military. Wait a minute. I'll call. Washington wants to know about two of the M-19s. . . ."

"Washington wants to know, Washington wants to know," chanted Jerry Harrison.

"Hey listen," said Baca, "that's why we've all gathered here. Because Washington wants to know. So do we, remember? Asencio is a member of *our* bowling team. Jerry, keep calling the embassies, would you? Washington—"

"Wants to know?"

"—why we don't have a firm list of who's inside yet."

"Because when we call to find out," said Jerry, "we get five guesses for every one fact. 'Gee, no, our guy isn't a hostage—but we think so-and-so from the Venezuelan embassy is. . . .' "

"Jerry . . ."

"Right. I'm going down the hall. We're short a couple phones in here I'd say."

"We're short some phones, a typewriter, a cleaning lady . . . look at this mess!" said Baca.

"Is anybody doing anything about it?" Jerry asked.

"Yeah. I asked for a typewriter and was told to go fuck myself. And one of the communications guys upstairs, he says we're using too many batteries on this open telephone line. 'We will use only one battery a day.' Do you believe it? Where does he think Asencio is? Out sick?"

Baca sighed and called CIA agent Evan Thomas.

"Thomas? Richard Baca. Washington says a Teheran newspaper printed a story about two of the M-19 guerrillas. We need to know if there's any Iranian connection here. What do you guys have on them? It's the same two on the front page of *El Tiempo* today. Oh, and listen Evan, we're flooded over here from all sides with the rumor that the army is going to attack. Can you guys get a reading on that?"

Baca hung up the phone and headed for the coffee machine. Welcome to Camp Bananas. There hadn't been any contingency plans for what had happened—A for ambassador, K for kidnap, now here's what we do, fellas. After two days of utter confusion, three round-the-clock teams had been set up to try to get some control over the information coming in and going out. Because the Peace Corps could easily spare him, and because Frank Crigler trusted him, he was in charge of one team, George Thigpen another, and Ken Keller, the consul general, the third.

Each team, besides the leader, had five members. Jerry Harrison was his "office" manager, running back and forth to the fifth floor every five minutes to collect and deliver the constant cable traffic. John McIntyre was the main contact for the ministries and helped write the three or four sitreps—situation reports—per shift. Emi Yamauchi, a junior officer with USICA, kept a log of all phone calls with Washington. Patt Lindsey and Nellie Woodward were the team's secretaries.

The fourth-floor conference room had been converted into the operations center. Everything, and everybody, was routed into Frank Crigler's office through the conference room. The team leaders were the traffic cops. A rope, in fact, had been put across the corridor leading into the ambassador's office, where Crigler now sat, so that the only physical access to him was through the operations center's sieve.

"Why are the goddamn windows open?" Boles said. "Haven't I got enough trouble?"

"The windows are open," answered Baca, "because we'd all rather die quickly from a bullet than suffocate slowly to death."

"Well, let it be noted," said Boles, "that it's against my orders. What's new?"

"What's new?" said Baca. "You're one of our chase-down-the-rumor sources. What about the army? Everybody and their mother wants to know."

"It's quiet," Boles said. "They have every piece of equipment out there that they've ever bought. But it's all hidden from view—or at least from the view of anyone in the Dominican embassy."

"Frank?" Baca asked. "Give us an update. What is it we know or don't know?"

"All right," said Crigler. "You know that we know that the guerrillas are M-19s . . ."

"I told Diego five months ago," said Boles, "that the M-19s were not 'decimated.' He threw me out of his office."

Crigler stared at Boles and then continued.

"We know they want the release of three hundred and eleven political prisoners."

"Aren't some of these prisoners M-19s who were rounded up in that army crackdown?" asked Baca.

"More than two hundred of them are," answered Crigler.

"They want fifty million dollars," continued Crigler, "publication of their revolutionary manifestos, whatever those are, and safe passage from the country.

"We also know that there are maybe a dozen other ambassadors in there with Diego. Along with, we think, the Papal Nuncio. They are supposed to start releasing the women hostages this afternoon. Maybe, finally, we'll be able to get a firm list then. The Red Cross has offered to deliver food and supplies. The guerrillas will probably accept that offer."

"What don't we know?" asked Baca.

"The army is what we don't know," Crigler sighed. "They are the volatile component here. President Turbay assures me that he won't give an attack order."

"But of course," finished Baca, "this is Latin America. What army waits for the president's order?"

"Well," said Crigler, "this army's better than most, on the one hand. On the other, the president before Turbay purged the army of all their bright people, for fear they'd take over his government. And now the army is not exactly a thinking man's organization. They're recruited from the most conservative area of Colombia. They're poorly educated, poorly paid."

"This is all good news," Baca said wryly.

"I'm talking to General Leyva," said Crigler, "whenever he lets me. He wants to know, What's the American position on this? What's the American position on that? Don't attack, is what I keep telling him. Don't jeopardize the hostages' lives. Stay cool. That's the American position. So far, so good. That's all we can tell Washington."

"Thomas, what do you have?" Baca asked.

"Here's the stuff on those two M-19s."

"Washington wants to know how the municipal elections are going," said Emi Yamauchi. "What should I tell them, somebody?"

"Tell them army tanks line Bolívar Square, army sharpshooters are in the cathedral tower and most of the voters are in the whorehouses, horizontal," Thomas said, straight-faced.

"Psssst." Nellie Woodward was trying to catch Baca's attention from across the room. She had her hand over the phone.

"It's the ambassador."

"Ours?" Baca mouthed.

Nellie nodded yes.

Baca's eyes went wide. Completely rattled, he fumbled around with the buttons on the tape machine next to his desk. Emi finally pushed his hands away and started the recorder herself.

"Where did Crigler go, Nellie?" whispered Baca.

"Upstairs to the scrambler phone."

"Go get him."

Sergeant Blake rested his shotgun and his elbows on the shoulder-high parapet. He and three other marines had been on the roof for over an hour. Boles had even asked for Colombian police, and four "greenies" were walking two-by-two outside the embassy gates.

Sergeant Blake looked out at the nearly empty streets. So much for any election-day violence. Nobody was coming to take the embassy. Bogotá was a piss-pot of rumors. Who would want a goddamn embassy without a goddamn ambassador in it? It'd been only four days since Asencio had been taken, and the CYA shit had already begun. That's all that happened in embassies, thought Sergeant Blake. CYA. Cover your ass.

Boles was running around telling everyone that he had a "secret document" dated last September that said the Colombian army had rounded up only twenty percent of the M-19s. And the CIA. Their story was that they'd gotten a tip the day before, but the informant wanted so much money—ten thousand dollars—that the station chief had to ask permission from Langley. The Soviet-bloc people had paid the money right away and that's why all the communist diplomats left the reception early, before it was attacked. "If it weren't for the damn money-tight, overly cautious Watergate mentality in Langley" . . . blah, blah, blah. Bunch of drunks playing kids' games.

Sergeant Blake aimed his shotgun at a Mercedes Benz. Probably just a drug trafficker, anyway.

That's what those fuckers drove. He fondled his gun as if it were a steering wheel. He felt out of place up here, armed to the teeth and dressed in jungle fatigues, watching the traffic.

Jungle fatigues. Jesus. That had been Boles's idea. "It's an advertisement," he'd said. "I want people to know that we'll defend this place." He'd even asked Sergeant Wherly for a set of fatigues his size. Good old Top. He'd told Boles to fuck off. "You chose to leave the marines thirteen years ago," he'd said.

Sergeant Blake wondered how long Boles would keep them out on the roof this time. Really, he didn't care. He preferred watching traffic any day to watching those huge, screaming rallies during his last couple of months' duty in Teheran. Two hundred fifty thousand people together in one place. "And they all hated me," Sergeant Blake said out loud.

At five minutes after six, Frank Crigler walked into Richard Baca's living room, sat down in a chair especially prepared for him with pillows and blankets, dipped his thumb into the glass of Scotch on the table next to him and sucked on it. Back and forth between the Scotch and his mouth his thumb went, while Baca and Bettie Crigler burst out laughing.

"Hours getting to you, Frank?" said Baca.

Bettie started giving her husband a back rub.

"You're doing fine," Baca said. "You know that. Everybody is impressed.

"Just one piece of business," he added. "I was kind of thinking. Will the army attack if they are provoked? You know, get pissed off about something and just rush in, risking everybody's lives? Do you know whether the troops are being rotated? So that nobody's out there too long, and they don't get tired and they don't get angry?"

"That's a good point," said Crigler. "When I get back to the embassy later I'll call General Leyva and pass it on."

"That occurred to me earlier today," Baca said.

"So why did you wait until now?" asked Crigler.

"Because my presence is not appreciated at the embassy," said Baca. "You know that. It's not only that your people think of Peace Corps directors as gym teachers—it's that I'm not State Department. There are a lot of people very unhappy with the fact that you picked me to be a team leader. You remember yesterday a cable arrived that I wasn't cleared to read? The communications guy made a big deal out of it—'We have a problem here.' I could feel the whole room gloat."

"Okay, but didn't you come straight to me and I said in front of everybody 'Baca can read anything'?"

"Yes, but I'm just not going to ruffle any more feathers if I don't have to. There's enough penny ante around, without my adding to it. I'd rather make any suggestions to you informally, at least for a while."

"All right."

"Is there anything you can do about Ingrid? She is insisting, since she was, er, is, the ambassador's secretary, that she should see all the incoming cables because she could make a decision about who else should see stuff better than us team leaders. Which may or may not be right. She's become a huge bottleneck. Can you say something to her?"

"I don't know. She cringes every time she walks into Diego's office and sees *me* sitting behind his desk," said Crigler. "Can you make nice with her for a while?"

"No choice, right? Do you want a ride back to the embassy after dinner?" asked Baca.

"What are you going back for?" Crigler said. "I thought you did the morning shift today."

"Right. But tonight I switch into the midnight shift. It was somebody's great idea that no one team should be stuck with the off-hours, when nothing happens."

"I'm the somebody."

"Great idea, like I said."

"Thanks for the ride offer," laughed Crigler. "But I've got to make a stop at Mike Kristula's tonight. Press conference. Ugh."

"Isn't this the first one?" Baca asked. "Jesus!"

"You sound just like Kristula."

"All right," said Frank Crigler, "it's after eight o'clock and I've got to get back to the embassy, so let's get this thing started."

Crigler walked over to the fireplace in Mike Kristula's living room while about a dozen American reporters found folding chairs to sit on.

"I think I'll sit down too," said Crigler, "I couldn't possibly stand."

"Let me get you a chair," Kristula said, but Crigler waved him away and sat on the floor, cross-legged. Typical, Kristula thought to himself. It was a rare State Department officer, he'd learned over the years, who was comfortable with the press. He knew what Crigler intended by sitting on the floor: the look of relaxed casualness that he didn't feel. He looked instead like an idiot, sitting there in his three-piece navy suit looking up at the guys on the chairs instead of having them look up at him. Kristula walked to the back of the room.

"Mike has already told you who I am and what the ground rules are, I presume," Crigler began. "No attribution to the American embassy or to the government. I don't want to jeopardize getting the guy I love out of that embassy. I happen to know when these M-19s get exercised they take it out on Ambassador Asencio."

"Did Ambassador Asencio help put that M-19 flag

up on the roof of the Dominican embassy? *El Tiempo* said the guerrillas forced some ambassadors to help put it up."

Crigler couldn't tell who'd asked the question. He really couldn't see past the first row. It didn't matter. He didn't know many of these people. He doubted very much if ABC News or *Newsweek* knew where Bogotá was before last Wednesday.

"I don't know. I do know he's part of a group of ambassadors serving as a sort of special committee. They are being kept downstairs near the entryway. He helped carry the wounded Paraguayan chargé to the door this afternoon. And the body of the dead guerrilla."

"Have you spoken with Ambassador Asencio?"

"Yes. I talked to him today. He sounds fine."

"What's happening with the demands?"

"Both sides are jockeying to establish direct contact," Crigler said, starting to play with the cuffs on his pants. "The United States is not involved in any way in the negotiating process."

"Is there still a fear that the army will storm the embassy?"

"I'm not worried about any sudden act of the authorities. They are very cool people. These Colombians have a very humane character."

"Are we, I mean, is the U.S. doing anything?"

"We do not pay ransom," said Crigler to the spot in the room the question came from. "We are not involved in tactics and negotiations."

"Then who is this guy from Washington?"

Crigler recognized that voice. That was Chuck Krause from the *Washington Post*, who'd caused him all that grief with his goddamn beef story. Crigler stared at him in stony silence.

Mike Kristula, standing in the back of the room, rolled his eyes toward heaven in a silent prayer. "Not now, Lord. Wrong time, wrong place, wrong war."

"Who is the guy Washington sent?" Krause repeated.

"That is Frank Perez—"

"Spell that, please?" came from the other side of the room.

"F-R-A—"

"Got the 'Frank,' thanks. What's the Peretz?"

"P-E-R-E-Z," answered Crigler. "Frank Perez is from the counter-terrorism department at State. He reports to me, and just generally helps me out."

"What kind of information are you getting from the Colombian Government?"

"They are briefing us infrequently," said Crigler, playing with his pants leg again. "But I'm satisfied."

"Have you talked to President Turbay?"

"Yes."

"More than once?"

"Yes."

"Do you have any information on the guerrillas?"

"They seem tough and disciplined. We know they're young, in their early twenties. Ambassador Asencio was leaving the reception when they attacked."

"Do you have any reading on public opinion?"

"No. I'm not exactly spending my time on the streets. But I think the Colombian Government does have its act together."

"Are they still threatening to kill the hostages one by one if their demands aren't met immediately?"

"I heard that rumor," said Crigler to the whole room, "about a ten P.M. deadline tonight. It scared the hell out of me. If it's true, the Colombian Government hasn't been told the news."

"People say the government invited this with the crackdown on the M-19s after the arsenal robbery."

"I don't think that's right," said Crigler, craning

to see who had spoken. "The M-19s are very poorly regarded by the public."

"One more question," said Kristula from the back of the room.

"How long can this go?"

"It's too soon to say," answered Crigler, getting up off the floor. "There hasn't even been any direct contact between the Colombian Government and the guerrillas yet."

"A list of hostages!" someone yelled.

"Forgive me for rushing out," Crigler said, already moving towards the door. "We'll do this again."

"Not likely," muttered Mike Kristula under his breath.

Tears were streaming down Emi Yamauchi's face.

"To the right!" she screamed. "Move to the right!"

"Fuuuuuuuck!" yelled Richard Baca. "Hang on! Hang on! Hah! I missed it!"

"To the left! The left!" Emi screamed again.

"Fuuuuuuuck!" Baca yelled again. "Too late! Here we go!"

And the big, white station wagon's left front wheel dropped into a hole the size of a soup pot.

"I'm losing it!" Baca said. "I'm losing it! Get your hand over the light, Emi!"

As Baca's door swung out into the street the car's ceiling light flashed on.

"Emi, goddammit!" Baca said. "I thought you said you were good with your hands! Cover that god-damn light! The guerrillas will get us!"

"Oh God, I can't," Emi wailed. "I gotta hold my stomach." She was doubled over with laughter in the back seat.

"All right," Baca said. "I've got my door back.

Now let's get this thing organized! Shit! Here comes another one!"

The car lurched, the door opened, the light went on and Baca had trouble seeing, he was laughing so hard.

"Goddammit, Yamauchi!" said Baca, when he'd caught his breath. "I give you one job to do—look for potholes. I can hold this door closed if we don't hit any potholes."

"Yeah, but then you stick me in the back seat behind Jerry," laughed Emi. "You're lucky I can see the mountains!"

"Wheeeeee!" Jerry Harrison sang out, as Baca swerved and missed a beaut. "And to think we passed up a ride to the embassy in a locked van with Chuck Boles and his merry marines."

"Better sorry than safe!" yelled Baca as he swerved successfully again. "I didn't know the door was going to break. I'm writing a letter to the mayor about the condition of the streets in Bogotá.

"Listen dears, you really gotta, while I tell you the tale of the midnight ride of Richard Baca . . ."

"To the right!" screamed Jerry. "Goddaaaaaam- mit!"

Baca was laughing too hard to even try to catch the door before it swung out.

"How about a song for Chuck?" Baca said, as he grabbed the door and pulled it shut.

"If you could see us now," began Baca in a roaring baritone, "me and this gang of mine . . ."

Randy Malley looked at his watch. Three o'clock in the morning. Christ, it'd been a long day. He'd started it at 8 A.M. at the airport, picking up Romero, a fat, jovial, curly-headed Latin type that the CIA had sent down to help out. They'd spent the rest of the day with the Colombian intelligence brigade. A lot of them were trained and equipped by Langley, and the Agency had good access to the information they collected. Not that the Russians didn't, but the Colombians were supposed to let the CIA in on any request for information the commies made. In turn, of course, the CIA shared their stuff. Some of it—a lot of it, in fact—albeit slightly filtered, went straight to President Turbay. It was not an unusual way to operate in a friendly country, but it could sometimes be terribly unwieldy. The control for all the information, and all the CIA agents and informants, was not in Colombia. The ambassador didn't know who was working for whom all the time. Neither did the station chief, for that matter.

It had been around midnight when Malley had given Romero his house keys and gone on to the Dominican embassy with three communications experts. They'd put up more directional mikes and repeaters. Every piece of eavesdropping equipment they could think of was now covering every orifice the building had. If only half this stuff worked, they would know a lot about the movement of people inside. A green-beret colonel had arrived from Panama—incognito, of course—to see if the Dominican embassy was attackable. Officially, the U.S. was "not involved in tactics and negotiations." Unofficially, Turbay was taking all suggestions.

Malley drove into his garage, shut the door and locked it before entering his house. He froze for a split second, listening. And then he pulled his gun. Somebody was groaning something godawful!

Malley moved slowly toward the sound, through the kitchen and into the living room. The groaning got louder as he neared the guest bedroom. The guy sounded as though he was dying. Either that, or—

Malley kicked open the door. Jesus Christ! There was Romero in bed with, from the looks of the clothes on the floor, some goddamn Colombian soldier.

"You goddamn fucking twits!" Malley yelled. "I oughtta kill both of you!

"Get outta here!" Malley screamed at the Colombian, who was gathering up as much of his uniform as he could, while staring at Malley's gun and running backwards out of the bedroom.

"You too!" And Malley started kicking Romero's formidable bare ass. He just managed to grab his boxer shorts before he landed rather unceremoniously on the front doorstep. His army captain was nowhere in sight.

Malley sank onto his couch. Three-thirty in the morning and there was this faggot pounding on the door in his drawers, yelling and screaming to be let back in.

"Covert." What a fucking joke.

12

"I'M FINE, I'M FINE," Nancy Asencio mumbled to herself as she roller-skated around the flagpole that stood in the middle of the residence's circular drive.

She just needed a little exercise, that's all. The other ambassadors' wives were calling and crying all the time. She hadn't cried yet. She was fine. Maybe there were bags under her eyes, down to her knees. But she wasn't on any medication. Her mind was clear. Clear enough to know that this whole thing had been going on for too long now. They'd had Diego for almost a month!

"I'll be fine," Nancy told herself again.

Secretary of State Vance had called. Jimmy Carter had called. She'd been patient with them. Okay, Jimmy boy, she should have said, relax the U.S.-does-nothing policy. This is not Iran. There are fourteen other countries involved.

"What gives?" Nancy said aloud.

Those people are not going to be able to get out unless there's some compromise. There's a time to pray and a time to act.

Pray. Father Bean was nice to come to the residence every day to say Mass. He gave an absolution at the beginning so everyone could receive communion together. She just invited a few friends. That's all she had, a few friends.

She'd told Father Bean she wasn't giving up anything for Lent. She'd already given up her husband.

Nancy laughed at her own joke and then looked

down at her spreading hips. Maybe she should give up something, though. She was putting on weight. Everybody was sending over food and she was eating it.

"I guess I eat when I'm nervous," Nancy giggled.

Diego was losing weight. Whoever was cooking the food that was delivered by the Red Cross was just awful. One hot meal a day, and it was awful. She hoped the roast beef she'd fixed this morning got there all right. She'd called the embassy liaison with the Red Cross, some economics officer, to get the delivery schedule. The stupid woman had screwed up. She'd had to call the Egyptian ambassador's wife to find out what was going on.

"Oh God, how much longer?" Nancy said aloud.

She had to keep her spirits up. It just seemed that nobody was paying any attention. What had happened to those hordes of press people who used to hang around at the gate?

"Not that I'd ever talk to them," Nancy said. "Wouldn't trust myself."

But where were all the stories? Had everyone forgotten about her husband? Eileen Heaphy had told some Colombian reporter in Washington that the crisis in Bogotá hadn't gotten as much attention as Teheran in the United States because Asencio was a Hispanic name and the public was confused as to whose ambassador he was. How could Eileen say something like that?

Her daughter Ann had been furious. She'd been in Bogotá when the interview had been published. Ann had written a letter to Assistant Secretary Bowdler asking for some kind of public balance to Heaphy's damaging comments, for the sake of Diego's reputation and his mental balance as a hostage.

The U.S. was wasting time and energy now, Nancy thought, appearing to be hard with this kidnapping. Should have put some energy into preventing the thing in the first place. It was the guerrillas against the establishment. On the one hand, they were fanatics. On the other, they did have reason for becoming what they were. She could see why. But they had her husband!

She wondered what time Diego would call today.

Better try to think of a joke or something. Better not tell him one of the kids needed to borrow a big chunk of money that they really couldn't spare. She wasn't bothering him with family problems. She kept telling him that she was fine, the kids were fine, everything was fine. It was important to keep his spirits up.

Yesterday Comandante Uno got on the phone and thanked her for all the Spanish omelettes she'd sent over. She'd cooked ten of them, twelve eggs each, with potatoes and ham and onions. Diego loved them. They were delicious, Comandante Uno had said—when was she sending over more? Not until my husband is free, she'd answered.

"I guess I told him."

"Op center," Richard Baca said, answering the phone.

"The U.S. Marines have landed at El Dorado airport," said a male voice. "And if you don't believe me, check about thirty minutes from now at the Hilton Hotel. That's where they're gonna stay."

"Who are you?" asked Baca.

"It doesn't matter."

"Where are you?"

"It doesn't matter."

"How many marines are there?"

"Maybe eighty to a hundred."

"Thank you for calling," said Baca, "we appreciate your concern.

"See you around, asshole," he added as soon as he'd hung up.

"Hey you guys!" Baca addressed the room. "A

hundred marines are on their way to the Hilton Hotel!"

"That's a hell of a way to spend our tax money," said John McIntyre.

"Better call and check."

"You've got to be kidding!"

"You never know," laughed Baca. "Let's start a 'best rumor' bulletin board—right there under the Snow White and Seven Dwarfs poster."

"Hi, I'm Grumpy!" said Emi Yamauchi.

"Hi, I'm Sleepy!" said Baca.

"Hi, I'm Dopey and I'm going to answer this ringing phone," said Patt Lindsey.

"You're looking for who? Top? Sergeant Wherly? Who's calling? Post One? Post One, could you describe him to me?"

Patt Lindsey had the whole room riveted. She knew who Top was.

"He's a little guy," Patt was saying into the phone, "I see. Balding? Right. And he's wearing green jungle fatigues? Oh God. I thought he was a tree. I just watered him."

Everybody was howling with laughter when Jerry Harrison came into the room.

"Cables! Cables! Get your cables, here!" sang Harrison, catching the mood. All of a sudden he took two running steps and turned a perfect somersault. The cables went flying.

"Bravo! Bravo!" yelled Baca, and he started to applaud.

It was something to do. He'd begun bringing books to read or Peace Corps work he'd fallen behind on. It was like a shift change at a hospital.

How's the critical patient today?

Nothing to report.

That's cool.

The crisis had turned cuddly, not really much good for anybody's career. Asencio was calling three

times a day, telling jokes, asking for his favorite
food to be sent in. He'd called one day and said that
he'd told Nancy to fix him some of her spaghetti
sauce, but that he was having trouble finding anybody who could get some Parmesan cheese. Could
they find him some Parmesan? He'd be real popular
with the boys inside if they could. They did.

Life had settled into a routine. Frank Crigler was
dealing with the big boys in the United States Government, the Colombian Government, a coordinating committee of four of the fifteen embassies
involved, the full committee of fifteen itself and Diego.

The team's function was to get information that
Frank wanted from wherever he wanted it. Sometimes Washington. Sometimes from some other embassy. Sometimes from within the American embassy.

At first there had been a dearth of information.
Then there had been tons of it. Pounds and pounds
of bullshit. Everybody was talking: Asencio, Comandante Uno—the guerrillas' siege leader—all the
other embassies, their governments, Washington,
Colombia. Everybody was talking to goddamn everybody.

Everything they said was screened for Crigler into
piles of "Must See"—a Washington instruction, for
instance; "Look At When You Have Time"—an
alleged interview with Comandante Uno; and
"Straight to the Trash Can"—the marines on their
way to the Hilton.

Washington had sent a shitload of people down to
hold—officially—Frank Crigler's hand, and—unofficially—Colombia's. Frank Perez had arrived first
from the anti-terrorist bureau at the State Department. Then, when the negotiations started between
the guerrillas and the government, a shrink came
down quietly to help the Colombians out with "the

psychology of negotiating." He was "Top Secret," since the U.S. was not supposed to be doing anything but praying for Ambassador Asencio and hoping things turned out all right. Assistant Secretary Veckey, the ex-ambassador to Colombia, came to cheerlead the embassy staff, congratulate the Colombians on keeping their cool and remind everybody that the U.S. does not pay ransom.

"Hello, honey?" Frank Perez said into the phone. The whole room went quiet. Patt Lindsey started mouthing the words as Perez drawled them.

"Is Mommy home?

"She's not? Where is she? You don't know? What time will Mommy be home, honey?

"Okay. Tell Mommy Daddy called, and I'll call back."

Every day Frank Perez came in to use the open line to Washington to call his wife. Baca's team guessed she was number two or three, and half Perez's age. She was never home for the first call. But every day Perez would return to call again. When he finally got her on the phone there would be some sweet French nothings and then he'd ask how the construction of the backyard swimming pool was going. The conversations had become such a joke that each team did a sitrep for the next shift on the progress of the Perez pool.

Chuck Boles threw his .38 on Baca's desk and sat down next to it. "I'm tired," he said. "There are so many alligators at my ass, I don't even know I'm in a swamp. Was up till twelve-thirty last night. Everybody's getting bomb threats. Not just us. A lot of the other embassies, too."

"Found any bombs yet?" Baca asked.

"Nope. But you have to run all that stuff down, you know. Ninety-nine out of a hundred won't be anything. But you have to catch that one. I went to bomb school. Dismantled seven out of nine bombs. I was 'killed' twice. They had this dynamite that went off above your head. It rattled the brain."

First Frank Perez, now Chuck Boles. Ah. And there was a trickle of people reading the posted sitreps and latest cables. Must be about the end of today's negotiating session, Baca thought. When some news was about to arrive, people started to gather, as around an accident. Maybe it was a way to put some excitement in their lives. Patt Lindsey called it "circle jerking."

"It's Asencio on line five," said Emi.

That would be the first report on how the negotiations went. The second would follow within the hour from one of Chuck Boles's Colombian employees who was pumping the driver of the van in which the talks were held. The third report of what was said came, unbeknownst to him, from one of the government's negotiators himself. He had a habit of running through each session afterwards with a friend of his in the military, who just happened to be in the employ of the CIA. The last report on the negotiations would come half a day later from the Colombian Government, who had the van wired.

Emi Yamauchi transcribed all the tapes of Asencio's and Crigler's conversations. They were always the same. Asencio would ramble on and on, in Spanish, of course—the only language Comandante Uno allowed the hostages to speak on the phone—and Crigler would just keep saying "Uh-huh, uh-huh, uh-huh."

Baca stared at the turning reel of tape. Then he caught Emi's eye and said, "Uh-huh, uh-huh, uh-huh."

Emi was still laughing when Crigler stuck his head around the door.

"Richard?"

Baca followed him into his office.

"Richard, can you come by the house tonight? Late. Maybe ten-thirty or so?"

"Uh, sure, Frank."

"Good. Thanks. See you then."

Baca was sitting at his desk wondering what Crigler had on his mind when Ken Keller walked in.

Shift-change time!

"Hey!" said Keller. "Did you guys see the signs on the op-center door? One sign says FRANK CRIGLER WILL HAVE A SEIZURE IF THE WORD 'SIEGE' IS MISSPELLED ONCE MORE. And then there's a sign right underneath that says SIEGE—THAT'S EASY: I AFTER E EXCEPT AFTER C. OR IS THAT . . .

"You've seen them," said Keller, spotting the Cheshire grin on Baca's face. "Did you write that second one, Baca?"

"It's the best memo since the crisis began. Hey Ken, what's this I hear about you moving into town? Did you have trouble out at your *finca*?"

"Yeah. Came home to find a car parked down the street one night. No license plates. Two guys sitting in the front seat, smoking, reading a newspaper. It gave me the heebie-jeebies. Same thing happened to Don Roberts, only the car was parked in his driveway. By the time Don went and got Boles's assistant, Bruce Witter, the car had gone. I mean his wife and two baby boys were inside the house!

"Ah, well. What's to report?"

"Nothing. Today's negotiation stuff is just coming in."

Keller sighed.

"Hey, look," said Baca, "We can't get grim about this. We have to be patient. We have to be reasonable. We have to be calm."

"What have you ever got from being those things?" asked Keller.

"I got laid once."

Keller didn't crack a smile. He just started his usual down-to-work striptease. First he hung up the jacket of his three-piece suit. Then he took off the vest and tie. He got the whole room's attention, however, when he started unbuttoning his button-down shirt. Pretending not to notice everybody's stares, Keller nonchalantly turned around to hang up his shirt next to his jacket.

Across the back of his white T-shirt was a big, red "Dracula Sucks."

"Do you mind if I just talk at you awhile?" Frank Crigler asked.

"Whatever you want, Frank," answered Baca.

Crigler sat slumped on the couch in his bathrobe and socks, just staring at the glowing coals in the fireplace while he absentmindedly stirred the ice cubes around in his Scotch.

"You look exhausted," Baca said.

"More frustrated than exhausted. Goddammit, I need some solutions. I know what the problems are."

And there are plenty of them, thought Baca. Nobody has to tell Frank Crigler the ambassador's a hostage and how the deal made for his release will affect American-Colombian relations for years. Nobody has to tell Frank Crigler the future of Colombia's democracy is at stake. If the military gets its hard-line way, everybody will be killed inside that embassy. Fifteen countries will have dead ambassadors and Colombia's left will have twelve new martyrs. And it's not just the military. Who knew better than Frank Crigler the problems with the other embassies? The Mexicans are telling Colombia that they've fucked up: Pay the goddamn money! Get them out! Fuck your democracy! You guys don't have any skills. Let us negotiate.

Half the committee of fifteen says, Get them out—

the longer you wait, the more somebody's temper, or whatever, will lead to bloodshed. The other half says, You have to stop this kind of thing whenever it happens. Don't pay. Don't negotiate.

"I feel like a tap dancer." said Crigler. "I want it to end quickly, who doesn't? The guerrillas want it to end quickly, figuring they'll get more of their demands met. That's why they let the ambassadors call their embassies so much. Pressure to end it fast. On the other hand, I recognize the government's concern. They want this thing to move slowly. They want to just wear the guerrillas down. If they meet too many of the demands the government takes a risk of exposing itself to a takeover by an angry military.

"So I tell General Leyva to stay flexible and I call and congratulate Turbay whenever he says publicly that we must all be reasonable, this isn't Nicaragua."

"And you're trying to manipulate the other diplomats, right?" said Baca. "When the army has Turbay's ear you try to send over to the Foreign Ministry the guys who will say, 'We care about the lives of our ambassadors. The lives of our ambassadors are foremost. Anything you do to jeopardize that, we will be over you like stink on shit.' When Turbay is in his we'll-wait-them-out-forever mood you try to activate the diplomat types who will say, 'You're dragging your feet. All you give a shit about is your petty-ass so-called democracy.' "

"Scatological," smiled Crigler, "but fairly accurate. Now the Colombians are getting the feeling that there are individual negotiations going on. And they're understandably angry. 'In public, you guys are saying it's our responsibility to deal with this thing, and then every one of you is going around behind our backs making separate deals. How are we supposed to negotiate? They don't have to talk to us if they're talking to you!' "

"Can't say I blame them—Colombia, I mean," said Baca.

"Richard, you were the first one to write a memo that said maybe these guerrillas were not as sharp as we first thought. That they didn't seem to have any firm ideology. That they didn't know what they were doing. I forget your line about the attack. . . ."

"Well, how slick had the takeover been?" said Baca. "Twelve well-armed guys overwhelmed three under-armed bodyguards. Big shit. And then came the tough part inside. All those fat people eating canapés and drinking Scotch. No, I didn't think they were that impressive. And they gave up so much—the amount of money, the number of prisoners—in the first negotiating sessions."

"But Colombia will not let even one political prisoner go," said Crigler. "They have, of course, no 'political' prisoners. That's where it's stuck. Any ideas? You were a big-time lawyer. Don't lawyers negotiate for a living?"

"Okay," said Baca. "Up the ante. Replace those two Colombian gopher negotiators in the van. Send in a heavyweight. Demand to talk directly with Comandante Uno. Then let them sit there and dicker until they get a deal. Not a deal that Uno's got to check out with the M-19 prisoners in La Picota prison. If he's gotta check with his mama, then maybe he's not quite the reb we thought he was. And then deal with him like—the classic example is the car dealer. 'Okay, I got a deal for you. I can hold it till five o'clock today. I can't be holding it while you check with your mama or Picota or the central party or whatever shit. You the boss or not? The fuckin' plane leaves at five. I'll give you guys this much money and move you out of here. Take it, and be safe and free, or leave it, and sit inside that stinky place getting fat on capitalist-cooked spaghetti.' "

Crigler was laughing so hard his Scotch was

sloshing over the rim of the glass onto the rug.

Let it spill, Baca thought, and he just sat there enjoying what he knew was a rare moment of relaxation for Frank Crigler.

He was glad to be able to cheer the cheerleader.

Emily Roth woke up in a sweat. She'd been dreaming. She'd been looking for the embassy in Bogotá, but everything was strange and she couldn't remember where it was and she hadn't felt as though she belonged there. No taxi would stop and pick her up, so she'd started walking. She'd passed lots of foreign currency just lying in the street. British pounds, French francs and American dollars. And then she'd passed Colombian currency. Sheafs of pesos, all ripped up.

What did that mean? thought Emily. No values, there are no values in this country. That's what it meant.

Finally, in her dream, she'd arrived at the embassy. She was standing at a window looking up at the sky outside, when she saw garbage flying toward her. That's not possible, she'd stood there thinking, the sky is where God is. Why is there garbage in the sky? Then all of a sudden a piece crashed into the window and stuck there. Garbage in the embassy.

She knew what that meant. Everything had turned sour again. It was all over with Miguel. She'd gotten out of crisis duty that first weekend so she could go to Cartagena with him, and what a disappointment—especially in bed. So much for Latin lovers. She'd felt like a contestant on that old TV game-show, "Beat the Clock."

They'd finally had lunch together yesterday, after weeks of almost total silence. He'd been distant and had cut off any discussion of personal things.

Maybe she'd made a mistake with this foreign service thing. Maybe she should have stayed married and had 2.2 children and 2.1 cars—or whatever the current American ideal was.

There was no purpose in her life. She wasn't in on any of the operation center stuff and the econ job didn't matter. She wasn't important to anybody personally, either.

And to top it all off, she'd received notice from the State Department today that they were docking her three days' pay for all the security violations she'd been charged with before the access door had been put up.

Enough. She would put in a curtailment request tomorrow. If it was okayed by Washington, she would be out of this place by December.

13

"Bogotá! Bogotá! This is Washington, Bogotá!" Eileen Heaphy leaned toward the speaker phone on the table.

"McIntyre probably went to the bathroom," said Marty Berman, a staffer from the State Department's anti-terrorism unit, who was assigned to the Special Colombia Working Group for the duration of the crisis.

"Look at this ad in today's *Post*: $23.99 for an egg poacher! And that's the sale price, for Christ's sake! My wife wants one of these things. What's the matter with you modern women? Can't you drop an egg in a pan of simmering water?"

"Bogotá! Bogotá! This is Washington, Bogotá!"

"Oh, let the poor guy take a shit, Eileen," said Berman. "How long has he been on the job now?"

"Frank Crigler disbanded the teams more than a month ago," said Heaphy. "So that's how long John McIntyre's been 'special assistant to handle crisis-related matters.' Jesus, which means Asencio has been a hostage for almost two months. That's a record. Terrorist acts in Latin America have never lasted this long."

"Will Asencio stay in Colombia, do you think?" asked Berman.

"I doubt it. That's too long a time as a hostage. Who knows what shape he'll be in when he gets out? Although he sure sounds good on those telephone tapes."

"Good!" laughed Berman. "He sounds great! Like

a one-man band! 'I told Comandante Uno to forget about getting any prisoners freed. . . . Well, I think the guerrillas will accept this. . . . I've told Comandante Uno that's all the money he'll get. . . .'

"There's a letter here somebody from Arizona sent to Senator Charles Mathias asking, for the thousandth time, why the Russians left the Dominican Republic's reception early. You want to handle it?"

"The policy line, right?" asked Heaphy.

"Right. There is no evidence that the Soviet bloc knew about the attack—"

"—They left early to attend the credentials-presentation ceremony of the new Chinese ambassador at the presidential palace," finished Heaphy.

"Let me tell you the latest Bogotá joke," Berman said. "You know the ambassadors take turns opening the front door for the Red Cross deliveries. Well, when it came the Israeli ambassador's turn, he said through the closed door, 'No thanks, we already gave. . . .' "

Eileen groaned.

"I'm going back to my office. Call me if you hear anything from the OAS."

"I will," said Heaphy. What a riot. How perfect! All these State Department types who can't force themselves to say the words "human rights" out loud are now panting after the OAS's human rights group. The Organization of American States had long ago scheduled an April trip to Colombia for its human rights unit. More than 216 M-19s were about to go on trial en masse. Instead of releasing them, as the guerrillas wanted, the Colombian Government said it would be willing to guarantee a free trial witnessed by any goddamnbody the guerrillas agreed to. If the OAS people would meet with Comandante Uno and if Comandante Uno agreed to their participation, maybe the siege would finally come to a happy end.

It never should have had a beginning. How many times had she asked Asencio what kind of people the Colombian army was really rounding up in their M-19 crackdown? "They're arresting the guerrillas," Diego would say. "There aren't any more M-19s." Bullshit. If he'd done his human rights homework down there he wouldn't be a hostage now.

Eileen Heaphy looked around the room. There was the usual assortment of yesterday's tea bags in the ashtrays, and yesterday's ashes in the tea cups. At one end of the room were eight clipboards of "Top Secret" and "Confidential" cables from Bogotá. The CIA was reporting its guts out.

"It's about time," Heaphy said out loud.

Across the room from all the classified paper was the unclassified blackboard—full of working group staffers' home phone numbers and lists of names to call at the various embassies in Washington for any news about the other hostage ambassadors. The most important thing on the whole blackboard, as far as Heaphy was concerned, was the parking pass number. A parking space in the State Department garage! She was the envy of her peers. Thank you, Diego.

Eileen had been eating lunch in the cafeteria the day Asencio was taken hostage. She'd been telling a friend how much she liked being a desk officer, except for writing bullshit memos about the birdshit islands. One more Quita Sueño memo and she was going to scream. When she'd got back to her office after lunch, her boss, Dick Barnabey, was waiting for her. "Where've you been! Diego's a hostage! Get upstairs to the operations center!"

By the time she'd gotten upstairs, the open line to Bogotá had already been set up by the anti-terrorist unit. "Well, Eileen," they'd said, "you thought you were rid of us when Richard Starr was released. I guess you can't stand being without a hostage in Colombia, huh?''

Those were long, hectic days, trying to sort out what had happened, and then how to deal with it. The Colombia working group shared a kitchen and sleeping area with the Teheran working group.

But that's all they shared. Eileen had had a terrible time trying to explain to the Asencio kids that there was no comparison between the crises. Iran was fifty Americans, oil, the Mid-East. Colombia was one American whose name sounded Colombian, marijuana and South America. Twice she'd had to suggest maybe Jimmy Carter should call Mrs. Asencio. He finally did.

But nobody remembered she'd done that now. All they could remember was that stupid conversation she'd had with that Colombian—who never mentioned that it was, in fact, an interview that he intended to publish. She was quoted publicly saying what she'd been telling the Asencio kids privately about the difference between Teheran and Bogotá.

It had been horrible. Deputy Assistant Secretary Sam Eaton had taken her out of the operations center for five days after that article appeared in Colombia. He wanted to remove her from the desk job too! It had been the worst moment of her career. Frank Crigler had been responsible. Heaphy would never trust him again.

Crigler had felt so bad when she was removed from the working group that he had called her and admitted that his cable saying what a ruckus the interview had caused in Colombia was just him covering his ass. If he hadn't reported it, and Washington had found out about the interview some other way, he would have been in trouble.

Eileen had worked for Frank in the political section of the U.S. Embassy in Mexico City. She'd liked and admired him then.

She hoped the whole thing had blown over. Although she still felt ashamed every time she talked to Nancy Asencio, or any of the kids, she really would have liked to get a meritorious award for her work as a member of the Colombia group. She'd never had one of those. It's not that I don't care about Ambassador Asencio, Heaphy thought, it's just that I'd like to get something out of this too.

Eileen wondered how Crigler was doing with his new staff. He'd asked to have a political officer, John Hamilton, someone they'd both worked with in Mexico, come to Bogotá temporarily to follow him around and do memcons of all the conversations Frank was having with Colombian ministers and the diplomatic committee members. That's how much he thought of his political section. He went and imported somebody from Greece. And then Crigler had named Ken Keller, the consul general, as acting deputy chief of mission. He gave the job John Simms and Frank Ravndal were dying for to his visa officer!

It was either a gutsy or a stupid thing to do. Right or wrong, thought Eileen, it must have caused a lot of bad feeling in Bogotá.

"Do you know how Crigler told me?" John Simms asked incredulously. "He said, 'I can do without a visa officer, but not without a political officer. That's why I've made Ken Keller my DCM.'"

"That's odd," said Don Roberts. "I could have sworn he'd forgotten he had any political officers."

"I'm just not his type," said Simms. "That 'management by objective' crap of his means eleven cheap-shot reports in five days and a schedule into September of reports coming up. Who knows what's going to be going on in September?

"You know the problem with Crigler? Foreign policy in Washington is paper. But in the embassies human beings are involved. He's not much of one."

"His paper isn't very good either," said Roberts. "Remember that cable—the two A.M. gem he sent saying there would be an early solution to the crisis, that the Colombians were going to release the prisoners?"

Simms started to laugh.

"Maybe his friend Mr. Hamilton, whom he brought in 'to work the ministerial corridors,' will improve his judgment."

"Crigler is still cutting all references in my cables," said Roberts, "to the fact that the M-19s—no matter how this all ends—have increased their influence and popularity with Colombia's youth."

"Crigler only reports what Washington wants to hear," said Simms. "He's a dangerous man."

"I did a cable yesterday," said Roberts, "about how the man on the street admires what the M-19s have done. They hate bureaucrats. They love to see something like this happen to the people they feel push them around all the time. You know what happened to that cable? He returned it to me today with 'Nonsense!' scribbled across the top. 'The man in the street has had thirty years of violence in this country. He's sick and tired of it.' "

"Wonder where Crigler found *his* man in the street?" Simms said. "Let's leave the crisis to glory-boy and get on with business. Have you told Washington that one of Turbay's new ministerial appointments is a known drug trafficker?"

"That's in the typewriter now," said Roberts.

"All right. I'll handle the Quita Sueño stuff."

"What exactly is that all about?" asked Roberts.

"*Alternativa*, our favorite leftist magazine, has a story this week saying the State Department has asked for the indefinite postponement of Senate consideration of the 1972 treaty, in deference to Nicaragua."

"The dung has hit the fan," said Roberts. "Again."

"It's gotten a lot of attention, you might say. And all negative. The usual: if this is how the U.S. treats its friends then . . ."

"Life does go on, doesn't it?" said Roberts.

"No goddammit, it doesn't." Simms slammed his hand down on his desk. "I'm curtailing because of Crigler. If that's the kind of guy the foreign service wants, they can have him. I'm getting out. Since 1950 my wife and sons and I have spent all of two years in the States. I'm fifty-six years old, Don, my career with the State Department is finished. It's obvious, even to me, that I'm never going to be an ambassador. I'll do better on the outside.

"I remember when I was DCM in Barbados. I ran that embassy for seven months. There were no staff meetings. No CIA. No USICA. We had a great time." Simms started to laugh. "There was this one embassy guy, very high ranking, who wasn't there but a couple of months before he knocked up a local bigwig's daughter— God! What's that noise?"

"Emergency exercises," said Roberts.

Patt Lindsey leaned into Simms' office. "One if by land! Two if by sea! What do the bells mean?"

"If it's one long bell, we go outside," said Roberts. "If it's a broken bell, we go up to the secure room."

"Isn't it the other way around?" asked Simms.

Patt opened the access door and looked down the corridor. "Everybody's going every which way. The instructions must have been classified."

"Welcome to the beautiful U.S. Consulate in beautiful Barranquilla! What did you think of Consul Thomas Gustafson?" asked DEA agent Torre Shutes.

" 'It's not my war on drugs,' " mimicked fellow agent Megan Rafferty. " 'I'm just the scorecard.' "

"And did you see the 'scorecard'?"

"You mean that book of his? Registration No. N1300; Cessna 310; March 27; 8 A.M. crashed; clandestine airstrip, Guajira; U.S. Citizen John Doe, killed, etcetera, etcetera, etcetera. The Aircraft/Vessels Accidents and Detentions book."

"Did you see the cover?" asked Torre.

"Yes," Megan laughed. "A World War II drawing of the U.S. Marines defending a beachhead under attack. The air is full of enemy planes. The sea is full of enemy ships. He says that's how he feels here in the Barranquilla consulate. Besieged."

"Did he tell you that this consulate had been closed for years?" asked Torre. "They had to reopen it in 1976 because of the drug boom."

"What a horrible job he has," Megan said. "He identifies decomposing bodies. He handles irate U.S. owners of confiscated boats and planes who say they didn't know what their craft were being used for. He refuses drug traffickers visas to the United States—telling them that something else is wrong with their application so they don't shoot him on the spot. He carries a gun with him whenever he leaves that dreadful office on the tenth floor to go out into this hot, sticky, dreadful city. Ugh."

"Did you know he was a foreign service classmate of Ambassador Asencio's?"

"No," said Megan. "You're kidding! How did he get stuck with this consulate?"

"He once told me," laughed Torre, "that his mother thinks he has enemies in Washington."

"I did ask him why he stayed here, what with his feelings about the drug thing. He said, 'I'm here because I don't have another retirement plan.' "

"Rumor has it that he may not be able to retire from the foreign service."

"What do you mean by that?" asked Megan.

"Rumor has it that there have been visa irregularities here in the Barranquilla consulate."

"Hm," was all Megan said. "That's why he's still alive."

"All I know," added Torre, "is that Chuck Boles was here sniffing around not too long ago."

"Oh, don't tell me any more," said Megan. "I feel sort of sorry for Gustafson."

"Well, then. What did our consul in question tell you about the state of the drug program?"

" 'Who cares?' was his first comment."

"Ah yes. Who does, indeed?"

"Gustafson said that in his last cable he described the program as having its 'ups and downs'—"

Torre Shutes howled with laughter.

"But that on the whole, mounting a drug 'war,' and getting President Turbay involved, was a good thing. Without the public statements against trafficking and traffickers, the business would go above ground. As it is, the marijuana is grown high on the mountains to escape detection and the mules and trucks that bring it down to the airstrips and ports must use the back roads. The government's pronouncements and the army's activity have kept the lid on, to some degree, and deprived the traffickers of any respectability."

"So the farmers who do the growing and the Guajira Indians who do the moving and the loading have felt a squeeze. The big boys are, as usual, untouched—and crying about their loss of respectability all the way to the bank.

"But you know and I know, Megan, that all that is going to change if the government pulls the army out. They were threatening to do it months ago, but I think Asencio was stalling them. With him out of the picture now for two months . . ."

"That's what Gustafson said. Only he was more precise. He sees signs already that the army has cut its patrols and the druggers are 're-thriving.' The five Colombian families that handle the marijuana trade are branching out into cocaine and Quaaludes. Rumors of audaciously open parties, with bowls of cocaine as hors d'oeuvres, are circulating again. Having a lot of girl friends as a symbol of status, and the banking outside of Colombia that their women do for them—none of that ever changed.

" 'The wild west' Gustafson calls it, 'where every man walks around in fear of self. Does every man have a price?' he asked me."

"What else?" asked Torre.

"The confusion of policies. On the one hand he's supposed to be looking after U.S. citizens' interests. On the other hand, the U.S. has asked Colombia to make war on drug traffickers, some of whom are U.S. citizens. Gustafson said his tendency is to sit and snicker while the rival agencies in Washington go after each other—one protecting, the other prosecuting. But every time he finds himself handing over incriminating evidence on an American citizen to the Colombians . . . He says he couldn't have survived in Barranquilla without Asencio. It was impossible not to step on State Department toes. Diego defended him.

"The most incredible thing happened while we were talking." Megan shivered. "All of a sudden there was this flap of wings and the room fell into shadow. I must have looked startled. Gustafson laughed and said 'It's just a condor on the windowsill.' *Just* a condor! My God, I've never seen anything so evil!"

"The vulture of the Andes," said Torre. "Let's quit sitting here in this van like two Americans doing a drug deal and I'll drive you to condor territory. Twenty, thirty of them are always flying in great huge circles above this particular part of Bar-ranquilla."

"Do you mean there's a part of town that looks worse than this?" asked Megan.

"This is the center of downtown. See the small square across the street there with—"

"The ever-present statue of Simon Bolívar," finished Megan. "Didn't Bolívar die disgraced and penniless somewhere on the north coast here?"

"Santa Marta. A murder-a-minute city run by druggers. Poor Bolívar. If he had lived to see what's happened . . ."

"Oh, he wouldn't have been surprised," said Megan. "In the nineteenth century Simon Bolívar, South America's greatest revolutionary hero, wrote: 'For us [Latin] America is ungovernable; whosoever works for the revolution is plowing the sea; the most sensible action to take is to emigrate. [The region] will ineluctably fall into the hands of a mob gone wild, later to fall under the domination of obscure small tyrants of every color and race.' "

Torre drove around the edges of the Magdalena River delta, which led out eventually to the Caribbean Sea. Next to huge tanks of Exxon fuel were clusters of crumbling, tin-roofed shacks with naked babies in the front yards playing in the dirt.

"This is like some caricature of poverty!" said Megan.

"Wait. I'll turn right. Watch what happens to the neighborhood as we go back toward town. Keep your door locked and the window at least halfway up."

The open, scruffy land, pitted with mounds of garbage and pools of dark, stagnant water, slowly gave way to huge cement warehouses whose signs, once brightly painted, had long ago faded and flaked in the heat of the sun. The street suddenly narrowed, and was lined on both sides with hundreds of people and dozens of vendors' carts. Three-days-past-fresh mangoes were stacked on top of the carts. Burst, rotting mangoes, black with flies, lay underneath. Flies crawled across faces unnoticed.

"I'd go into drugs, too, to get out of this," said Torre.

"It looks like a B-movie set of Shanghai," said Megan. "And the smell!"

"Look up through the windshield. See the condors circling?"

"God, Torre what are we doing here?"

"Saving U.S. youth from 'moral corruption,' " said Torre.

"Is this what you wanted to do when you grew up?" asked Megan.

"I wanted to be an L.A. cop," said Torre. "But my eyesight was bad. What's your excuse? What is a pretty woman like you doing in an ugly business like this?"

"I like it," said Megan. "And, so far, I like Colombia. How long have you been here, Torre?"

"Only a couple of months."

"You sound disillusioned already."

"If the DEA left tomorrow, nobody would notice. It wouldn't make any difference. What *is* my job? My job is to make things happen. I come to Barranquilla from Bogotá a couple times a month to work informants, to pass on any good tips to the F2—who can't be trusted; or to the agents who work for the attorney general's office—who are floundering with no money, no equipment and no support from Bogotá; or to the army, which lies and bullshits me eight ways from Sunday. Their latest request is for more 'information money.' Information, my foot. I live in a small, unreal world of little successes—a pill press here, two kilos of marijuana there—that add up to nothing.

"In Colombia drugs are a political football. So we have an ambassador who comes in for two or three years all gung ho. Agencies are created, empires are built and then the ambassador leaves. They'll never let Asencio stay—if he's ever released. The army lacks will, the attorney general's people are half-assed, and now they want to create a new agency—a six-hundred-man police force! Bullshit! A year's time and millions of dollars will be wasted getting that into motion—for what? It's a joke! A pipe dream!"

"Gustafson thinks Frank Crigler will lose the drug program," said Megan.

'As soon as the army goes, it's lost. They need armed patrols up here."

"What Gustafson doesn't know," said Megan, "is that Frank Crigler *wants* to lose the drug program."

"I'm not surprised."

"He thinks Colombia should legalize marijuana. That would 'eliminate corruption.' "

"Jesus."

"As Dave Burnett says, 'what can you expect from a music major?' "

Torre laughed. "The sixteen million dollars is in limbo because Crigler can't get a letter of agreement signed by the Colombians. The time limit on the appropriation is running out. If they all keep fighting over who gets what part of the money, they'll lose it altogether."

"Poor Dave," Megan said. "Crigler snubs him and has cut him off from any Colombians higher than law-enforcement types. He's 'just a cop.' And while the bureaucratic war on drugs remains in a stalemate, the traffickers are gaining ground every day. Burnett thinks we're back to where we were four years ago. He's begun to talk about 'decreasing DEA presence' in Colombia."

Torre just sighed. "Well, I'll drive you over to meet General Guillermo Jaramillo Narioso, commander of the Second Brigade. First he will show you all the pretty equipment the army has captured from the druggers. And then he will tell you that the army bought him his new cream Mercedes. And then he will say that his predecessor wasn't crooked and that, of course, there is no connection between guns and drugs. If he ever admitted that publicly, the army would have to stay in the drug program and they don't want that.

"Oh," added Torre. "I bet he asks you if you're married."

General Guillermo Jaramillo Narioso sat small under three five-foot-high oil paintings. One was of Simon Bolívar, one of Jesus on the Cross and one of the Blessed Virgin Mary.

"So look what we are fighting. Here," and he threw a gold-handled revolver on the desk. "We have captured Blazer trucks with special motors and armor. We have confiscated hundreds of small light submachine guns and communications equipment I have never seen before. Look, see this little thing? It's a radio receiver with a telephone dial. A communications expert taught me how to use it. Now I use it like they did. Here. I will call my wife."

Megan could hear the phone ringing.

"Hm," said the general. "Not home.

"I have seven battalions on the north coast. Our main job is public order. We don't know how to fight traffickers.

"What we have done is to capture some manifestation of the drug problem. Planes, pilots, truck drivers and a lot of product. But we have not touched the big heads. They are in the United States. They have the money to buy the ships. They have two or three trucks against my one.

"Some of my people have received money. We've punished them. It's not bad now, but if we continue in this, corruption will win. It's a terrible risk. A nation needs an army that is correct, honest. That's why we've asked the government to relieve us of this mission.

"Everybody says everybody else is a trafficker. I don't trust you. You don't trust me. Three days ago I got my new Mercedes from the army. Already people are saying, Where did he get that new car? I am honest. So was my predecessor.

"We have been successful enough to push the traffickers south. So one day soon—if we are not removed from this duty—all army brigades will be fighting drugs. Six months we were supposed to do this. It's now a year and a half. Everybody is so afraid there are guns for drugs. Bah! Everybody should be afraid instead of a dishonest army!"

Megan opened her mouth to speak.

"The government needs to build programs for people," the general continued. "Jobs, other sources for money. The governor of the Guajira says to me, 'If we didn't burn these tons of marijuana, we could sell them to the United States and we could build schools and roads.'

"I don't know about the governor.

"It's very difficult to see the future. The problem is so profound. I have one radar in the Guajira, which doesn't work. Do you know how I spot planes? Men on mountaintops with binoculars. Sometimes I think it is a joke.

"Do you know what I found the other day? A letter dated 1556, from the governor in Cartagena to the King of Spain, asking what to do about all the contraband gold in the Guajira. I sent the letter to Bogotá. You see? Drugs today. Tomorrow another thing."

Finally General Guillermo Jaramillo Narioso ran out of breath. To keep command of the room, he stood up and walked around to the front of his desk, twirling his blue-tinted aviator glasses in his hands.

"I am a great friend of Diego Asencio's. I have been to Miami and Washington, D.C. I fought in Korea with the Americans. Did you know Colombia sent a battalion? Of course not.

"I like Americans. But I feel you are beginning to lose in many things. It's a problem for the free world. The communists are separating the Americas. The only people who care about human rights are the democracies. All the time we tie our hands. The M-19s are communists.

"Colombia was not a colonized country like the United States. We were conquered. The Spanish came to take our gold and our emeralds to Europe. People here were slaves. Plunder is still a way of life. And the Catholic Church? The Spanish brought that too. The clergy try to put in the hands of God everything that happens. We call God 'fate.' There is no God—only good luck and bad luck. There is no feeling that work makes any difference. Only luck. That is why drug trafficking is so successful here. Easy money is good luck."

The general sat down on the arm of Megan's chair.

"Tell me, dear, are you married?"

Emily Roth fixed herself a batch of piña coladas and got out the family Christmas tape from 1977.

She could picture the scene. Her sister Rose and Rose's husband, Ernie; her sister Alice, Alice's husband, John, and their daughter, Amy, were all sitting around the dining room table at Rose and Ernie's house. It was the first Christmas she'd missed with them. She had been in Greece, so they had sent her a tape recording.

"Merry Christmas, Emily!"

That was Ernie's voice.

"Merry Christmas, Aunt Emily!"

That was her niece, Amy. She was seven years old and wonderful. Emily had started writing short stories for her about children in other countries—Greece and Colombia, to be exact.

Everybody in turn wished Emily a loud Merry Christmas and then there was the sound of ripping paper.

"We're opening your gifts first, Emily," Ernie said. "Oh, look at that! That's beautiful. Thank you, Emily!" And then Emily could hear Ernie lower his voice: "Rose, the mouthpiece is on sideways. I think somebody smoked this pipe before I got it."

Emily started to laugh.

"Oh!" came a squeal. That was Rose. "What beautiful copper!

"What is it?" Rose muttered to somebody.

"It's a wall plaque." That was Alice.

In the background Emily could just make out Ernie saying, "It'll be okay. It's just bent a little. We can hammer it out."

Emily took a sip of her piña colada. God, she missed them.

"It's a chess set!" John said. "Look at that onyx!"

There was a whole minute of silence.

"We're looking to see if any of the pieces are broken, Emily!" Ernie said.

"Only two." That was John now. "But they're broken just right. They'll be easy to fix."

"Don't say anything is broken on the tape," Alice snapped.

"It's too late. It's already on the tape," Ernie said, and then somebody leaned over and switched it off.

Emily was laughing so hard tears came to her eyes. And then she started to cry.

"You know we really shouldn't be having a party," said Jeannie Kuhlman. "With Asencio still a hostage and all . . ."

"It's not a party!" said Phil Ferris. "It's a wake!"

"A toast!" said Jim Welch, raising his glass of beer in the air. "To the decline and fall of the American embassy!"

"Correction," quipped Ferris. "The decline and fall of the American 'mission,' as in 'moral.' "

"Or is it 'post'?" said Welch. "As in 'listening.' The place has gone sour the last couple of months. I don't know if it's just the psychological fallout from the hostage thing, and the fact that there's no place to release the tension, or whether it's . . ."

"Frank Crigler," finished Ferris.

"There's something almost—embarrassing—about Crigler," said Welch, "I can't put my finger on it. . . ."

"Maybe it's that few Colombians have ever heard of him," said Hadia Roberts. "The minister of justice asked Don the other day who was running the embassy now. Don told him, Frank Crigler, the chargé. 'Oh, is he new?' asked the minister? New! He's been here eight months and nobody's ever heard of him!"

"Tsk, tsk," said Ferris. "What's Don talking to a minister for? Not allowed now, you know. Must have permission from Frank Crigler."

"Not under Diego," Hadia said. "If Don hadn't asked long ago to curtail because of the security problems here, he would be asking now because of Crigler. He feels like a schoolchild, writing reports that are constantly corrected."

"Half the embassy is curtailing because of Crigler," said Welch. "I know what I mean by 'embarrassing.' Frank Crigler believes that we have *palan-*

ca. I don't think the United States is so important to Colombia anymore. We can't sell them sophisticated weaponry. So they get their fighters from France and their ships from Germany. We can't sell them guns. So they buy those from Brazil. We are no longer the free world's only source of advanced technology, and as we move into a position of equality in the bear pit of foreign trade, we are going to have to change—or ignore—the holier-than-thou no-bribe laws of our yahoo Abscam congressmen."

"I hadn't even noticed Crigler's version of foreign policy," said Ferris. "I can't get past his personality. He's a hollow man, a martinet. Even when he says the right words, there's no heart behind them. Do you believe his going after George Thigpen the other day in front of everybody?"

"What did Thigpen do?" asked Hadia.

"He talked to a minister without permission."

"Jerry, what about this Chuck Boles–Bruce Witter thing?" asked Hadia. "Is Crigler involved?"

"No. Distinctly not," Jerry Harrison answered. "He's letting Ken Keller handle it. Keller has split the embassy."

"I've only heard bits and pieces of this," said Jeannie. "But I know almost everyone in this room has written Keller a memo of support for Bruce. What's the story?"

"Well, there's been bad blood between them from the beginning," Harrison began. "You all know what Boles is like. Bruce has been telling Frank Ravndal for months that he's having trouble working with Boles. Ravndal did nothing. Well the whole thing came to a head last week when Boles accused Bruce of desertion of post—"

"What post?" asked Jeannie.

"Remember how afraid everybody was of more violence from the M-19s on April nineteenth, their eleventh anniversary? Boles had the marines on alert, and he put Bruce in charge of guarding Nancy Asencio at the residence. According to Bruce, he was supposed to use his 'discretion' about how long to stay. Well, Boles called about five-thirty in the afternoon and found Bruce had gone home. There hadn't been a hint of trouble anywhere in the city all day. Boles hit the roof.

"When Bruce came into work the next day, Boles was grinning and bouncing a tennis ball against his office wall, saying 'I'm gonna get you Bruce, I'm gonna get you.' "

"Captain Queeg!" said Welch.

"Bruce went to his desk," continued Harrison, "and found a copy of a memo Boles wrote to Keller charging him with desertion, calling him 'criminal' and 'dangerous.' He could see his whole career going down the drain. That new job he wants in Chicago. Everything was in jeopardy. And do you know what Keller told him? He said there seemed to be a 'personality conflict' between a senior and a junior officer and, he said, if Bruce couldn't prove that Boles was incompetent, it would be Bruce's ass. That's when Witter came to me for some help."

"What did you do?" asked Jeannie.

"Well, the first thing we did was write an answering memo to Keller saying Bruce did what he was told, used his discretion, and then returned to the residence when Boles ordered him to and stayed until after midnight. And we made up a list of people in the embassy who would vouch for Bruce's work. That was an interesting experience. All of a sudden nobody of any senior rank wanted anything to do with Bruce, including Crigler."

"What about Sergeant Wherly?" asked Jeannie. "He's not exactly a fan of Boles's."

"Top said that Boles had already gone after his job once, and if Bruce was relieved of duty, he would be next on Boles's shit list, especially if he helped Bruce in any way.

"I should also add that Top felt Bruce brought on his own problems. True, Boles may be a little nuts, but Top thinks Bruce is a little lazy. Anyhow. It now stands at a stalemate. So Keller has asked for an outside referee. A security guy from Panama is coming in next week to hear both sides and make a decision.

"That's not all. Rumor has it that Boles got himself into trouble in Barranquilla."

"What was he doing *there*?" asked Hadia.

"He was investigating charges of visa finagling against the consul, Thomas Gustafson."

"Who brought the charges?" asked Jeannie.

"A junior officer in the consulate, who happens to be a friend of mine. He says Gustafson was handing out visas to drug traffickers. Boles had been there 'investigating' only a couple of days when my friend came home late one night to find two mafiosos waiting for him. He hot-footed it to a hotel and Washington shipped him off pronto to an embassy in Germany."

"Dear God," said Jeannie. "Is everything rotten in Denmark?"

"Don't know about Denmark," said Welch. "But everything seems rotten in Colombia."

"Security problems are up," admitted Jeannie. "A new arrival, Sue Williams, noticed she was being followed by a Colombian man while she was window shopping in El Chico the other day. When she returned to her car, the man got into the car in front of hers, and proceeded to ram her—back to front—three times before driving away, leaning out the window and laughing."

"To live in this place is to die by inches," said Hadia.

"My wife is worried about me," Harrison said. "She says I picked a fight the other day. Some Colombian bastard was blocking my car! He'd parked behind me, and I couldn't get out. I tooted the horn politely. Twice. And then I got out of my car and asked him whether he happened to notice that he was in my way. He said, Yes. Do you believe it? I said, Well, why don't you move then, buddy. He finally did, but Michele was scared. She said the guy could have had a gun and they shoot people around here for less."

"This is an ugly country," said Welch, "full of ugly people."

"Michele and I have talked about it," added Harrison. "We've agreed I should take one more post and then decide whether I want to stay in the foreign service or not."

"Well, you're a better man than I am, Gunga Din," said Patt Lindsey. "Every time I drive to work past that block-long visa line I think how many of those little bastards won't come back to Colombia after their visa expires. But they're easier to take than the State Department. I've written a letter of resignation. The secretary's job is dull, dull, dull. I crocheted my way through this embassy. And at night I'd go home, close the curtains, play a movie on my Betamax and try to forget where I was."

"What did you put in your letter?" asked Jeannie.

"I said that I had been impressed with the rigid qualifications which must be met prior to acceptance into the foreign service. I have been equally disappointed, I said, with the utilization of these same qualifications.

"With twenty years' experience, I was given the duties of a clerk-typist—and, I said, I found the manner in which I was treated very demeaning. Unless the phrase 'just a secretary' was eliminated from the thinking and vocabulary of most officers, they will find themselves—the officers—doing more and more clerical work, and less and less effective diplomatic work."

"Damn right," said Ferris.

"When I get home to Texas," Patt added, "I'm going straight to my congressman about the foreign service!"

14

"FRANK," SAID RICHARD BACA, "the embassy is rudder-less."

"You asked me to lunch to tell me that? Rudder-less," Frank Crigler snickered. "It's not rudderless, Richard, it's sick."

"I would have said 'flat,' not 'sick.' I mean Asencio is free. The guerrillas only got two and a half million dollars and a free trip to Havana. Their comrades in prison have had their trial switched from a military to a civilian court. Colombia is still a democracy. Everybody is happy. But there has been a letdown in the embassy. You know, Watergate is over, it's back to covering traffic accidents."

"I worked hard on Richard Starr's release, didn't I?"

"Of course, Frank."

"And I worked hard on Diego's release, too."

"Yes."

"We turned our heads on Starr and the FARC got two hundred and fifty thousand dollars," Crigler said. "But we were tougher on the no-ransom line with Diego. That was hard to get across to him. I mean Diego was calling out with negotiating suggestions one to three times a day. And I'd been told by Washington to disregard him. He was a prisoner under duress as far as we knew.

"All that reporting to Washington. Ninety-five percent of my time was spent informing Washington. I couldn't do anything to solve the problem. Washington didn't need all that paper. They were not making any decisions. They just wanted to use what amounted to trivia to compete with each other at staff meetings. You remember how it was, Richard. On my way back from the meetings with the diplomatic committee, Washington would want an oral report on the open line right away, and then they'd want it written.

"I'm paid to solve problems, not to be a reporting agency. There wasn't any time to be creative or resourceful. We're a press service. Three hundred and sixty-five days a year. A press service.

"And after all that reporting—all that work—Diego went back to Washington to tell everybody how he got himself out."

Baca didn't say anything. If Frank only knew. There had been a feeling during the long negotiations that Asencio was mucking things up from the inside—playing soft with the M-19s—while calling the embassy and asking for more action. Baca had been assigned to escort Nancy Asencio to Miami to meet her husband. The kissing and hand-clasping were hardly over before Asencio asked Baca why Frank Crigler had sat on his ass. Baca told the ambassador that Frank had been around working all the time. When Diego started thanking Frank in his welcome-home press conferences, at least, Baca thought he'd headed off any further unpleasantness. Asencio was quiet for the moment, vacationing with his family in Florida.

"Frank, uh, do you think you've been too quick to put your mark on the embassy? Asencio has been out of the country barely a month."

"What do you mean?"

"Bettie, for one thing. She's been running around, even during the crisis, saying her husband was the only officer in Bogotá who could write. She just added to the growing feeling of neglect. All those unremunerated hours, all that work while Asencio was hostage—and so little recognition."

"You know how I feel about that what's-in-it-for-me attitude, Richard."

"And you know how I feel about Bettie. She was one of the few people who constantly volunteered to help during the crisis. To people who have complained about her to me, I've just said, 'Can't you handle Bettie Crigler, for Christ's sake?' But it's not just Bettie, Frank, and you know it."

Frank Crigler slumped back in his chair.

"I know I'm on the shit list. I do care what people are saying about me."

"It's everything from you and your wife and daughter tying up most of the embassy cars every day to you as a Jekyll and Hyde—humiliating staffers publicly and kissing Washington's ass privately."

"Have I humiliated people? They have a lot to be humiliated about. I'm sorry, Richard." Crigler sighed. "I worry a great deal about this."

"At first I just thought it was resentment," said Baca. "I remember the first job I ever had as a lawyer. I walked in the goddamned door and two months later my boss gave me the two biggest cases we had. There were people there who'd been born in that office, but I got the two cases. And I ran 'em like a mother-fucker. People started talking bad about me, bad about my mama, bad about every place I'd ever been, for reasons that had nothing to do with me."

Crigler started to smile.

"But I've never seen resentment like this."

Crigler's smile froze.

"I have no problem with the Ken Keller promotion."

"He's acting DCM because he ran the best section," Crigler said.

"No, I know that," agreed Baca. "He ran the best crisis team, too, except for mine, of course. I have no problem either with the handling of the clash between Boles and Witter."

"I was too close to that to get involved," said Crigler. "I'm sorry Bruce had to go, he was a good man. But they couldn't work together. Chuck's on thin ice at the moment. He's a loser."

"It worked out all right in the end. Bruce got his job in Chicago with nothing nasty put in his personnel file forever, and Chuck Boles got Bruce out of the country and out of his hair."

"What *do* you have a problem with, then?" Crigler asked.

"It's not just resentment," Baca said, looking straight at Crigler's face. "It's hate, Frank. And a lot of it is focused on the evaluation reports. You were rough on people."

"Maybe I overreacted when did the OERs," admitted Crigler. "But I think I'm honest. Not brutal. I didn't go into all of everybody's faults. You know it's funny, Richard. I got my ambassadorship in Rwanda by attracting the attention of a very influential assistant secretary in Washington. And the way I attracted his attention was to suggest reforming the annual officer evaluation reports. I suggested oral 'exams.' Instead, we got reviewing panels and more paper work. And now a whole handful of people know who said what about whom."

Crigler started stabbing his chicken and rice "crepe" with his fork.

"Killing amoebas, Frank?" Baca laughed.

"I'm forty-six years old going on ninety." Crigler looked past Baca. "I had a reputation before this place for getting people to cooperate. To work well. I haven't succeeded here. People I count on aren't working for me. That hurts."

Crigler put his fork down. "I know everybody wants to leave this embassy. Everybody hates everybody else. Latin America is the garbage dump of the foreign service.

"I like people who are good. Asencio didn't know diddly shit about running an embassy. By the time I got here this staff had atrophied for two and a half years. He completely discouraged initiative. He ran a one-man show. Why not? Diego could sell an Alaskan ice. Well, I can't. I don't have those talents. I need input. I need people, good people.

"What do I have? Good writers who have no ideas, people with good ideas who can't write. And, all right, I forced George Thigpen, John Simms and Frank Ravndal to curtail by making it damned unpleasant to work for me. You can't fire people in the foreign service. You can only get them transferred.

"You know what, Richard?" smiled Crigler. "I've asked to be made ambassador here."

"That's not usually done, is it?" asked Baca. "I mean, the deputy chief of mission elevated to ambassador in the same embassy he DCM'ed."

"No. I probably won't get the job. But I'd love to turn this place around."

"You've already begun that, Frank."

"It's GORM time—Goals, Objectives, Resource Management." Crigler's face lit up. "At the top of my objectives is Caribbean basin security. I want to get Colombia more involved, and not view everything as black and white—communist, non-communist. America is somewhere in the middle now. Carter's policy in Nicaragua and Salvador is the best handling of this hemisphere we've ever done.

"And I want to encourage more international human rights organization activity here.

"At the bottom of my GORM list is drugs. It's my own personal belief that little can be done as long as there is a market for marijuana and cocaine in the States."

"I agree," said Baca. "If we don't care, why should Colombia care?"

"I hated sitting on Emil Castro's drug economics report," Crigler continued. "It was good. I sat on it because of Asencio. They ought to legalize marijuana here. That would solve the corruption problem, which is the only serious consequence of narcotics prohibition.

"The policy from Washington as well as it can be ascertained is to do 'something.' Diego took that Washington policy to the sixteenth degree. His sixteen-million-dollar shopping list of military goodies came from his own forehead. That drug program was his personal podium. You can always buy foreign policy programs. But can you persuade a country to do it on its own? That's diplomacy!"

"Won't you lose more than a third of your staff if you cut back the drug thing?" asked Baca.

"Doesn't really matter. We don't need an embassy this large anywhere. It's not just the drug program. So many things are built into the bureaucracy—same as in Washington.

"You know what I've done to get around the section heads?" smiled Crigler. "I've asked John Simms and George Thigpen to designate a GORM 'representative' from their staffs to send to my meeting later this week. I mean, I know pretty much what I want to say. The staff meeting could only change my GORM plan a little. But by getting people together, everybody would feel they're contributing.

"Decisions aren't made in meetings, Richard. People can talk forever. Management is done most effectively by memo. That's how ideas are set."

"I hate to change the subject," said Baca, enjoying Crigler's sudden animation. "It all sounds interesting. I don't know from memos and GORMs. How's your daughter doing? She picked a strange couple of months to come visiting. Is she liking Bogotá?"

"It's happened," said Crigler, grimacing.

"What?"

"She's 'involved' with some guy."

"From the look on your face," said Baca, "he must be Colombian."

"Yes. They're nice people, but you wouldn't want your daughter to marry one."

"I can't place your accent," said Emily Roth. "Where are you from?"

"I was born in Europe," said portly Dr. Franz Kunderecz. "What used to be Transylvania."

He smiled with big yellow teeth. "Then I went to New York. No like. California was just like New York. People always hurrying. So now I live here and teach atomic physics at Gran Colombia University. Here is quieter. Now let us begin. What is your date of birth?"

"April seventeenth."

"That's good! Aries. Is very dynamic."

Emily smiled.

"And how old are you?"

"Thirty-five."

"Okay. Give me your left hand.

"Hmmmm. You have very large life line in chain form. Means you have to work. You are realistic. Not romantic. Not a dreamer.

"Now give me your right hand. Oh! You are very emotional! See the islands on your heart line?"

Emily watched Dr. Kunderecz pick up a magnifying glass.

"Now, look straight at my eyes. I can see by your iris and tell you—oh! The colon is inflamed! The liver too! Because you are under tension, no?"

"Why yes," said Emily.

"See?" Dr. Kunderecz turned to his desk and started writing. "Now I give you some names of enzymes you can buy to help. The altitude here is a problem. Is not 'medicine.' Is not 'prescription.' Is just to help.

"Your left hand again. Ah. There is your luck line and—ah!—you have a double destiny life."

"Will I be a writer when I'm older?" asked Emily.

Dr. Kunderecz ignored her.

"Your right hand again. You were deep in love when you were about twenty-two, no?"

"Yes," said Emily, very impressed.

"You have a little trouble after this. An incapability with marriage."

"Yes."

"What sign was your husband?"

"Capricorn."

"No good! Is not stable. I have a hypersensitivity just looking at you. Your hand confirms it. Ah! You're impulsive. Defensive. You have never been stimulated emotionally or sexually."

Dr. Kunderecz smiled his yellow smile. "You can be a tyrant after you are stimulated. You have passion."

Emily laughed.

"I know personally the Dalai Lama. The yogis, they have no tension. They use sound to find the center of meditation. Listen to the vibration.

"Ohhhhhhhhhhmmmmmmmmmmmmmmmmm," hummed Dr. Kunderecz. "That is the 'ohm' sound."

"Ohhhhhhmmmmmmmm," repeated Emily. "I can feel it! What are these little papier-mâché pyramids on the shelf with the razor blades hanging on them?"

"The pyramid, if built just right," explained Dr. Kunderecz, "is a source of energy. Strong enough to sharpen the razor blades I shave with."

Emily looked at the stubble on his chin.

"Ah. And next door I have built a pyramid tent.

That is where I meditate and where I sleep. It is best to face your back to the north."

"That's how I sleep!" said Emily.

"In a pyramid?"

"No. With my head pointed north."

"Good. Now let me see your right hand again. So. You must use your head more than your heart.

"I see three possibilities more in love. Before you are forty years you will have a man."

"Oh good." Emily breathed a sigh of relief. "Let's see." Counting off on her fingers, she said, "That gives me four or five more years. I can relax."

Dr. Kunderecz was staring at her.

"Yes. You will live together more than twenty years. Look, here you can see."

Emily bent over her hand.

"If you will have patience. Is better late than never," Dr. Kunderecz laughed.

"The economical is not bad either. See, your right hand has three lines. Is better than one.

"Ah." His nose was less than an inch from Emily's palm. "And you have the ring of Apollo. You will never be poor.

"Oh. But you do have sometimes little depressions." Dr. Kunderecz turned to his desk and started writing. "This is a little something for anti-depression. It is not habit-forming. After one half hour, you are free from depression."

"Wonderful," said Emily. "I can sure use some help with that."

Dr. Kunderecz grabbed her left hand.

"You are practical and strong."

"I am!"

"But you are doing first, and thinking later."

He grabbed her thumb. "You are dominating! Your husband will take the belt to you!"

"Yes," said Emily. "But I am sensitive."

"You are a psychic person," Dr. Kunderecz

agreed. "Hold your hands together like this," and he held his hands as if in prayer, thumbs uncrossed, fingers parallel to the floor.

"Oh. The magnetism is out to here," and Dr. Kunderecz waved his hands more than a foot from Emily's.

"You can expand that with yoga. Breathe quickly six times in and out. Now slowly three times. That is yoga respiration. Now close your eyes.

"Oh. You have a very good aura. I see a little yellow, some blue—that's devotion. Oh. And green for vitality. Very nice.

"Give me your left hand.

"You are not very ambitious. Not materialistic. You are very idealistic."

Dr. Kunderecz turned her hand over.

"Lots of perseverance."

He grabbed her little finger. "Oh, you are very convincing!"

Emily laughed. "I'm convincing, all right."

"Seventy-six years you will live. After that you will have difficulty with the heart. You will live past your husband. But then there will be a neighbor.

"Watch trouble with your kidneys. Drink no more than four cups of coffee a day.

"Ah. Money and love you will always have."

"Will I have children?"

"Give me your right hand. Oh yes. See these vertical lines?

"You have to have confidence in yourself," said Dr. Kunderecz. "That is the principal thing."

"What country will I go to next?" Emily asked.

"Venezuela. You should see Venezuela."

"No, no," said Emily. "I mean my work. Where will I go next?"

"Oh. I cannot tell you that."

"I'm gonna have my own Fourth of July party, Bobby, that's what."

"You do that, Clay," customs agent Bobby Herrera said, glancing nervously around The Den. "Just keep your voice down, would you?"

"Goddamn Crigler canceled the embassy's Fourth of July party, Bobby." Clay carefully lifted his glass of vodka to his mouth and then changed his mind and banged it back down on the bar. "The United States is afraid of the M-19s, is that it, Bobby?"

"That's enough, Clay," Bobby cut him off. "Pipe down."

"He's gonna let the drug program rot, Bobby. Crigler's gonna let it rot. 'Drugs are not my hang-up,' he says. Do you believe that, Bobby?"

"Guy can't be too smart," said Herrera. "If he drops drugs, he's going to lose half his embassy staff."

"God, Bobby, Crigler asked me to stay in Bogotá. To extend my tour. He doesn't even know what customs agents do!" Clay stared forlornly at his drink. "He sends Keller to the narc staff meetings and Ken says, 'How's your project? What's going on in your shop?' Wittenberg says maybe we can buy a Cobra with some of that sixteen million. I fell off my chair! Ever seen a Cobra, Bobby? That's how you start World War III! Keller says, 'We'll see about that.' Jesus.

"I went with Crigler to General Leyva's office yesterday to see if we could get him to sign that letter of agreement for the sixteen million dollars. Crigler says, General the Congress of the United States has put certain limitations on how the money can be spent. And then Leyva says, I think you should give us the money with no limitations. Why should Congress dictate? Back and forth they went. There's still no letter. . . . I miss him, Bobby."

"Diego?"

"Yeah. We coulda got him out early, Bobby. You know that? Then maybe they would have let him stay here as ambassador. The CIA knew where the hostages were all the time, Bobby. When they were in rooms together. When they slept. They had a scenario for every contingency. Even Crigler didn't know all of them. Only Washington. We were ready to send in our troops. A SWAT team coulda been on alert just fifteen minutes away. Turbay said no. He didn't think our surgeon's plan was any better than his guys' smear-'em-up shotgun approach.

"And we couldn't just sneak in like the Israelis. Not us Americans, no. Whenever we move, we move with all this fuckin' equipment. First we need to open a commissary.

"Shit. So Turbay nixes the military types and negotiates. Two months! And what does Crigler do? He brings in this kid from Greece! Hamilton. A fish out of water. He had Frank's trust, but that was it. And Simms. He cuts Simms off from the ministers! John knew the ministers like the back of his hand! We needed all the intelligence—every scrap of information we could get. And Crigler cuts the embassy's expert off! Frank was too young, too unknown. Nobody was listening to him."

"Did you send over to the embassy that DEA report on Magangué, Clay?" asked Herrera. "The one that said Cubans had been spotted working with the FARC?"

"I asked those guys if they were gonna," said Clay. "It was their report. They said no. 'We, in the DEA, don't assert ourselves—especially since Crigler doesn't like Burnett.' I made sure the CIA saw it.

"Colombia is setting up an operation called Group Ten. It's gonna be run by an army colonel working up near the north coast. They're keeping it real quiet. They don't want to admit they have a problem with drug money and terrorism. But they know they do, and they have some reports of their own about Cubans working in the small villages up there. The CIA is trying to spring some covert money for Group Ten.

"Grab my briefcase, Bobby, let's get out of here. Let's go home. Is Doña Helena in my briefcase Bobby? Did you put her in?"

"Yes, Clay. I've got your gun. Now shut up and let's go."

"I mentioned the Magangué report to Crigler, Bobby," Clay said, sliding off the bar stool. "Frank said, 'Do you believe that, Clay? I'm not impressed with the guerrilla groups here.' Jesus, Bobby, he's kindergarten."

"Time . . ." sang a resonant man's voice. "Time . . ."

"Time on my hands," chimed a chorus of high-pitched women.

"*La hora en fantasia*"—the male—in singsong Spanish.

"Fuck." Sergeant Blake reached over and pushed the off button on the portable radio. He didn't need to be reminded that he had time on his hands.

Sergeant Blake looked at his watch. Two A.M. Post One was a small pool of light between the embassy's lobby and the first-floor elevators. He had the rolling front-grill gates halfway down so he could sit in his glass cage and rot in private. For the next four hours, the U.S. Embassy in Bogotá belonged to him. He glanced at the three TV screens. All quiet at the front gate. All quiet at the back garage entrance. All dark on the third screen. It hadn't been working for a month.

He had a couple of gas grenades at 50/50 strength for indoor use. He had a button to press that would open four gas valves in the lobby ceiling. Riot control. Below the waist-high bullet-proof glass windows there was a billy club and a twelve-gauge police rifle. There were eight alarm systems scattered around the building. When they were set off by infrared sensors, they lit a button on the console next to the TV monitors. Also, there was an alarm system that was connected to the ambassador's car. The alarm activated a tape recorder—or it did when it was working.

Sergeant Blake sighed. He had a lot of equipment to keep him company, and if he got bored he could look through the big red mug-book of known international terrorists. Or the little green book of incident reports.

The sergeant smiled. It was the greatest feeling to step off the elevator on rover duty—Post Two—and watch the State Department jerks turn to run down the corridors to see if they'd left classified stuff on their desks.

The embassy had been locked up tight since 10:30. The Post Two marine had escorted the charwomen through the secure areas, burned any classified wastepaper and done one last security inspection before deserting him at Post One for the long, lonely night.

Sergeant Blake tried to remember how he'd gotten himself into this boring embassy duty in the first place. He'd wanted to be a marine since he was eight years old, when he'd put on a plastic helmet, filled a canteen full of water and marched down to the marine recruiting office in Rome, Georgia. He'd sung the Marine Hymn and asked to be sent to Vietnam. When he was finally old enough to join up, there wasn't any war. Since he wanted to travel, he took the embassy security job.

He had all this equipment and nothing to use it on. He'd never fired a gas grenade, except in training; he'd never pushed the lobby ceiling gas-valve button. He had caught a few mail bombs with his metal detector, and he'd helped sweep the embassy for bombs and bugs quite a few times, but the bombs hadn't materialized and the bugs were getting harder to catch.

Even the embassy off-duty was unpleasant. Cars and cycles were not allowed. And though the marines didn't wear their uniforms or carry guns on the street, Colombians still picked them out and yelled *gringo*.

Sergeant Blake glanced around his glass prison. In one wall box were all the embassy car keys, eleven cars. Only five of them ran. Colombian mechanics were no good, and there was trouble getting parts. In the other wall box were keys to the embassy kingdom. The ones with red tags were handed out to Americans only. The ones with green tags could be given safely to Colombians.

Post One had been exciting once. Sergeant Blake had been on duty the morning Ambassador Asencio was released. Frank Crigler had had trouble using the radio. "This is AK5, uh . . ." Sergeant Blake called upstairs and asked if he could help. Security Chief Chuck Boles and Colonel Carl Wittenberg were in separate cars, both assigned to follow the bus carrying the guerrillas and hostages from the Dominican embassy to the airport. He heard Wittenberg say, "I'm lost, I'm lost! Where is the Dominican embassy, anyway?" When they got there, Boles kept asking Wittenberg if he could see anything. "Not much," Wittenberg answered. Sergeant Blake was in stitches. When the hostages and their guards were loaded on the bus, Boles and Wittenberg started to follow, until Wittenberg yelled, "I've just gotten cut off by a police van! Can you pick them up?" When the bus broke down, Boles and the colonel did a radio play-by-play of the cops beating off the newsmen, until another bus was brought. Crigler tried to break in to say that someone had called the embassy. They'd heard Asencio interviewed on the radio. Did that mean that the ambassador was not going to be one of the hostages taken by the M-19s to Cuba? Could Boles or Wittenberg see him at the airport? Had he boarded the Cuban plane? Boles said they couldn't see him. They would try to find him. Crigler had somebody call the radio station. The manager said they had interviewed Asencio. Then Crigler called the foreign ministry. He was told Asencio was on the plane; the interview on the radio station had been an old tape. Boles and Wittenberg drove back. As they walked in the embassy, Sergeant Blake had no sooner said, "Nice job," when a phone call came in, saying Asencio was at the residence. Boles tore over. And, of course, the ambassador wasn't there.

15

Eileen Heaphy got from her in-box the latest cable from Tom Boyatt, the new United States ambassador to Colombia. The M-19s who had taken the Dominican embassy, who had held a couple dozen hostages for two months, and had then flown free and rich to Havana, had just tried to mount an invasion of Colombia by boat. The army was waiting for them. Some were dead. Comandante Uno was in jail, weeping.

Eileen looked at the "Merit Award" she'd taped up on her office wall. It was no more than a thank-you memo—a Xerox of a thank-you memo. Thanks to the Colombia working group for the long hours, thanks for a happy ending. Thanks for the memories.

"To everything there is a season. And a time to every purpose under the heaven." She hated to admit it, but maybe she was starting to think President Reagan's way—that Cuba, and therefore Russia, was behind all the trouble in Latin America. Fidel Castro was getting too adventurous. The captured M-19s said they had received training in Havana. How can any government sit by and take that?

The M-19s were down, but nobody would say they were out. The embassy in Bogotá wasn't making that mistake again. There were reasons for guerrillas. Colombia was not exactly a paradise.

Eileen picked up another cable on her desk.

Summary: This cable responds to telephonic requests from certain elements in Washington whose interest can only be described as prurient. The murder of the Dominican Republic's ambassador was an old-fashioned case of passion and sex. End summary.

The Dominican ambassador to Colombia, Eduardo Antonio Garcia Vasquez, was shot and killed across from the new Dominican Chancery in Bogotá, in front of the house of the Dominican consul, Raphael Augusto Sanchez.

Initial reports of the incident were sketchy, indicating only that the ambassador had been shot, which led to much uninformed speculation, including that he had been assassinated by one of Colombia's several terrorist groups. It was reported that the consul was upstairs taking a bath when the shooting occurred and that it was he who discovered the body of the ambassador on his front steps. One fact was clear: the ambassador had been shot seven times, which, as most Colombians realized, immediately ruled out accidental shooting as the cause of death.

The diplomatic corps heaved a sigh of relief when it was reported in the press two days later that Consul Sanchez had, in fact, shot the ambassador, rather than terrorists. In this version of the story, Sanchez was upstairs sleeping, was awakened by his wife's cries for help, descended to find the ambassador making *galanteos* to his wife, and shot him. The accompanying front-page photos of the uncommonly comely Mrs. Sanchez lent immediate plausibility to this story. The police, however, were reportedly troubled by certain anomalies in this version, specifically, that Sanchez should have been sleeping when his superior was visiting, and second, that Sanchez managed to hit the ambassador seven times and miss his wife completely despite their reported relative proximity.

Once the basic ingredients of sex, violence and intrigue became known, it was probably inevitable that this story would be played first as soap opera, then as melodrama. Local commentators publicly tried, and indignantly acquitted, Sanchez of this "crime of passion," declaring it to be a clear case of justifiable homicide. The fact that it occurred during a slow news period also contributed to the wide press coverage.

The latest version to emerge, although more detailed, contains significant variations. It now appears that Sanchez and the ambassador spent the better part of the day together fulfilling certain diplomatic obligations which entailed the drinking of alcoholic beverages. They returned to Sanchez's house about eight in the evening to talk and listen to music. The conversation reportedly turned argumentative about 10:30 and resulted in Sanchez's kicking and slapping the ambassador, and requesting him to leave the premises. The latter, ignoring clear indications as to the excitable nature of his subordinate, chose this inopportune moment to declare that he felt great attraction for Señora Sanchez, and allowed further as to how he thought Sanchez was a homosexual. In retrospect, his statements were viewed as inappropriate to both their superior/subordinate relationship, and to the occasion—bad timing. In any case Sanchez, reacting immoderately to these ill-chosen words, then shot the ambassador seven times in sundry parts of his body with a 9mm pistol, from what is termed point-blank range. . . .

It was a cinch something that lively hadn't been written by Simms or Roberts, Heaphy thought. Simms was serving time on the board of foreign service examiners in Washington, while looking around for a job in the private sector. Don Roberts headed up the one-man political section in Mali. Jerry Harrison had stayed, by request, in consular work and had been assigned to a desert African country. Frank Ravndal was the new admin officer in Jakarta. Ellis Glynn had retired to Colorado

Springs. Clay Allison was teaching customs work to new agents in Georgia. Thomas Gustafson, cleared of all charges, was still in Barranquilla.

Heaphy started to laugh. After months of checking and double-checking to make sure there were no drug traffickers involved in the building's financing, the consulate staff had finally moved into a new high rise in Barranquilla, out of the orbit of the circling condors. But they'd forgotten to check the construction design and the building had just been declared structurally unsound. The U.S. Consulate in Barranquilla was now located over the laundry room of the El Prado Hotel.

Ambassador Diego Asencio, after some months' rest in Florida, had started working as assistant secretary for consular affairs in Washington. He'd switched from a drug war to the green revolution. As he put it, in the year 2020, when the green revolution has reached its peak and the world's population is at an unfeedable six billion, there are going to be islands of prosperity surrounded by havoc. It has started to happen. The richer countries realize this, but are not sharing their wealth, so an increasing number of poor people are moving to where the wealth is. Technology has always saved us before, Asencio says, but who knows now? It's a horrible thought, and there's no vision around to prevent it.

Asencio is pretty sure he'll survive in his job through the Reagan changeover. They need a well-placed Hispanic as much as Jimmy Carter did.

He had been offered the Buenos Aires embassy after his hero's welcome at the State Department. He'd said no, although he'd always coveted the post. Nancy Asencio did not have the stomach to go back out—and so far away from the States—and Diego had felt B.A. would be a bad job. He'd be stuck bringing nothing but negative human rights news to the Government of Argentina. It had looked then as though Carter would get a second term. The consular job wasn't much fun, but it meant power, and no one understood power better than Diego.

Asencio had asked to review Frank Crigler's evaluation report when he'd gotten back to work. Crigler had been upset about that. Frank wasn't very happy with his new assignment either—deputy assistant secretary for Mexican affairs. It was a position of some influence, considering Mexico's oil, but it wasn't an embassy. Crigler wanted an embassy.

Heaphy picked up her draft of the letter that outgoing President Carter was sending to President Turbay. "As my term in office draws to a close, I am writing you to express my satisfaction with the current state of U.S.-Colombian relations. The relationship between our two nations has been strengthened and broadened in a spirit of mutual respect and cooperation. . . . I also want to thank you for your personal role in the success of our mutual efforts to halt the traffic of illegal drugs between Colombia and the U.S."

Asencio was gone, and the "war" was over. The army was out, the police unit was in. They were doing okay. Ambassador Boyatt was requesting only $2.7 million in assistance for next fiscal year. It was moot in any case. It looked as though Congress was going to repeal the Percy Amendment, which meant that paraquat could be sprayed—destroying the marijuana in the fields. The DEA would get its wish: eradication.

The question was, would Turbay do it? The U.S. would offer to pay to spray, but Colombia had grown understandably fond of its drug income. It was money for a rainy day, or a coffee-bean frost.

Nothing had happened about Quita Sueño. The current reason for delay was all the new faces on Capitol Hill.

Heaphy was fascinated by Ambassador Boyatt.

He ran a different sort of embassy, with a management approach to foreign policy. It certainly was different from Diego's. Asencio would look at an agency like A.I.D., and even though it had been invited out of Colombia, he would try to figure a way to keep some of it in—working with the Guajira Indians, perhaps, as a piece of his drug war. That was the Latin approach. Boyatt says Colombia has a five-billion-dollar foreign reserve. Let *them* assist their Indians.

"A time to be born . . . a time to die . . . a time to laugh . . . a time to weep . . ."

Eileen still had a few months left on the Colombia desk, and then wouldn't it be nice to go to Europe next? That's where everybody wanted to go. She suspected that the career counselors at State maneuvered those plums for themselves.

Richard Baca lay flat on his back with a book balanced on his belly. Fuck. Maybe it was time to write a letter to his friend in Texas. Remember when you said, When you and I grow up, let's do law together? Well, I think I've grown up. The Peace Corps was going out of business in Colombia, and everybody was trying to figure out how to say goodbye. It was the first time the corps was leaving a country for economic, as opposed to political, reasons. What the United States was saying was, You don't need us anymore, you're only underdeveloped where you want to be; which was true. But the economic reasons were, really, primarily Richard Starr economics. What the United States wasn't saying was, We don't need that kind of ransom crap anymore.

It was all the same to him. Life was so exciting now that he would arrive home from the office at 5:16, take two packages of M&Ms up to bed at 5:17 and be asleep for the night by 5:30.

The Colombians did not deserve a Peace Corps; they didn't deserve a country, either. Christ, they could fuck up anything. They could make chicken shit out of chicken salad. They are the way they drive: every man for himself. What could you say about a people who urinated in the streets?. Who grazed cows in the middle of the best neighborhoods?

Colombians were incompetent. Emeralds were selling for four times as much a carat as diamonds. Colombia had 90 percent of the world's supply, and they were still not making it. They could be a major coffee exporter, but they weren't. Their marijuana is technologically passé. The stuff with all the THC, and the higher street price, was coming from Hawaii and California.

Colombian guerrillas can't work together. The stupid M-19s were all locked up. What had Diego said about the M-19s? Fuzzy philosophy. Not terribly serious. Concerned about starving babies, sure, but not clear what they were going to do about it. Do we care if this country goes communist? All of South America, for that matter? The war between the two powers is not going to be fought here. And if we do care, then we train their military in the United States, turn our backs, and let them make their country secure. Then we shove whatever we want down here: contracts for dams, color TV. We don't ask nice.

Baca laughed remembering a conversation he'd had with Frank Crigler. He'd told Frank one drunken night that American foreign policy had to be more reflective of the American people. Frank had said, What the hell does that mean? You know, Baca had explained, we're into self-awareness. Good ejaculations and strong climaxes. Very individual. Crigler had just stared at him and then asked how one fashioned a foreign policy for that. It had been the end of a promising conversation. What was he going to tell Frank about his foreign service decision? He just wasn't sure how he felt about joining anymore. Going back to practicing law looked more attractive to him now.

It wasn't until Asencio had been taken hostage that Baca had started dealing on a regular basis with a lot of the embassy people. Before, he'd just worked mainly with Asencio and Crigler—both top-notch. At the start of the crisis, one guy's job had been to get desks into the conference room. What kind of job is that for a grown person? Another guy's job had been to hook up telephones. Some people had been involved in strategy, had dealt with substance. But others were just making rules about how many batteries to use, or making up duty rosters. A competent secretary can do a duty roster. You don't need someone making forty-plus a year. Some of them were as good as their jobs. Some were disasters: incapable, drab lifers.

It had been Baca's good fortune to practice law in California's legal service, and then in the Civil Rights Commission, with people who he felt were as good as he was, or better. So many of the embassy types were disillusioned people; they were victims of their own brightest and best myths. They knew it and they knew that it didn't matter.

Maybe he'd still be tempted if he could come in somewhere in the middle level—an FSO4 or 3. But all those dues at the bottom of the ladder—he couldn't do duty rosters for two minutes, much less two years.

Of course Baca would be glad to join up if they'd make him an ambassador right away. That was one of the things that had frustrated Crigler about Asencio's staff. They didn't care if they made it to the top. What did they want? The foreign service only made sense if you made it a career. As just another job, it wasn't great. A lot of hassle for very mediocre money.

Maybe what was happening to the foreign service was what was happening to a lot of organizations. It had happened in legal services too. There came a time when the legal services program started to exist more for the benefit of the employees than it did for the clients. And that's when lawyers and secretaries and everybody else started worrying about working conditions, unions, promotional opportunities, salaries. All of those things. What had changed in America?

"Top, I need to talk to somebody." Chuck Boles grabbed Sergeant Wherly's arm. "Can you just listen? I'm so tired, Top."

All of a sudden Boles grimaced and doubled over. Top could feel the blood stop in his arm, Boles's grip had got so tight.

"Chuck, you're not supposed to be drinking with that ulcer of yours. How many beers have you had? What are you doing at a Marine House happy hour anyway? You ought to be at home taking it easy. C'mon. That's where I'm taking you now."

"But there's nobody there, Top. Junie . . . Can you stay with me and talk? Just for a little while."

"Sure. Let's go."

Boles doubled over twice more during the walk to Top's car. What had happened to him shouldn't have happened to a dog, Sergeant Wherly thought. Whether you liked Chuck or not, it wasn't fair for life to be this unfair. Ambassador Asencio was no sooner safe than Boles's wife died.

"It was maybe eleven-thirty at night, Top," Boles said. "And Junie and I—we'd just made love. She felt fine. And then she didn't. And then she was gone."

Boles leaned his head back on the car seat. "You know it's funny, Top. I killed all those stupeheads in Nam. It didn't mean anything to me. Now my brother—he's a cop—is dead. My wife . . ."

"Chuck," Sergeant Wherly grasped at a change of

subject. "How did you get into the security business, anyway?"

"I was in the marines for nine years two months and two days. But there was nothing to be said about my future. I didn't want to be regimented, uniformed. I didn't want to go back to Vietnam. So I became a security officer for a computer software company. Then I met a guy who worked for the foreign service. Seemed like the thing to do at the time. At first I did domestic detail. Secretary of State Rogers' protection team in 1973. Kissinger's in 1974. I went from one year in El Paso to one year in Peking. And then I went to Afghanistan.

"My career is hanging by a thread, Top. I think I'm going to get fired. When I investigated that Gustafson visa thing in Barranquilla, I broke a few laws. . . . I told people things I shouldn't have. It was heart over head. . . . I'm in trouble, Top. So what if I went after Witter's job? Anybody who says eight A.M. to four P.M. is enough . . . It was dangerous what he did at the residence. I got a phone call April nineteenth saying the M-19s were coming after the hostages' wives, so I sent Witter out to the ambassador's residence to stay with Mrs. Asencio. I sent a couple marines with him and they had orders to shoot to kill. You know that. Well, at five fucking thirty he deserts post and leaves those marines there. Christ, Top, what if they'd shot the gardener!

"Washington thought the shoot-to-kill order was a little heavy-handed." Boles tried to laugh.

What an awful sound, Sergeant Wherly thought.

"I'm going nuts, Top."

"Why don't you just quit, Chuck? Get out."

"I'm not gonna quit. I keep thinking something I do will make a difference. It won't, but . . . What about my kids? What kind of world are they going to live in?

"The U.S. has to change. We're losing. Always running around like crazy after the fact. Our CIA is de-fanged. Human rights is the biggest fucking millstone. . . .

"We never know enough, Top. Do you know what I mean? I mean . . . the only thing we know is that we don't know. No embassy can protect itself from determined assault. Three countries I've worked in now . . . I never knew who the 'they' were who were coming to get us . . .

"We have to play by the same rules as everybody else, Top. Or us good guys are going to get killed. The U.S. has maybe five more years to change its ways . . . just five. . . .

"You know what the shrink told me in Washington after I buried my wife? He said if I got my shit together I could have another overseas post. I want to stay overseas.

"I didn't screw up, Top. That Asencio thing . . . it could've . . . could've . . . happened . . . to . . . anybody."

Sergeant Wherly looked over at Boles. He had finally fallen asleep.

Emily Roth felt great. Outside the plane there was not a mountain in sight.

"I've just left Heathrow Airport in London," she wrote in her diary. "I'm on my way to Rome, where my life will begin again, where I'll get a new contract with myself and start all over.

"It has such a clean ring about it—so refreshing, really. It's so nice to feel that you can put everything behind you and start all over again, new. I suppose that's a feeling we should always have, saving the most memorable experiences. Moving every couple of years certainly makes it easy to put things behind. Bogotá seems very far away right now—thankfully."

Emily was so excited. Rome! What an assignment! She would be working in the economics section again, but Rome! Lovely piazzas, beautiful fountains, the Colosseum, and pasta!

She'd had two wonderful weeks with her family in Chicago. Then she'd had six weeks of language training in Washington. *A rivederci*, Bogotá!

Emily wondered whether Rome would change her mind about the foreign service. She'd just have to see what happened. It was anybody's guess.

She felt a sudden rush of happiness. Rome had to be a good post. Maybe she would stay in the foreign service. Maybe she would not. Perhaps Rome would be a nice post to end her foreign service career.

The Italians in the plane looked tall, dark and sexy, dressed in those close-fitting European-style suits.

"I wonder what Italian men are really like," Emily said out loud, and then caught herself and smiled.

The sun was shining brightly up above the clouds. It was very appropriate to the way she felt. Something smelled wonderful! Oh my God, they're giving out food! Fettucine Alfredo!

Emily had such a feeling of well-being and good fortune. This was going to be a great tour.